ONWARD
MUSLIM
SOLDIERS

ONWARD MUSLIM SOLDIERS

How Jihad Still Threatens America and the West

Robert Spencer

Since 1947
REGNERY PUBLISHING, INC.
An Eagle Publishing Company • Washington, DC

Library of Congress Cataloging-in-Publication Data
Spencer, Robert, 1962-
Onward Muslim soldiers / Robert Spencer.
p. cm.
Includes bibliographical references and index.
ISBN 0-89526-100-6
1. Jihad. 2. War-Religious aspects-Islam. 3. Terrorism-Religious aspects-Islam. 4. Religious tolerance-Islam. 5. Islam-Controversial literature. I. Title.
BP182.S64 2003
297.7'2—dc22

                       2003017604

Published in the United States by
Regnery Publishing, Inc.
An Eagle Publishing Company
One Massachusetts Avenue, NW
Washington, DC 20001

Visit us at www.regnery.com

Distributed to the trade by
National Book Network
4720-A Boston Way
Lanham, MD 20706

Printed on acid-free paper

Manufactured in the United States of America

10 9 8 7 6 5 4 3 2 1

Books are available in quantity for promotional or premium use.
Write to Director of Special Sales, Regnery Publishing, Inc., One Massachusetts Avenue, NW, Washington, DC 20001, for information on discounts and terms, or call (202) 216-0600.

Acknowledgments

For many reasons, including the unpleasant prospect of reprisals against innocent people, there are more people who helped make this book a reality than I can thank here. However, I am able to single out Dr. Andrew Bostom and Bat Ye'or for alerting me to important sources, Theresa Barger for help with French, and many others for their enormously valuable advice, information, and support, including Jeffrey Rubin, Dr. Walid Phares, Fr. Thomas Steinmetz, Paul Weyrich, and Dr. Farajollah Parvizian. I am grateful also to the indefatigable and resourceful Steve Lilienthal of the Free Congress Foundation, and to my editor, the protean and insightful Harry Crocker. As for the others, I trust you know who you are, and to all: Shukran.

Dedicated to the victims of jihad and dhimmitude worldwide
Your sufferings are not forgotten

Table of Contents

Introduction

JIHAD TODAY

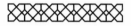

"Get out your weapons," commanded Jaffar Umar Thalib, a forty-year-old Muslim cleric, over Indonesian radio in May 2002. "Fight against [Christians in Indonesia] to the last drop of blood."[1]

I T WAS JIHAD.

Christians, Jaffar explained, were "belligerent infidels" (*kafir harbi*) and entitled to no mercy. This designation was not merely a stylistic flourish on Jaffar's part. On the contrary, *kafir harbi* is a category of infidel that is clearly delineated in Islamic theology; by using it, Jaffar not only incited his followers to violence, but gave that violence the legitimacy of Islamic doctrine.

His usage and reasoning resonated with his followers in the now-disbanded Laskar Jihad. Thousands heeded his call with ferocious single-mindedness. Some estimate the death toll among

Indonesian Christians to have been as high as ten thousand, with thousands more left homeless.[2]

Hamas, the Palestinian terrorist group that has set itself up as the chief roadblock on the latest road map to peace in the Middle East, also sees itself as fighting a jihad. The Hamas charter of August 1988 declares: "Nothing is loftier or deeper in Nationalism than waging Jihad against the enemy and confronting him when he sets foot on the land of the Muslims."[3] When will it end? "It is a Jihad until either victory or martyrdom," declares the Hamas Qassam Brigade at the end of each of its communiqués.[4]

Meanwhile, across the Atlantic Ocean, aspiring warriors of jihad were invited to enroll in Ultimate Jihad Challenge: "a two-week course in our thousand-acre state-of-the-art shooting range in the United States." This was not a course for effete intellectuals. "The course emphasis is on practical live fire training. You will fire between two to three thousand rounds of mixed caliber ammunition. Class theory is kept to a minimum." The British-based website advertising the course explained that, "due to the firearms law of the UK all serious firearms training must be done overseas."[5] That is, in the United States.

The website's owner, an English convert to Islam named Sulayman Zain-ul-Abidin, denied operating anything less innocuous than a training center for security guards. However, police charged that he had received and erased e-mails containing evidence to the contrary, including one that read, "Let me sacrifice myself for jihad—send details."[6] Investigators probed links between Zain-ul-abidin and "Camp Ground Zero" in Alabama, where they found mannequins, buses, and even police cars that had been used for target practice. Marion, Alabama, police chief Tony Buford said that "it was rumored that the camp here was used as a training site for possible people [sic] that were sent here to do bodily harm to Americans."[7]

Enrollees in the Ultimate Jihad Challenge at Camp Ground Zero would no doubt have agreed with the Saudi sheikh Nasser Muhammad Al-Ahmad, who preached a sermon on jihad in 2000 at the Al-Nour mosque in Al-Khobar, Saudi Arabia. Speaking of Jerusalem, sheikh Nasser declared, "There is no solution to this problem, and to any problem to which the infidel enemy is party, except by waving the banner of Jihad....The sites holy to Muslims will be regained only by Jihad for the sake of Allah....When true Islamic Jihad is declared, the balance of power will shift."

The sheikh rejoiced that the West perceived jihad as a threat. "What frightens the West more than anything else is the word 'Jihad,' because they understand what it means."[8] A sweatshirt spotted among Muslim radicals at pro-Iraq rallies in the Middle East in spring 2003 bore a similar legend: "JIHAD is the language they understand!"

Sheikh Nasser and the sweatshirt manufacturers could be certain that the West understood what they meant by jihad, because their view of the term has ample support in Islamic theology, tradition, and history. Theirs isn't the only Muslim understanding of jihad, but it's well enough established in Islam to enable radicals to recruit and mobilize Muslims in Egypt, Palestine, Pakistan, Turkey, Nigeria, the Philippines, Indonesia, and around the world—including Western Europe and the United States. Jihadist movements are able to gain followers around the world not by calls for political or economic justice or by twisting and abusing Islamic theology, but by preaching the old-time religion of jihad as holy war, which has always been attractive to a significant sector of Islamic populations. Samuel Huntington puts it bluntly in *The Clash of Civilizations*: "Some Westerners, including President Clinton, have argued that the West does not have problems with Islam but only with violent Islamic extremists. Fourteen hundred years of history demonstrate otherwise."[9] Jihad constitutes an ongoing and global threat to the

West—a threat that, as Huntington points out, key Western analysts and policymakers persistently refuse to face on its own terms.

That is what I report about in this book. In doing so, I give not my own conclusions but draw on Islamic sources themselves, beginning with the Qur'an and ranging through Islamic tradition and law from the earliest centuries to the present day. Whenever possible I have quoted these sources verbatim, in order to emphasize that these are not my words or mere reconstructions of what they have said, but their actual statements.

Muslim controversialists often try to silence critics who quote uncomfortable passages from Islamic sources by maintaining that they can be truly understood only in Arabic. This claim, however, is palpably absurd. Muslims around the world preach Islam and attempt to make converts in languages other than Arabic. If the Qur'an's message can be understood only in Arabic, why do they do this? Also, most Muslims in the world today are not native speakers of Arabic; the most populous Muslim country is Indonesia, hardly an Arab land. With ancient and populous Muslim communities existing outside the Arab world, from Bosnia to Iran and Pakistan to Indonesia, Muslims have always translated the Qur'an, if only for private spiritual edification. I have relied in this book on Qur'anic translations written by Muslims for Muslims—chiefly *The Meaning of the Holy Qur'an* by 'Abdullah Yusuf 'Ali and *The Meaning of the Glorious Koran* by Mohammed Marmaduke Pickthall. I shall also quote copiously from the writings of influential Muslim radicals.

There are many variants in the way Arabic names are rendered in English; I favor one system, but those I quote favor others, so I might refer to the "Qur'an" while someone I quote refers to the "Koran." I ask the reader's patience in this. Please note also that English translators of the Qur'an and other Arabic texts like to insert parenthetical words and phrases to bring out the meaning of the text. So except where I noted otherwise, the parenthetical material in quotations is in the original.

In using this material, I do not present my own findings or opinions about what Islam teaches or what jihad means. I am certainly not saying that one version of the religion is correct and another isn't. Islam has no central authority; consequently not even a Muslim can credibly claim that his understanding of the Qur'an and Islamic law is definitive. But I am pointing out that radical Islam is not as eccentric and circumscribed as many have claimed. It exists, and it is widespread. Obviously not all Muslims in the United States or around the world—indeed, not even a majority—subscribe to the Islam of modern-day terrorists. Most Muslims, like everyone else, want to live their lives in peace. But that fact doesn't change or mitigate another fact: that terrorists and militants around the world today are using the Qur'an and the teachings of Islam to recruit and motivate terrorists, making principal use of the doctrines surrounding the concept of jihad.

The issues here are too important to be relegated to politically correct silence, wishful thinking, or lies of intimidation or politeness. It is incumbent on us to look squarely at the truth.

Part One

JIHAD NOW

Chapter One

ARE WE ALREADY FIGHTING A JIHAD?

How Radical Muslims Use Jihad as a
Modern-day Rallying Cry

"You guys are coming into our countries, and you're going to rape
our women and kill our children."[1]

THIS STATEMENT WAS MADE early in the Iraq war of 2003—
but not by Saddam Hussein, Tariq Aziz, or any other Iraqi.
Rather, these are the words of Sergeant Hasan Akbar, an
American engineer from the 101st Airborne Division. Akbar was
accused of killing Captain Christopher Scott Seifert, Major Gre-
gory Stone, and wounding fifteen others in a grenade and small-
arms attack in northern Kuwait on March 22, 2003.[2]

Analysts routinely dismiss religion, particularly the Muslim religion, as a possible motivation for violence. This incident was no different. Doug McLeroy, a chaplain at Akbar's stateside base in Fort
Campbell, Kentucky, assured the world, "This is an isolated, indi-

vidual act and not an expression of faith."[3] He didn't seem to have any evidence to back this assertion beyond his own assumptions about Islam and the workings of Sergeant Akbar's mind. A Pentagon official ventured just a bit farther out of political correctness by explaining: "He's a Muslim, and it seems he was just against the war."[4] When Akbar's trial opened, his defense team did connect religion with violence, but not to explain their client's actions; instead, they focused on reports that American Muslims had faced discrimination in the military. Akbar's mother reportedly worried that he had been accused of the grenade attack in the first place because of his Islamic faith.[5]

It's reasonable to assume that Akbar might have had misgivings about the war in Iraq, and not solely because of fears of discrimination. He was probably aware of the verse in the Qur'an that forbids a Muslim from fighting against his fellow Muslims: "It is not for a believer to kill a believer unless (it be) by mistake" (Sura 4:92). A well-attested Muslim tradition quotes Muhammad: "He who pointed a weapon towards his brother the angels invoke curse upon him even if he is his real brother so long as he does not abandon it (the pointing of weapon towards one's brother Muslim)."[6]

Did Sergeant Akbar decide that it was his religious responsibility to switch sides? After all, he did reportedly shout out, "You guys are coming into *our* countries . . ." Who is "our"? He is not an Iraqi, and in any case he referred to "countries" in the plural. His family charged that he was a victim of racism, but Iraq isn't populated by blacks, so he couldn't have meant "countries with a majority (or even significant) black population."[7] No, however much Doug McLeroy or anyone else might want to believe that Akbar's attack stemmed from his anger at racism or discrimination or his misgivings about the war, certainly Akbar meant "our *Muslim* countries," and was repositioning himself not as a warrior of the United States, but as a well-known and celebrated figure of Islamic history and culture: a *mujahid*, a warrior of jihad.

What jihad means

Jihad is a central duty of every Muslim. Modern Muslim theologians have spoken of many things as jihads: defending the faith from critics, supporting its growth and defense financially, even migrating to non-Muslim lands for the purpose of spreading Islam. But in Islamic history and doctrine violent jihad is founded on numerous verses of the Qur'an—most notably, one known in Islamic theology as the "Verse of the Sword": "Then, when the sacred months have passed, slay the idolaters wherever ye find them, and take them (captive), and besiege them, and prepare for them each ambush. But if they repent and establish worship and pay the poor-due, then leave their way free. Lo! Allah is forgiving, merciful" (Sura 9:5). Establishing "regular worship" and paying the "poor-due" (*zakat*) means essentially that the "idolaters" will become Muslim, as these are two of the central obligations of every Muslim.

Such verses are not taken "out of context" to justify armed jihad; that is how they have been understood by Muslims from the beginning of Islam. *Sahih Bukhari*, which Muslims regard as the most trustworthy of all the many collections of traditions ascribed to Muhammad, records this statement of the Prophet: "Allah assigns for a person who participates in (holy battles) in Allah's Cause and nothing causes him to do so except belief in Allah and in His Messengers, that he will be recompensed by Allah either with a reward, or booty (if he survives) or will be admitted to Paradise (if he is killed in the battle as a martyr)." Muhammad emphasizes the value of this military jihad in the strongest possible terms: "Had I not found it difficult for my followers, then I would not remain behind any *Sariya* (an army-unit) going for *Jihad* and I would have loved to be martyred in Allah's cause and then made alive, and then martyred and then made alive, and then again martyred in His Cause."[8]

One classic manual of Islamic sacred law is quite specific and detailed about the meaning of jihad. It defines the "greater jihad" as "spiritual warfare against the lower self" and then devotes eleven pages to various aspects of the "lesser jihad" and its aftermath. It defines this jihad as "war against non-Muslims," noting that the word itself "is etymologically derived from the word *mujahada*, signifying warfare to establish the religion."[9]

This manual stipulates that "the caliph makes war upon Jews, Christians, and Zoroastrians... until they become Muslim or pay the non-Muslim poll tax." It adds a comment by Sheikh Nuh 'Ali Salman, a Jordanian expert on Islamic jurisprudence: the caliph wages this war only "provided that he has first invited [Jews, Christians, and Zoroastrians] to enter Islam in faith and practice, and if they will not, then invited them to enter the social *order* of Islam by paying the non-Muslim poll tax (jizya)...while remaining in their ancestral religions."[10] The caliph was the successor of Muhammad as the leader of the Muslim community; the caliphate was abolished by the secular Turkish government in 1924. But the manual also states that in the absence of a caliph, Muslims must still wage jihad.[11]

The requirement that non-Muslims first be "invited" to enter Islam and then warred against until they either convert or pay the *jizya*, a special tax on non-Muslims, is founded upon the Qur'an: "Fight those who believe not in Allah nor the Last Day, nor hold that forbidden which hath been forbidden by Allah and His Messenger, nor acknowledge the religion of Truth, (even if they are) of the People of the Book, until they pay the Jizya with willing submission, and feel themselves subdued." (Sura 9:29)

This verse has been used in Islamic history and jurisprudence to establish three choices for non-Muslims that Muslims are facing in jihad: conversion to Islam, submission under Islamic rule (which involves a carefully delineated second-class status centered around but by no means limited to the jizya, the tax on non-Muslims), or death. The goal of jihad is thus the incorporation of non-Muslims into Muslim society, either by conversion or submission. The laws that consider non-Muslims *dhimmis*, protected people, and enforce their submission to Muslims are thus inextricably bound up with the concept of jihad.

Dhimmitude is a direct challenge to the idea that all men are created equal and are endowed by their Creator with certain unalienable rights. Non-Muslims in the *dhimmi* system of Islamic law are not given the choice or the opportunity to live in Islamic society as equals of Muslims. While Jews, Christians, and other non-Muslims are allowed to practice their religions, they must do so under severely restrictive conditions that remind them of their second-class status at every turn.

The Qur'an contains numerous exhortations to fight; virtually every major collection of the traditions of Muhammad (Hadith) contains an extensive section on jihad. Muhammad himself expands upon the three choices of Sura 9:29 in a tradition found in one of the collections considered most reliable by Muslims: *Sahih Muslim*. It depicts the Prophet of Islam appointing generals and exhorting his troops:

> It has been reported from Sulaiman b. Buraid through his father that when the Messenger of Allah appointed anyone as leader of an army or detachment he would especially exhort him to fear Allah and to be good to the Muslims who were with him. He would say: Fight in the name of Allah and in the way of Allah. Fight against those who disbelieve in Allah. Make a holy war; do

not embezzle the spoils; do not break your pledge; and do not mutilate (the dead) bodies; do not kill the children. When you meet your enemies who are polytheists, invite them to three courses of action. If they respond to any one of these you also accept it and withhold yourself from doing them any harm. Invite them to (accept) Islam; if they respond to you, accept it from them and desist from fighting against them. Then invite them to migrate from their lands to the land of Muhajirs [the Muslims in Arabia] and inform them that, if they do so, they shall have all the privileges and obligations of the Muhajirs. If they refuse to migrate, tell them that they will have the status of Bedouin Muslims and will be subjected to the Commands of Allah like other Muslims, but they will not get any share from the spoils of war or *Fai'* [the proceeds from taxes and other levies on non-Muslims] except when they actually fight with the Muslims (against the disbelievers). If they refuse to accept Islam, demand from them the Jizya. If they agree to pay, accept it from them and hold off your hands. If they refuse to pay the tax, seek Allah's help and fight them.[12]

Out of all this material Muslim jurists have constructed an elaborate legal edifice that is without parallel in any other major religion: a codified, detailed mass of laws for the conduct of warfare in the name of God.

Within Sunni Islam, which comprises roughly 85 percent of Muslims around the world, there are four schools of jurisprudence: the Shafi'i, Hanafi, Hanbali, and Maliki. Most Sunnis belong to one of these schools, and most popular commentaries on the Qur'an and guides to Muslim behavior elaborate the perspectives of each. There is actually not much significant difference between them; they agree on about 75 percent of all questions on Islamic law, including the broad outlines of the doctrine of jihad.

The legal manual quoted above is a product of the Shafi'i school. A Hanafi manual of Islamic law repeats the same injunctions. It insists that people must be called to embrace Islam before being fought, "because the Prophet so instructed his commanders, directing them to call the infidels to the faith." It emphasizes that jihad must not be waged for economic gain, but solely for religious reasons: from the call to Islam "the people will hence perceive that they are attacked for the sake of religion, and not for the sake of taking their property, or making slaves of their children, and on this consideration it is possible that they may be induced to agree to the call, in order to save themselves from the troubles of war."

However, "if the infidels, upon receiving the call, neither consent to it nor agree to pay capitation tax [jizya], it is then incumbent on the Muslims to call upon God for assistance, and to make war upon them, because God is the assistant of those who serve Him, and the destroyer of His enemies, the infidels, and it is necessary to implore His aid upon every occasion; the Prophet, moreover, commands us so to do."[13]

Ibn Khaldun (1332–1406), a pioneering historian and philosopher, was also a Maliki legal theorist. In his renowned *Muqaddimah*, the first work of Islamic historical theory, he notes that "in the Muslim community, the holy war is a religious duty, because of the universalism of the Muslim mission and (the obligation to) convert everybody to Islam either by persuasion or by force." In Islam, the person in charge of religious affairs is concerned with "power politics," because Islam is "under obligation to gain power over other nations."[14]

The great medieval theorist of what is now known as radical or fundamentalist Islam, Ibn Taymiyya (Taqi al-Din Ahmad Ibn Taymiyya, 1263–1328), was a Hanbali jurist. He directed that "since lawful warfare is essentially jihad and since its aim is that the religion is God's entirely and God's word is uppermost, therefore according to all Muslims, those who stand in the way of this aim must be fought."[15]

Violent jihad is a constant of Islamic history. Calls for jihad went out in the seventh century against the Christians of Egypt and Syria and the other areas of what is now known as the Muslim world. Such calls sounded innumerable times against the Christians of Europe until 1683.

After that, although jihads became less common (particularly in Europe), at no point did Islamic theology evolve beyond the legal manuals and medieval theorists just quoted. Jihad remained part of Islamic thought and practice, but as the Islamic world went into economic and cultural decline, so did jihad. Jihad is not a suicide pact; those who fight must have some reasonable chance of success, and such success became less assured as the West gained military predominance.

Still, Indian Muslims declared jihad against their colonial occupiers, and the Ottomans did so against their enemies in Europe as late as 1914. Turkish Muslims proclaimed jihad against the secular state that was ultimately established by Kemal Ataturk. Yasir Arafat and Hamas have both called for jihad against Israel, just as Saddam Hussein and Osama bin Laden declared jihad against the United States.

Muslims received these latest calls with varying degrees of enthusiasm. When a call to jihad is self-serving and comes from a less-than-solid Muslim like Saddam, it is naturally met with skepticism.

But the simple fact that jihad remains a vital part of Islamic theology is insufficiently appreciated in the West. In stark contrast to the apologies for the Crusades issued by the Pope and various Protestant groups, no major Muslim group has ever repudiated the doctrines of armed jihad. The theology of jihad, with all its assumptions about unbelievers' lack of human rights and dignity, is available today as a justification for anyone with the will and the means to bring it to life.

The idea that non-Muslims must be fought, and that the ideal state of peaceful coexistence between Muslims and non-Muslims is predicated upon the subjugation of non-Muslims, affects the overall prospects for peaceful coexistence between the Muslim world and non-Muslims. Can non-Muslims ever be full citizens in states that obey Islamic law (the Sharia), either in whole or in part? They are not so today in large part and on account of the doctrines of jihad and the Qur'anic injunction to make non-Muslims "feel themselves subdued" (Sura 9:29), and because of the complex of laws and institutions that are founded upon these teachings.

When modern Muslims like Jaffar Umar Thalib and Osama bin Laden declare jihad, Muslims take them seriously, even if they don't always act upon the call. For these men not only bill themselves as mujahedin, warriors of jihad; they are widely seen as just that. In a 2002 interview with Qatar's celebrated TV network, Al-Jazeera, Saudi Sheikh Mohsin Al-'Awaji, former imam of the Great Mosque at King Saud University in Riyadh, criticized Osama for (among other things) targeting "innocent people, and I refer to the innocents on the face of the entire earth, of every religion and color, and in every region." Nevertheless, he still found himself able to praise the mastermind of the September 11 attacks as "a man of honor, a man who abstains [from the pleasures] of this world, a brave man, and a man who believes in his principles and makes sacrifices [for them].... The Saudi people love every jihad warrior, every fighter, and every man of honor, whether in Afghanistan, Chechnya, Kashmir, or southern Sudan."

Another sheikh, Dr. Muhammad Al-Khasif, opined, "There are dozens, even millions, who lift up their eyes to Osama bin Laden as a savior."[16]

Many of these are in the United States right now.

Extremist Islam in America

Was Sergeant Akbar one of them?

Few dare to ask this question. Obviously other Muslims served in the forces that went into Iraq, and there were no other such incidents. Most people make choices with complex motivations, such that it's impossible to predict how anyone will react in a particular situation. But the Akbar case suggests that forces that hate the United States and the West make use of Islam to further their cause, and there's no rational basis for assuming that Akbar was the only young Muslim in the United States who may have absorbed their ideas. Yet to what extent jihad is actually a motivator for young Muslims around the world and in the United States, and how many calls for jihad can be used to recruit and motivate terrorists here and abroad, is a taboo subject in these politically correct times. In the trial of Omar Abdel-Fatah Al-Shishani, who was suspected of smuggling money into the United States on behalf of al Qaeda, the defense managed to have a number of terms declared off-limits, including *al Qaeda, terrorism, terrorist groups, Osama bin Laden, Muslim*, and—of course—*jihad*. The prosecution was also forbidden to quote any verse from the Qur'an.[17]

Yet Akbar might have heard that his primary allegiance was to Islam, not to the United States, in his mosque. The Bilal Islamic Center in Los Angeles was built with a pledge of up to eight million dollars from King Fahd of Saudi Arabia and an additional $295,000 from the Saudi Islamic Development Bank for the mosque's school. The Islamic Development Bank states that it works "to foster the economic development and social progress of member countries and Muslim communities individually as well as jointly in accordance with the principles of Shari'ah, i.e., Islamic Law."[18] Presumably this would include the Sharia's full teaching about the impermissibility of a Muslim fighting another Muslim, and the necessity of jihad against non-Muslims.

According to news reports, "Bilal is just one of many black mosques funded by Saudi. Most of them, including Bilal, are associated with Imam W. Deen Mohammed, head of the Chicago-based Muslim American Society, or MAS, which has been credited with helping convert more than a million U.S. blacks to Islam."[19]

W. Deen Mohammed himself has acknowledged that Saudi money comes with strings. He told the *Los Angeles Times* that "in Saudi Arabia it's the Wahabi school of thought... and they say, 'We're gonna give you our money, then we want you to... prefer our school of thought.' That's in there whether they say it or not. So there is a problem receiving gifts that seem to have no attachment, no strings attached." When asked if he himself had taken Saudi money, he replied like a nervous schoolboy caught red-handed in a bit of mischief: "Well, I don't receive any money now, but I have received some and I lost it." However, he added, "I suspected some strings were attached. I said I can't accept this kind of relationship. They were choosing my friends for me, too. The enemy of the friends who were giving me money was supposed to be my enemy, too."[20]

The Wahhabis' enemies list

The Wahhabis are generally considered one of the most extreme—and to unbelievers, dangerous—Islamic sects. They are also the majority sect in Saudi Arabia, and their teachings are dispersed around the world via mosques and schools bankrolled by the Saudis.

Who are the enemies of the Wahhabis?

Wahhabi imams routinely identify the enemies of the Muslims as "Jews and Christians."

This has been going on for years. As long ago as 1986, at the Qaaba mosque in the holy city of Medina, Sheikh Abd Al-'Aziz Qari assailed the Jews. "In ancient times, the Jews, the enemies of Allah, killed the prophets unjustly.... Afterwards they became the enemies of all humanity and they [termed] non-Jews 'gentiles,' and used all means to destroy them by starting wars among these gentiles, destroying their beliefs, and corrupting their moral values."

Preaching in a mosque in Al-Damam, Saudi Arabia, Sheikh Muhammad Saleh Al-Munajjid agreed with Sheikh Abd Al-'Aziz Qari and also expanded the enemies list. "It is impossible ever to make peace with the Jews.... The Jews are defiled creatures and satanic scum. The Jews are the helpers of Satan. The Jews are the cause of the misery of the human race, together with the infidels and the other polytheists. Satan leads them to Hell and to a miserable fate. The Jews are our enemies and hatred of them is in our hearts."

The Sheikh's prescription? Jihad. "Jihad against them," continued the Sheikh, "is our worship... Muslims must... educate their children to Jihad. This is the greatest benefit of the situation: educating the children to Jihad and to hatred of the Jews, the Christians, and the infidels; educating the children to Jihad and to revival of the embers of Jihad in their souls. This is what is needed now...."[21]

In a 1997 sermon at the Al-Salaam mosque in 'Al-Unayzah, Saudi Arabia, Sheikh Abd Al-Muhsin Al-Qadhi denounced dialogue and cooperation with Christians. "Regardless of [Christian] deviations from the path of righteousness, it is possible to see many Muslims... who know about Christianity only what the Christians claim about love, tolerance, devoting life to serving the needy, and other distorted slogans.... After all this, we still find people who promote the idea of bringing our religion and theirs closer, as if the differences were minuscule and could be eliminated by arranging all those [interreligous] conferences, whose goal is political."

Likewise, Sheikh Adnan Ahmad Siyami on May 11, 2001, at a mosque in Mecca, Islam's holiest city, said, "[Islam] believes that only Islam and the 'Camp of Kufur' [unbelief] exist, and that there is no way to reach Paradise and to be delivered from Hell except by walking in the path of our Prophet Muhammad and joining Islam. Any other way leads to Hell. . . . In light of this, my believing brethren, how can it be claimed that Judaism, Christianity, and Islam are all paths leading to Allah?!"[22]

Sheikh Adnan also denounced peaceful coexistence and called Christians "murderous wolves"—especially Pope John Paul II because of his efforts to promote harmony between Christians and Muslims. Far milder talk would get someone charged with hate speech and incitement to violence in many Western countries.

It is important to note that these sermons were preached in mosques all over Saudi Arabia, contrary to Saudi spokesman Adel al-Jubeir's contention that "a lot of these clerics are underground. A lot of these clerics issue their fatwahs, which are really their opinions, on the Internet, and that gets bandied about." Al-Jubeir is anxious to prove the Saudi government's probity in combating Islamic extremism and terror, but radical Muslims were preaching hatred and jihad in Saudi mosques at least as late as spring 2002, and quite frequently before that.[23]

Did this overheated Wahhabi invective make its way, along with all those Saudi millions, into Sergeant Akbar's mosque?

It certainly made its way into Muslim schools in the United States. Recent revelations about textbooks used in Islamic schools indicate how the same hate that is retailed in Saudi mosques is being taught to American young people. Muslim textbooks claimed that:

After telling the governor lies about Jesus and making him think that Prophet Jesus was starting a rebellion against Rome, the Jews were finally able to get an order for his execution. The Koran states that the Jews did not kill Jesus nor did they crucify him. Allah states, however, that the Jews thought they did it.

> *from "What Islam Is All About," IBTS*
> *[International Books & Tapes Supply, target*
> *readers: grades 6–8*[24]

Actually the Qur'an tells the "People of the Book," that is, not only Jews but also Christians and others, that Jesus was not crucified (Sura 4:171).

Allah revealed to Muhammed that the Jews had changed their Book, the Torah, killed their own prophets and disobeyed Allah. And the Jews did not want the Arabs to know about these shameful things.

> *from "Mercy to Mankind," IQRA [a*
> *publisher of Islamic texts], target readers:*
> *grades 5–6*

This charge is based on Qur'anic verses such as this one:

Some of those who are Jews change words from their context and say: 'We hear and disobey; hear thou as one who heareth not' and 'Listen to us!' distorting with their tongues and slandering religion. If they had said: 'We hear and we obey: hear thou, and look at us' it had been better for them, and more upright. But Allah hath cursed them for their disbelief, so they believe not, save a few.

> *Sura 4:46*

Other textbooks give more modern reasons to hate Jews:

Jews subscribe to a belief in racial superiority.... Their religion even teaches them to call down curses upon the worship places of non-Jews whenever they pass by them! They arrogantly refer to anyone who is not Jewish as 'gentiles,' equating them with sin.

from "What Islam Is All About," IBTS,
target readers: grades 3–6.

Many [Jews and Christians] lead such decadent and immoral lives that lying, alcohol, nudity, pornography, racism, foul language, premarital sex, homosexuality and everything else are accepted in their society, churches and synagogues.

from "What Islam is About," IBTS, target
readers: grades 3–6[25]

Other texts, distributed in the United States by Saudi-funded entities, including the Institute for Islamic and Arabic Sciences in America (IIASA) in Fairfax, Virginia, and the World Assembly of Muslim Youth (WAMY), in Alexandria, Virginia, echoed these sentiments. According to a text financed by the foundation of Ibrahim Ben Abdul Aziz Al-Brahim, father-in-law of King Fahd, "Judaism and Christianity are deviant religions." Consequently, a Muslim must not befriend them: "Befriending the unbelievers, through loving and cooperating with them while knowing that they are unbelievers, makes those who are their friends the same as them."

Yet another text declares that "whoever admires the infidels and polytheists is affected by them and prefers them. Thus the Muslim is forbidden to associate with idolaters, deviants and the misguided.... The unbelievers, idolators, and others like them must be hated and despised.... They cannot be supported against Muslims and must not be followed in anything.... We must stay away from them and create barriers between us and them.... [The] Qur'an forbade taking Jews and Christians as friends, and that applies to every Jew and Christian, with no consideration as to whether they are at war with Islam or not."[26]

This kind of hate appears even more often in Wahhabi materials in Saudi Arabia itself. According to a report by the Middle East Media Research Institute, "a textbook for eighth grade students explains why Jews and Christians were cursed by Allah and turned into apes and pigs. Quoting Sura Al-Maida, Verse 60, the lesson explains that Jews and Christians have sinned by accepting polytheism and therefore incurred Allah's wrath. To punish them, Allah has turned them into apes and pigs."[27]

Here the textbook was recalling the notorious passage of the Qur'an (in Sura Al-Maida, the chapter entitled "The Table") that refers to non-Muslims—principally Jews and Christians—as "apes and pigs":

> Say: 'O people of the Book! Do ye disapprove of us for no other reason than that we believe in Allah, and the revelation that hath come to us and that which came before (us), and (perhaps) that most of you are rebellious and disobedient?' Say: 'Shall I point out to you something much worse than this, (as judged) by the treatment it received from Allah? Those who incurred the curse of Allah and His wrath, those of whom some He transformed into apes and swine, those who worshipped evil; these are (many times) worse in rank, and far more astray from the even path!
> *(Sura 5:59-60)*

Saudi Wahhabi imams often favored images of Jews and Christians as apes and pigs. In his sermon in Medina, Sheikh Abd Al-'Aziz Qari explained that the conflict between Muslims on one side and Jews and Christians on the other would continue until

Judgment Day: "Two groups—the Jews and the Christians—are the main elements constituting the 'Camp of Kufur' [unbelief] and will continue to be its two foundations until Allah allows their downfall and annihilation at the end of days. . . . These two groups will continue to serve as the grindstones of the conflict and the war between belief and Kufur until eternity comes. . . . The Jews are the objects of Allah's [promised] wrath, while the Christians deviate from the path of righteousness . . . The Koran described the Jews as a nation cursed by Allah, a nation at which he was angry—some of whom he turned into apes and pigs."

Preaching in Mecca, Sheikh Mustafa Bin Sa'id Aytim also denied the very humanity of Jews and Christians: "It is no surprise that the Jews and Christians deny the Koran. What is amazing is that some ignoramuses and traitors from among the Muslims say: 'The Jews and Christians are our brothers.'...By Allah, who told you that wild animals can become human? Can wild animals give birth to anything other than wild animals?"

"We are not Americans. We are Muslims."

Interestingly, Sergeant Akbar's Muslim chaplain at Fort Campbell received his training and certification from organizations established by Saudi Wahhabis.[28] Akbar also seems to have been active in the Muslim Student Association (MSA) at the University of California at Davis.[29] Chapters of the Muslim Student Association have long been associated with radical Islam. Recently two speakers at an MSA meeting at Queensborough Community College in New York City expressed just the kind of hatred for America and transnational solidarity with their fellow Muslims that Akbar's statement about "our countries" betrays. Abu Yousuf, an American-born Muslim, called the United States' conflict with Iraq a "Christian crusade to rid the world of Islam." He also predicted, like

Sergeant Akbar, that American soldiers in Iraq would "starve, rape and murder our brothers and sisters."

"Our brothers and sisters." Again, not Americans, but Muslims. The next speaker, Muhammad Faheed, a twenty-three-year-old Muslim born in Pakistan who lived in America from the age of three, reinforced the idea that a Muslim's allegiance must be to the Muslim *umma* (the Muslim community worldwide), and not to the United States or any other nation. "We must not recognize any government authority, or any authority at all besides Allah."

In case anyone missed the implications of this, he spelled them out. "We are not Americans," he cried. "We are Muslims. [The U.S.] is going to deport and attack us! It is us versus them! Truth against falsehood! The colonizers and masters against the oppressed, and we will burn down the master's house!...The only relationship you should have with America is to topple it!"[30]

Less emotional but along the same lines was the statement of Muzammil Siddiqi, the former president of the Islamic Society of North America, who joined President Bush at the National Day of Prayer after the September 11 attacks. Said Siddiqi: "I believe that as Muslims we should participate in the [American] system to safeguard our interests and try to bring gradual change...We must not forget that Allah's rules have to be established in all lands, and all our efforts should lead to that direction."[31] Likewise, Ihsan Bagby, Associate Professor of Modern and Classical Languages at the University of Kentucky, stated in the late 1980s, "Ultimately we can never be full citizens of this country, because there is no way we can be fully committed to the institutions and ideologies of this country."[32]

Muslim children born in this country have imbibed these sentiments. Not long after September 11, 2001, *Washington Post* reporter Marc Fisher visited the Muslim Community School in Potomac, Maryland. There, "six young people, all born in this country, all American citizens, told me that no, they did not believe that Osama bin Laden was necessarily the bad guy the president says he is, and no, they did not think the United States should be attacking Afghanistan, and, no, they might not be able to serve their country if it meant taking up arms against fellow Muslims." An eighth grader said, "If I had to choose sides, I'd stay with being Muslim. Being an American means nothing to me. I'm not even proud of telling my cousins in Pakistan that I'm American." The school principal added, "Allegiance to national authority is one thing, but the one who gives us life is more entitled to that authority. This is the story of religion through all time. When national laws and values go counter to what the Creator believes, we are one hundred percent against it."[33]

A week before the grenade attack in Kuwait, a writer on a Muslim bulletin board website gave a hint of what might have motivated Sergeant Akbar. He advised American Muslim soldiers: "Learn how to make a bomb out of C4 plastic, and when your [sic] on the ship on your [way] to the middle east. . . . *BOOM* Or better yet, re-wire the missiles that are stacked on the ship and watch the 4th of July in the middle of the ocean!"

The same writer expanded on this idea in another post: "I always thought (and still think) it's a great idea to join the US ground forces for a simple reason: they're all getting shipped off to the Middle East for FREE! So, you go there, free, with US equipment and weapons, yada yada yada, then when you get there, you change sides and fight the kufar [unbelievers]! After changing your uniform of course! And while you're at it, you can sabotage some of their stuff from the inside!"[34]

This advice recalls the seditious language of Sami Al-Arian, a professor at the University of South Florida who, after years of investigations, was indicted on February 20, 2003, on federal charges of aiding the terrorist activities of Islamic Jihad—particularly by raising money for the group. Al-Arian wasn't a silent partner; he made the jihadist and Islamic character of his efforts clear as early as 1991, when he shouted at a rally, "Jihad is our path. Victory to Islam! Death to Israel! Revolution, revolution until victory!"[35] Also that year, he shouted: "Let us damn America, let us damn Israel, let us damn them and their allies until death."[36] He said these things, of course, while on American soil and enjoying the protections of American laws.

In Lackawanna, New York, on September 13, 2002, six Muslims, all American citizens, were arrested on suspicion of having acted on these ideas. In spring and summer 2001 they had traveled to Afghanistan to attend an al Qaeda training camp. There they were trained in the use of automatic weapons and a rocket-propelled-grenade launcher. Afterward they returned to the United States, where they might have been awaiting orders to carry out a terrorist attack.

Why did they go? Jihad. One of the men, Yahya Goba, explained in court that the group was recruited to go to Afghanistan by four unnamed men, two of whom "recruited the Lackawanna group to prepare for jihad," or, as prosecutor William Hochul delicately phrased it, "preparation for a possible battle against people not of the same faith." By March 2003, three of these men had plea-bargained their way out of being tried for treason, agreeing to plead guilty to charges including providing material aid to a terrorist organization.37 Another American, Earnest James Ujaama, also attended "violent jihad training camps, which were operated by al Qaeda" and was subsequently arrested and indicted.38 This Seattle native, who converted to Islam in 1997, entered a guilty plea to charges of providing material aid to the Taliban.39

Yet another group of American Muslims, which comprised Jeffrey Leon Battle, Patrice Lumumba Ford, Ahmed Ibrahim Bilal,

Muhammad Ibrahim Bilal, and October Martinique Lewis, was charged with "conspiracy to levy war against the United States." This involved trying to get to Afghanistan in order to fight with al Qaeda and the Taliban against American forces. Part of their preparations for the trip included training with shotguns, assault rifles, and semiautomatic pistols.[40] Also mentioned in the federal indictment is Habis Abdulla al Saoub, a Jordanian and a permanent resident of the United States who seems, unlike the other four, to have successfully made it into Afghanistan. His partners returned to the United States and are now in custody.

In Patrice Lumumba Ford's home, investigators found several articles downloaded from the Internet: some from the Internet journal *Taliban and Mujahideen News*, and others titled "Taliban and Jihad Against America," "Jihad Unspun," "Kurdish Jihadis," and "Every Piety: Jihad for the Cause of Allah." Jeffrey Leon Battle and October Martinique Lewis had also downloaded articles, including "Making the World Safe for Terrorism" and "Islam Ruling on Defending Muslim Land Under Attack." Meanwhile, they had stocked their bookshelves with *Jihad in Islam*, *The Qur'anic Concept of War*, and *Sacred Rage: The Wrath of Militant Islam*. Habis al Saoub had a document in Arabic entitled "A Martyr's Will," which called upon Afghanistan to "[keep] the jihad going" and quoted "the prophet Muhammad's seventh-century assertion that abandoning the cause of jihad is a disgraceful act tantamount to leaving the Islamic religion." Battle also had a copy of a book entitled *Join the Caravan*, an exhortation to jihad written by Abdullah Azzam, a friend and mentor of Osama bin Laden. We will examine this book closely later.

According to journalist John Perazzo,

Jeffrey Leon Battle spoke about the need for the Muslim community to fearlessly, single-mindedly carry on a jihad against the kaffirs (non-believers), as he called the American people. Stating that there could be absolutely no room for peace during jihad, he claimed that it was "stupid" for any Muslim to live in the United States. While his original intent, he said, had been to carry out terrorist acts against Americans living in the U.S., Mr. al Saoub had convinced him to instead join the jihad being fought against the United States in Afghanistan. Of the September 11 attacks and the recent bombings of two American embassies in Africa, Battle proudly said, "We accomplished a lot." He stated that those incidents had not only forced non-Muslims everywhere to take notice of Islam and the Koran, but had also caused many Muslims "to wake-up" and take a stand against the kaffirs. But alas, he lamented that because those attacks did not permanently destroy America's financial system, they were ultimately "not enough." Expressing his wish for the establishment of a true Islamic government, he said that while he is in the United States he considers himself an "undercover" combatant working to do damage "behind enemy lines."[41]

Perhaps the leader of their group thought of himself as another undercover agent. According to federal prosecutors, this was a Palestinian Muslim named Maher Hawash, a naturalized American citizen who worked for Intel Corporation and went by the nickname "Mike." If the charges are true, his involvement in this terrorist cell was particularly disturbing. According to the *Wall Street Journal*, he was just an ordinary guy, an average American who "had fully integrated himself into the mainstream community where he lived. In many respects he had attained the American dream. He owned his own home and was respected at microchip-maker Intel, one of the U.S.'s preeminent high-tech giants. He was exceptionally popular and known in the community for his volunteer activities."[42]

Perazzo notes that this entire group attended the Bilal Mosque in Beaverton, Oregon, during which time their commitment to Islam grew progressively more militant.

Similar to Hawash, in having appeared to have successfully united the obligations of being both a Muslim and an American, was Sami Omar al-Hussayen, a Saudi native who was studying computer science at the University of Idaho at Moscow. As the head of the university's chapter of the Muslim Students Association, al-Hussayen declared after the September 11 attacks that Moscow's Muslims "condemn in the strongest terms possible what are apparently vicious acts of terrorism against innocent citizens."[43] But now the FBI charges that such statements were just a cover for his terrorist activities; in February 2003 he was arrested and charged with visa fraud, as well as with helping to "establish Web sites that promoted violence against the United States."[44]

Likewise, the Global Relief Foundation, a Chicago-area Muslim charity, issued a statement on December 11, 2001, urging Americans "to remember the tragedy as we unite against terrorism and disaster worldwide.... To forget the tragedy would be acquiescing to terror, and to the misery it brings. We will join hands and fight against terror wherever it strikes."[45] Global Relief sued the U.S. government and several American news organizations, including the *New York Times*, for publishing stories alleging that it had ties to terrorism.[46] In October 2002, however, the Foundation was placed on the United Nations list of "organizations subject to sanctions," and its assets frozen to prevent them from going to al Qaeda and other terrorist groups.[47]

Partisans of Global Relief still insist that the organization was never anything more than a charity, and that it never funded terrorist activities. Yet if the organization was funding terrorism, at least one American Muslim is unlikely to have been surprised. An American convert to Islam, New York prison chaplain Warith Deen

Umar, asserted early in 2003 that "even Muslims who say they are against terrorism secretly admire and applaud" the September 11 terrorists.[48]

Which is more representative of the views of the majority of Muslims in America: the apparent loyalty to the United States of most of the Muslims who fought in the second Persian Gulf War, or the loyalty to Islam of Sergeant Akbar and the others discussed here? The relative absence of terrorist attacks since September 11, 2001, suggests that most American Muslims are like everyone else: they want to live quiet and peaceful lives. But no one really knows for sure how extensive Muslim radicalism is in the United States, because most people who are in a position to find out don't even dare investigate. The Council on American Islamic Relations (CAIR) and its allies have energetically tarred those who ask such questions as bigots and hatemongers. We are supposed to accept as a given that Hasan Akbar, Sami Omar al-Hussayen, Sami Al-Arian, James Ujaama, Mike Hawash, and all the rest are isolated cases, cut off from the mainstream of Islam and unrepresentative of the whole of American Muslims—and even to ask for evidence of this is to pass beyond the bounds of acceptable discourse.

Yet no matter how successful CAIR and other Muslim advocacy groups are in evading questions about the extent of Islamic radicalism in America, it is clear that Sergeant Akbar could have taken inspiration from any number of imams in America who, along with imams abroad, advocate violence in the name of Islam.

The latest jihad

This radical strain was particularly vocal at the onset of the second Gulf War. In late 2002 and early 2003, as the United States and Iraq edged ever closer to war, President George W. Bush repeatedly insisted that his conflict was not with Islam. He went to immense lengths to reassure the American Muslim community of his good will—even to the point of alienating many conservative Christians. But that didn't stop Muslims worldwide from presenting the war on Iraq as a war on Islam.

Saddam Hussein, whose credentials as a Muslim were always questionable, led this rhetorical attack, skillfully positioning his conflict with the United States as a religious war and himself as the defender of Islam.

He didn't set aside his Hitlerian personality cult ("Iraq is Saddam and Saddam is Iraq"), but he added a significant Islamic element.[49] When the American attack began, Iraqi television ran a speech in which Saddam quoted the Qur'an (Sura 22:39): "In the name of God, the merciful, the compassionate. Those who are oppressed are permitted to fight and God is capable of making them victorious. God is Greatest."[50] The Associated Press version of this speech omitted Saddam's Qur'an quotation without explanation or notice that the transcript was incomplete, but it did contain this: Saddam declared that Iraq was fighting for, among other things, "the sake of the banners of jihad and its (national) religion." Saddam also cried, "Long live jihad!"[51]

The Iraqi people, under the omnipresent threat of Saddam's security forces, fell into line. On March 18, 2003, the day before the war began, five thousand Iraqis took to the streets of Baghdad. Waving rifles in the air, they chanted, "Allahu Akbar, join the jihad!" and pledged their willingness to fight for Saddam to the death.[52]

A Muslim clergyman leveled one of the most serious charges of all, in the eyes of a pious Muslim. "These infidel sinners started their war against us in this country of Jihad. We witnessed with our own eyes Koran books being torn apart by their war fires and their abominable bombs." Another suggested that the burning Qur'ans were not just an unavoidable byproduct of burning the buildings that housed them, but were an actual American war objective. "The enemy wants to obliterate Islam, to obliterate Allah's edicts, to obliterate everything that Islam brought about.... He burned the Koran, and by that wanted to burn the faith of Muslims and their ties with Allah. This crime is no different than the rest of their crimes against Islam and Muslims."[53]

This kind of rhetoric might have been expected from Iraqi propaganda. It's clear to everyone now that Saddam was widely hated by his own people. He could have calculated that if the people of Iraq weren't inspired by cries of "Saddam Hussein is Iraq," they might still have been moved by the one common denominator shared by Sunnis, Shi'ites, Kurds, and almost everyone else in Iraq: Islam, and its theology of jihad.

International jihad

The Gulf War was seen as a jihad by Muslims not just in Iraq, but around the world. Numerous Muslim theorists placed the conflict in the context of the defensive jihad that becomes the obligation of every Muslim when an Islamic land is attacked.

Sheikh Omar Bakri Muhammad, the notorious London-based radical imam who held a rally in support of Osama bin Laden on the first anniversary of the September 11 attacks, issued a strong call in late 2002 for jihad in defense of Islam. He said that there is "ample proof from the sayings and the actions of the Messenger Muhammad (may Allah pray for Him) that non-Muslims have sanctity for their lives unless they are at war with the Muslims either determined by the Khalifah (caliph) in his foreign policy or (as in today's situation) they are violating the sanctity of Muslim land, honor or life."

In such a case, says Bakri, jihad is obligatory on all Muslims—"when the enemy enters Muslim land, such as Palestine, Chechnya, Kosova, or Kashmir." In that case, "all Muslims living within travelling distance of the aggression" must fight, with all possible support from Muslims worldwide.

Numerous important Islamic voices confirmed this interpretation. Among them was Sheikh Muhammad Sayyid Tantawi of Al-Azhar University in Cairo, Egypt. As Grand Sheikh of Al-Azhar, Tantawi is the foremost cleric in Sunni Islam; when he condemned the September 11 attacks, he was hailed by the Western media as "the highest spiritual authority for nearly a billion Sunni Muslims."[54] The *New York Times* gushed that Al-Azhar under Tantawi's direction "has sought to advise Muslims around the world that those who kill in the name of Islam are nothing more than heretics. It has sought to guide, to reassure Westerners against any clash of civilizations."[55]

But Tantawi's opinion about the clash of civilizations was different at the beginning of the new Gulf War. When it began, the Islamic Center for Research at Al-Azhar issued, with the Grand Sheikh's approval, a communiqué stating that "it is in accordance with logic and with Islamic religious law that if the enemy raids the land of the Muslims, Jihad becomes an individual's commandment, applying to every Muslim man and woman, because our Muslim nation will be subject to a new Crusader invasion targeting the land, honor, belief, and homeland."

The communiqué spoke clearly and definitely about the nature of the war as religious: "The Center for Research has studied the events... and realized that our Arab and Islamic nation, and even our religious faith, Islam, are a main target of all the military forces, who are targeting millions of people from among our nation, as well as our faith, everything sacred to us, and all the sources of wealth and power of the Arabs and the Muslims. The first manifestation of this will be the attack on Iraq, the occupation of its land, and the seizing of its oil resources."[56] Left unexplained is exactly how and why the military forces are targeting Islam itself.

Tantawi's position works from the rulings of Islamic religious law on invasions of Muslims lands; it is a careful exposition of the

Islamic theology of jihad. One manual of Islamic law that Al-Azhar certifies as conforming "to the practice and faith of the orthodox Sunni community" stipulates that "when non-Muslims invade a Muslim country or near to one...jihad is personally obligatory upon the inhabitants of that country, who must repel the non-Muslims with whatever they can."[57]

This is a venerable teaching of Islam. Ibn Taymiyya considered it an absolute.

> If the enemy wants to attack the Muslims, then repelling him becomes a duty for all those under attack and for the others in order to help them. God, He is exalted, has said: 'Yet if they ask you for help, for religion's sake, it is your duty to help them.' (K[oran] 8:72) In the same vein the Prophet has ordered Muslims to help fellow Muslims. The assistance, which is obligatory both for the regular professional army and for others, must be given, according to everybody's possibilities, either in person, by fighting on foot or on horseback, or through financial contributions, be they small or large.[58]

Calls to this responsibility have resounded throughout Muslim history. In modern times Muslims have fought colonial occupation by European powers as a jihad against unbelievers. In 1912, al-Sayyid Ahmad al-Sharif, the leader of the revivalist Muslim group the Sanusiyyah, called upon all Muslims to wage jihad against the Italian colonizers of Libya. "Abandoning jihad means leaving the Religion.... This goes for the jihad that is a collective duty and therefore *a fortiori* for the jihad that has become an individual duty because of an attack by the enemy."[59]

Likewise, the Ottoman Sultan and caliph of Islam Mehmet V issued a *fatwa* (religious ruling) calling for jihad at the outbreak of World War I. It answers yes to this question: "When it occurs that enemies attack the Islamic world, when it has been established that they seize and pillage Islamic countries and capture Moslem persons and when His Majesty the Padishah of Islam thereupon orders the jihad in the form of a general mobilization, has jihad then, according to the illustrious Koran verse: March out light and heavy [hearted], and strive with goods and persons [in the way of Allah; that will be better for you' (K[oran] 9:41)], become incumbent upon all Moslems in all parts of the world, be they young or old, on foot or mounted, to hasten to partake in the jihad with their goods and money?"[60]

For political reasons this Ottoman call for jihad met with little enthusiasm among Muslims worldwide. Many similar calls for jihad, including those issued by Saddam and Osama, have also fallen on largely deaf ears among Muslims. But since Tantawi's position was grounded in classic principles of Islamic law, it drew agreement from other Muslim leaders—including some who have never been considered "radicals" or "fundamentalists." According to Dia'a Rashwan of the Al-Ahram Center for Political and Strategic Studies in Egypt, "Now we have many calls to jihad, and those calls aren't only coming from what we usually call radicals or extremists."[61]

The Grand Mufti of Syria, Ahmad Kuftaro, whose official literature says that he is "actively striving to unite the human family" and who drew the ire of Muslim hardliners when he received Pope John Paul II at the Umayyad Mosque in Damascus on May 6, 2001, also affirmed that fighting against allied forces in Iraq was a religious duty for all Muslims.[62] Early in the war he issued a statement saying, "I call on Muslims everywhere to use all means possible to thwart the aggression, including martyr operations [that is, suicide attacks] against the belligerent American, British and Zionist invaders. . . . Resistance to the belligerent invaders is an obligation for all Muslims, starting with (those in) Iraq."[63] However, after the swift conclusion of the war in Iraq, the official Syrian government radio station broadcast these words from Sheikh Muhammad Habash in Damascus:

> Jihad began today, O brothers. But, as we said more than once and a thousand times, jihad has a thousand methods and doors. We are fighting with the great jihad, that of reason and proof.... I am not standing here on this pulpit for self-flagellation, but to announce a new jihad, the jihad of science and knowledge, the jihad of work and giving, and the jihad of culture and advancement. When you go to your university you are in jihad. When you go to your hospital as a nurse or doctor you are in jihad. When you go to your scientific center you are in jihad for the coming days. Our enemies defeated us this time by their scientific assets. We have to release our cultural energies and resurrect our past glories so that we can again become masters of the world, protecting ourselves, and our past, present, and future.[64]

As the war began, however, the call to the military form of jihad sounded from as far away as India, where the influential Imam Syed Ahmed Bukhari declared, "The war between right and wrong has begun. This is a jihad."[65]

Even in Canada, the imam of the mosque in Ottawa endorsed the call for jihad. "If I were there" in Iraq, said Imam Gamal Soleiman, "I would fight with them. I would fight the Americans with my nails and teeth." However, he parted company with bin Laden and other radicals by rejecting retaliatory attacks on American soil: "Not every American is against Arabs. So it is not open to go and kill Americans. No. The Americans who are coming to kill you, yes, you can face them to defend your country. When any Arab goes to America and makes mischief, that is totally objectionable."[66]

Hardliners, of course, endorsed jihad as well. In Pakistan, four-teen radical clerics issued a statement declaring that the Iraq con-flict was indeed a jihad. They called for the support of all Muslims and the participation of as many as were able. One of them, Mufti Mohammed Jamil Khan, explained, "We issued the statement to tell Muslims that the American war on Iraq is a religious conflict and not a political one. . . . It is up to the people to implement it. Allah will reward them if they fight in His name. Jihad is manda-tory and people should go to Iraq."[67] Shi'ite and Deobandi Muslim leaders in Pakistan noted that earlier fatwas declaring jihad on the United States were still in effect.[68]

The same sentiments were echoed in far-off Mindanao in the Philippines. Parouk Hussin, the leader of the Autonomous Region in Muslim Mindanao, agreed that the American action against Iraq was "one situation where the element of jihad [holy war] is justi-fied."[69] Habib Rizieq Shihab of Indonesia's Islamic Defenders Front (FPI) also declared jihad in Iraq, claiming that "we will send some, a number of Muslim people, going for jihad to Baghdad." However, other Indonesian Muslim leaders scoffed at this idea, saying that Saddam Hussein was not running a Muslim state and thus deserved no support from Muslims. Still, many Indonesian Muslims saw Sad-dam as "a Muslim symbol in the Middle East."[70]

By speaking of thwarting aggression and repelling invaders, all these leaders place the conflict squarely within the parameters of defensive jihad in Islamic law.

And what could be wrong with that? On the face of it, defen-sive jihad seems to be a reasonable concept. Some have compared it with the Catholic just war theory.[71] Muslim apologists in the United States, including the Council on American Islamic Rela-tions, have included in their explanations of jihad the idea that it can involve "struggle in the battlefield for self-defense (e.g., having a standing army for national defense)." Who could be against that?[72]

No one, but there are several factors that make defensive jihad less justifiable than it might first appear. Today the distinction between offensive and defensive warfare has become steadily more difficult to discern. No great feats of mental gymnastics are required to turn an offensive campaign into a defensive one, and vice versa. In his declaration of jihad against the United States and other messages, Osama bin Laden portrayed his struggle with the West as defensive; in the November 24, 2002, "Letter to the American People" that bore his name, he wrote, "Why are we fighting and opposing you? The answer is very simple: Because you attacked us and continue to attack us."[73] President George W. Bush responded to Osama's "defensive" strike at America on September 11, 2001, by sending troops first to Afghanistan and then to Iraq—both defensive actions, although they were portrayed as acts of aggression by the hostile press in the Muslim world as well as in the United States and elsewhere. And whatever their ultimate justification, they were certainly not defensive actions in the way such actions have been traditionally understood.

Similarly, Islamic law allows for preemptive strikes within the context of defensive jihad. The Muslims need not wait for the unbelievers to attack them, but need only have a reasonable certainty that they are going to attack. This distinction is based on several preemptive attacks initiated by the Prophet Muhammad himself, as we shall see.

More ominous is the insistence on framing the second Gulf War and other modern conflicts as jihads at all. Even in defense, jihad is a religious, not a political concept. As we have seen in the calls for jihad in Iraq from Egypt, Syria, and elsewhere, it transcends national boundaries and envisions by its very nature a conflict much larger than those between nations that have constituted warfare from time immemorial. Indeed, it envisions precisely a clash of civilizations, dividing mankind by creed.

According to some radical Muslim legal theorists, such a conflict would have no civilian casualties because no one would be considered a noncombatant. American forces in Afghanistan and Iraq were careful not to target civilians, even if they weren't always successful. Al-Jazeera and other Muslim news sources were quick to trumpet civilian casualties as proof of American perfidy. But Omar Bakri, for one, has no problem with warriors of jihad targeting civilians. Embassies have traditionally been considered safe harbors; Bakri, like the Iranian Muslim revolutionaries who seized the American embassy in Tehran in 1979, considers them fair game. "[F]oreign forces occupying Muslim land are legitimate targets and we are obliged to liberate Muslim land from such occupation and to co-operate with each other in the process, and can even target their embassies and military bases."

This doesn't mean that all non-Muslims would be targeted for death, as were those in the World Trade Center on September 11, 2001. They must be offered the traditional choices given to non-Muslims according to the rules of jihad established in Islamic law. In his postwar scenario, as in his considerations of the war itself, Bakri insists that "we cannot simply say that because we have no Khilafah [caliphate] we can just go ahead and kill any non-Muslim; rather, we must still fulfill their Dhimmah."[74]

That is, Muslims must present non-Muslims with the three choices of Sura 9:29 of the Qur'an: conversion, submission with second-class status under Islamic rule, or death.

International volunteers

All the calls for jihad made a difference: an unknown number of non-Iraqi Muslims made their way to Iraq—notably from Syria, Jordan, and Lebanon.[75] Some even volunteered for duty as suicide attackers. One of these men, an Egyptian named Muhammad Ridha, who on Iraqi television was billed as a "jihad fighter," explained that he had gone back to his native country after an initial stay in Iraq, but had since returned. "I returned to fight the Jihad, and left behind in Egypt four daughters and a son. . . . I came to fight [the war of] Jihad and I take an oath in front of the leader Saddam Hussein that I will die as a martyr and that I do not want to return to Egypt. I say to all the Arabs and Muslims that Jihad is our duty."

A Syrian named Abd Al-Karim Abd Al-'Azzam, who was called a "volunteer suicide fighter," declared, "I want to send a message to our Muslim brethren throughout the world. . . . Brothers, we are not defending Iraq only, but all the Muslim countries. It started in Iraq, but Syria, Lebanon, and other Muslim countries will follow. How long will we keep silent, how long will we wait? America and the Jews may decide next to bomb Mecca and Al-Medina, what are we waiting for? Are we waiting for them to enter Al-Medina?"

This man's suggestion that America had designs on other Muslim countries wasn't the only reason put forth for why non-Iraqi Muslims should fight for Saddam. Others echoed the words of Tantawi and Kuftaro about jihad as a religious obligation that transcends nationality. Another "suicide volunteer," an Algerian identified only as Abdallah, expressed this idea: "I call upon the entire Muslim nation to stand as one and defend the Muslim nation." Likewise, the Syrian Abd Al-'Aziz Mahmoud Hawash said, "We are here, and we left the wife and children in order to defend the Arab and Muslim nation. . . . We came as 'Shuhadaa' [martyrs] and we pray that Allah accepts our martyrdom for Him." Another warned that the American forces "want a crusade, but we will be the drawn swords in the hand of the Jihad fighter Saddam Hussein."

As the war broke out, anti-U.S. rallies were held all over the Muslim world in Bahrain, Egypt, Jordan, Lebanon, Sudan, Syria, the West Bank, Yemen, and elsewhere. According to news reports, in Yemen "tens of thousands of angry demonstrators marched on the U.S. embassy in Sanaa, chanting slogans against the United States, Israel, and Arab leaders as U.S. and British forces continued their advance into Iraq."

Of course there were similar antiwar demonstrations in the United States and Western Europe. But in Yemen there was a twist. Demonstrators shouted that secular and pro-Western governments in Muslim countries should "Leave office and open the door to jihad!"[76]

The idea of the mutual responsibility of all Muslims worldwide to protect the Muslim *umma* in whole and in part is so prevalent among Muslims that the government of Malaysia felt compelled in the early days of the war to issue hasty calls to its people *not* to journey to Iraq. Abdul Hamid Zainal Abidin, the Malaysian minister in charge of religious affairs, explained his stance with reference to jihad. "The concept of jihad is very wide. We don't have to go in the physical sense and fight along with the Iraqis while their country is being besieged by the United States. Both Malaysia and our Prime Minister have voiced their views against the war on the international stage and the whole world knows our stand on this matter. This is a form of jihad as well."[77]

Malaysia's Prime Minister, Mahathir Mohamad, made a more pragmatic appeal—but still made a bow to the idea of jihad. Going to Iraq, he said, was a "stupid idea. If we go to Iraq just like that, I don't see any benefit from it apart from merely venting our anger. We want to fight a holy war if we can win. If we go in just to be killed, that's not jihad. If we want to go to a war, we must have the strategy and strength."[78]

But another Syrian "suicide volunteer" seemed to think it was a good idea to go "just to be killed." He tied participation in the war in Iraq to the crown of jihad, martyrdom, and exclaimed: "Listen,

Oh Bush, and listen America...we are not the aggressors, you crossed the ocean and came here to slaughter our children and our women, and the most important thing that they came for is this religion.... We came to seek martyrdom and to raise the chant: Allah Akbar, Allah Akbar, Allah Akbar [God is great]."[79]

Muslim spokesmen in the West have sought to reassure non-Muslims by insisting that suicide bombing is forbidden by the Qur'an's words about suicide: "be not cast by your own hands to ruin" (Sura 2:195). It would indeed be reassuring if all Muslims thought this way; unfortunately, however, others have defended suicide bombing on the basis of other verses of the Qur'an: "Allah hath purchased of the believers their persons and their goods; for theirs (in return) is the garden (of Paradise): they fight in His cause, and slay and are slain: a promise binding on Him in truth" (Sura 9:111). They have pointed out that this is the only guarantee of Paradise given anywhere in the Qur'an: to those who "slay and are slain" in Allah's cause. The first suicide attackers of the war killed four American soldiers on March 29, 2003; other attacks followed.[80]

In portraying himself as the leader of a jihad against the United States, Saddam Hussein proved himself to have been just as cynical as Josef Goebbels, but also just as canny. Declaring his war a jihad could cost him nothing and would bring him only benefits. It would deflect attention away from the real causes of the war, at least in the Muslim world; gain him support (however grudging) among his political opponents; make fighting in the war seem to be a religious obligation for a great majority of his people; and give his actions an overlay of theological justification and theological nuance.

It also placed the second Gulf War within a larger conflict, one that was already raging worldwide when the war began.

How they do it

Terrorists and radicals don't just declare their conflicts jihads and expect Muslims to show up. On the contrary, they make sophisticated use of the Qur'an and other Islamic sources in order to identify their cause with concepts of jihad that Muslims worldwide accept as elements of their faith.

How they do this is instructive: the closer their expositions of jihad jibe with traditional understandings of it in the Muslim world, the more likely they are to gain adherents. One extraordinarily revealing example of how Muslim radicals use the rhetoric of jihad to give a theological cast and religious motivation to present-day political conflicts came in Baghdad's Mother of All Battles mosque on November 8, 2002. Even though the preacher, Sheikh Bakr Abed Al-Razzaq Al-Samaraai, was principally interested in solidifying support for Saddam on the brink of the new conflict with the United States, the arguments he used have a wider resonance—indeed, they are similar to arguments made by other jihadis around the world:

> Brothers, today more than ever before, we need the grace of Jihad of the soul . . . particularly in this difficult hour in which the Islamic nation [is] experiencing, an hour in which it faces the challenge of [forces] of disbelief of infidels, Jews, crusaders, Americans and Britons.

It may seem curious to twenty-first century Westerners to be referred to as "crusaders," but we have already seen this word used by Al-Azhar and a Syrian suicide bomber; it's a common feature of modern Muslim anti-Western rhetoric. An alternate name for Osama bin Laden's al Qaeda is the "World Islamic Front for Jihad Against Jews and Crusaders." To use the word "crusader" in this way is to evoke a host of vivid associations for the Muslim—chiefly the idea that American forces want to conquer Muslim nations and convert Muslims to Christianity; to resist them is to defend Islam. Sheikh Bakr expands on this idea in the same sermon:

[The opponents of Iraq] challenge Allah, His Book, His Prophet, they challenge you the believers. They believe that their castles will protect them from Allah. They think that with their bombs, planes, missiles and advanced [weapons] they will scare us. By Allah, no!!! You [the West] are the real terrorists. We will scare you with the help of Allah.

In this the Sheikh's words would probably have recalled in his hearers, well-versed as they were in the Muslim holy book, this passage from the Qur'an: "Remember thy Lord inspired the angels (with the message): 'I am with you: give firmness to the believers. I will instill terror into the hearts of the unbelievers: smite ye above their necks and smite all their finger-tips off them'" (Sura 8:12). Saddam himself alluded to this verse in a later address, promising that "Iraq will strike the necks" of their opponents and reminding his people that "You are ordered by Allah . . . hit them above the necks and cut (off) all the heads."[81] The Sheikh made other references to the Qur'an in his sermon:

We stand strong; Allah will not allow the infidels to overcome the believers. Who are you, Oh foreigners. Who are you, Oh descendants of pigs and apes, to scare Muhammad, who is supported by Allah, as well as by Gabriel and the [other] Angels?

Referring to Jews and Christians as "apes and swine" on the basis of Sura 5:59-60 has become commonplace among radical Muslims. We have already seen several examples of this usage, and there are many more. On an Egyptian TV show for Muslim women, the hostess coaxed a three-and-a-half-year-old girl to call Jews "apes and pigs." The hostess responded: "Who said they are so?" The girl dutifully replied: "Our God." Where? "In the Koran."[82] Sheikh Tantawi of Al-Azhar also said that Jews were "the enemies of Allah, descendants of apes and pigs."[83] While Jews are "descendants of apes and pigs," Muslims have a more exalted lineage. Sheikh Bakr identified it in his sermon at Mother of All Battles mosque: "Who are you, anyway, Bush [you] little dwarf to threaten Muhammad and his descendants!!??" He went on:

> Jihad, Jihad, Jihad, Jihad. Oh nation of the Koran, the nation of Muhammad, Oh Muslims: Jihad for the cause of Allah, and for defending Muhammad's holiness [sic]. Whoever does not defend Muhammad and the Koran, will not smell the aroma of paradise forever.... Today, after the capture of Jerusalem, and after the infidels defiled the Arabian Peninsula and are threatening Arabs and Muslims, the holy places, and especially Iraq—Jihad has become an obligation of every individual Muslim [Fardh 'Ayn]. Anyone who does not comply, will find himself lost in [hell], side by side with Haman, Pharaoh and their soldiers.

Note that he agrees with Al-Azhar's Tantawi that present circumstances make jihad "an obligation of every individual Muslim." The Arabic *fard ayn* is a term of the theology of jihad; it refers to a religious obligation that falls upon every Muslim in the world as an individual—in this case, the obligation to defend the Muslim *umma* when it is attacked. *Fard ayn* is a step up from *fard kifaya*: an obligation that, if taken up by some Muslims, is not incumbent upon the others.

Sheikh Bakr didn't hesitate to theologize the present situation, calling the Iraqi people "warriors of Jihad" and "Allah's chosen," contrasting them with Bush, Ariel Sharon, and the British, the "enemies of Allah." As he drew his sermon to a close, he framed the conflict in the most explicitly theological terms: "Oh Allah, raise the banner of monotheism, raise the slogan of monotheism." He sounded the historic war-cry of jihad: "'Allah Akbar' [God is great] to the criminals; 'Allah Akbar' to America, 'Allah Akbar' to Britain.... Oh Allah do not let the Jews or the crusaders overcome the Muslims.... Allah, help the Jihad warriors everywhere.... Oh Allah, for Thee we fight, we kill and are killed.... Our dead for the cause of Allah are Shuhada [martyrs] in paradise, while their dead are in hell."

With the cause being the defense of monotheism, Sheikh Bakr presented Saddam as the chief monotheist. "Allah, support the leader of the monotheists, the President, the Jihad warrior in the victorious—with the help of Allah—Saddam Hussein.... [Allah] hold his hand towards a crushing victory, that will realize the Muslims' might; Oh Allah, protect him on his left and his right, from above and below, from behind him and at his front."

Was all this just one man's opinion? The Sheikh himself thought otherwise, challenging his listeners. "These are not just words of a sermon delivered from the pulpit of a mosque with enthusiasm, they are religious law. Ask the jurisprudents, if you don't know that."[84]

Other jihads

Sheikh Bakr wasn't indulging in empty bravado. He knew he was on firm ground, working from traditional ideas of jihad that respected *ulama*—councils of Muslim theologians around the world—would endorse.

But even though Saddam's Iraq collapsed quickly once American forces entered the country, despite the presence of mujahedin from all over the Muslim world, jihad is still a force to be reckoned with. For it was always more than just a convenient tool for Saddam or the anachronistic preoccupation of a few fanatics and kooks. Evidence of that comes from the fact that jihad is today an international phenomenon. Besides Saddam Hussein and Osama bin Laden, who declared jihad against the United States in 1998, and Yasir Arafat and Hamas, who have declared jihad against Israel again and again, other terrorist groups around the world have used jihad rhetoric freely. And they continue to do so.

⊠ **Algeria:** Mustafa Bouyali's Algerian Islamic Movement waged jihad to establish an Islamic state ordered according to Islamic law. Bouyali was assassinated in 1987, but not before his cause attracted numerous jihad fighters who were veterans of the anti-Soviet campaign in Afghanistan in the early 1980s. The Islamic Salvation Front (FIS), which was also dedicated to establishing the Sharia in Algeria, made such gains that in 1992 it won a national election and was poised to take power but was headed off by the sitting government. After that the situation degenerated into a civil war that killed over 100,000 people by 1999, as Muslim radicals terrorized the populace in the name of jihad.[85]

⊠ **Ambon:** This Indonesian city was a key base of operations for the now-disbanded Laskar Jihad, which killed as many as 10,000 Christians during three years of bloody sectarian strife.[86] Laskar Jihad's leader, Jaffar Umar Thalib, issued numerous belligerent statements that made it abundantly clear that he regarded his struggle as a religious war.

⊠ **Bosnia:** Veteran jihadis from Afghanistan did their best to turn the bloody ethnic conflict in the Balkans into a jihad beginning in the 1980s. The flamboyant commander Abu Abdel Aziz, his two-foot-long beard dyed with henna after the example of the Prophet

Muhammad, declared that the Bosnian war "confirmed the saying of the Prophet, peace and blessings be upon him, 'Verily, the jihad will endure until the Day of Judgment.' A new jihad was beginning in Bosnia; we went there, and we joined the battle, according to God's will."[87]

In a 1994 interview for a Muslim newspaper in the United States, Aziz firmly rejected the prevailing view that jihad talk is just a cover for political motivations: "As to your question about the characteristics needed for someone to be a Mujahid [warrior of jihad], I say: Belief in Allah, praised be He [comes first]. He should be in our sight, heart and mind. We have to make Jihad to make His word supreme, not for a nationalistic cause, a tribal cause, a group feeling, or any other cause. This matter is of great importance in this era, especially since many groups fight and want to see to it that their fighting is Jihad and their dead ones are martyrs. We have to investigate this matter and see under what banner one fights."[88]

⚔ **Chechnya:** Muslim Chechens have been waging jihad against the Russians for over two centuries.[89] As long ago as the 1780s, a convert to Islam from Catholicism who called himself Sheikh Mansour led a jihad against the Russians in Chechnya on behalf of the Ottoman Sultan. Later, Ghazi Mullah, a disciple of the Naqshbandi Sufi Mullah Muhammad Yaraghi, proclaimed a jihad against the Russians and attempted to institute the Sharia in Chechnya. Ghazi's Sufi ties—and the Sufi army he raised—are interesting in that present-day Westerners generally regard Muslim Sufis as peaceful; this may be true, but it would be hasty to assume that they have all rejected the Islamic doctrines of jihad. His disciple, the Imam Shamyl, actually presided over what Chechens still remember as the "Time of Sharia in the Caucasus." In the 1990s,

Chechen struggles for independence took on a decidedly Islamic cast. With material and religious aid from Wahhabi Saudi Arabia, a disciple of Osama bin Laden named Omar Ibn al Khattab has positioned the Chechen independence fight as part of the global jihad.[90]

⊠ **Egypt:** The land of the pharaohs is also the birthplace of modern-day Islamic extremism, as we shall see in detail later. In 1981, members of a group called Islamic Jihad, an offshoot of the pioneering twentieth century radical Islamic group, the Muslim Brotherhood, assassinated President Anwar Sadat. In 1997, members of another group, Jihad Talaat al-Fath ("Jihad of the Vanguard of Conquest") were linked to the brutal murder of fifty-eight foreign tourists at the Temple of Queen Hatshepsut in the city of Luxor.[91]

⊠ **Kashmir:** Syed Salahuddin, the leader of the Kashmir Islamic Movement, has declared that the Indian government has "offered millions of Rupees to the youth to distract them from the course of Jihad. However, the Kashmiri people are determined to strive despite their captivity and regardless of the price, to liberate Kashmir from the hands of the Hindus, and will not accept less than this."[92] Maulana Fazal-ur Rehman of Pakistan's Jamiat-e-Islami, or Muslim Party, has declared his support for this jihad. Mahmood Ghazi, Pakistan's Minister for Religious Affairs, stated that the struggle of Muslims against Hindus in Kashmir was a jihad, and that it was "in accordance with the teachings of the prophet Mohammed."[93] Kashmir was wracked by violence in the spring of 2003, including several suicide attacks.[94] These attacks belied the widespread portrayal of the Palestine-based suicide bombing, mainly targeting Israelis, as the only resort of a people bereft of arms and support, rather than as a manifestation of Islamic radicalism. In Kashmir, militants have access to arms from many sources, including those that flowed into Afghanistan during that country's struggle against the Soviets, yet suicide attacks continue.

🔳 **Mindanao:** Imam Ustadz Salamat Hashim, leader of the Moro Islamic Liberation Front (MILF), issued a call through the Muslim news magazine *Crescent International* to the international Muslim community: "We would like to remind the Ummah of the promise of Almighty Allah and Prophet Muhammad, peace be upon him, that Islam will prevail and that the Islamic Ummah will have to assume the responsibility for leading and guiding humanity to the right path, whether the world likes it or not. . . . However, this promise of the Creator of the Universe and His Messenger, peace be upon him, can be realized only after an intense and long jihad in the Way of Allah which carries with it much sacrifice, suffering and adversity on the part of the Ummah. Your brothers and sisters in the Bangsamoro homeland are waging jihad in the Way of Allah against an oppressive and tyrannical kafir [unbelieving] government."[95]

🔳 **Sudan:** With material help from France, the Muslim regime in Khartoum continues to wage a bloody jihad against the Christians in the southern part of the country. According to U.S. Secretary of State Colin Powell, there is "no greater tragedy on the face of the earth than the tragedy that is unfolding in the Sudan." So far it has claimed the lives of two million Sudanese Christians and displaced five million more.[96] Countless Christians have been kidnapped and enslaved, and even forcibly recruited by the government to fight this jihad. According to International Christian Concern, "Sam [his real name is not given for security reasons], who is seventeen years old, has been discovered by the government of Sudan jihad recruiters. He was informed that he must report to the Jihad Center, where he will be forced to undergo Islamic jihad training, after which he would be made to serve in the all-Muslim military as a Jihad warrior. Most likely Sam will then be sent to the front lines to fight against his own Christian people in the south."[97] In spring 2003, radical Muslims burned a Christian pastor and his family to death while carrying out an unprovoked massacre of fifty-nine villagers.[98]

☒ **The United States:** Steven Emerson has done admirable work uncovering the activities of American Muslim terrorist groups in his book *American Jihad*. Recent events have confirmed his reliability: Sami Al-Arian, whose terrorist ties are exposed in *American Jihad*, was finally indicted by the Justice Department in February 2003. The indictment indicated that he used an Islamic religious center as one base of his operations.[99]

Al-Arian was not alone among American Muslims in aiding Palestinian terrorism. A Pakistani immigrant named M. Yaqub Mirza, owner of several businesses in northern Virginia, has come under suspicion of "funding the Palestinian Islamic Jihad, which targets Israeli civilians with suicide bombers. U.S. officials privately say Mr. Mirza and his associates also have connections to al Qaeda and to other entities officially listed by the U.S. as sponsors of terrorism."[100]

The al Qaeda cell in a mosque in Lackawanna, New York, and the money for al Qaeda that flowed from the al-Farooq mosque in Brooklyn, New York, during the 1990s are just two of the many other recent indications that jihad is alive and well in America.[101] Yet another indication of this came from the arrest of five Muslims in Michigan: Karim Koubriti, Ahmed Hannan, Youssef Hmimssa, Abdella Lnu, and Farouk Ali-Haimoud. On August 28, 2002, they were charged in federal court with providing material support to terrorists in support of an "international holy war, or *global jihad*."[102]

On December 23, 2002, a Qatari national named Ali Saleh Kahlah Al-Marri, who had studied in the U.S., was charged with lying to the FBI about his connections to a man who helped pay for the September 11 terrorist attacks. According to an affidavit sworn by FBI Special Agent Nicholas A. Zambeck, Al-Marri had on his computer "audio files containing Arabic lectures by Usama bin Laden and his associates, concerning, among other things, the importance of jihad... and that clerics who claim that Islam is a religion of peace should be disregarded."[103]

Rabih Haddad, a Muslim leader in Ann Arbor, Michigan, who was charged with also helping to fund terrorism, was questioned in court about "newsletters published by his charitable organization that talked of 'martyrdom through jihad.'" Haddad countered that jihad "can refer to doing good or a struggle for good, and that doing charity work was an example of that."[104] Haddad is right: jihad has many meanings, which we will examine in later chapters. But it's hard to see how "martyrdom through jihad" could refer to anything but the taking-up of arms. How exactly does one attain martyrdom through feeding the poor?

A more likely explanation of jihad in this context came from two other Muslims, Imran Mandhai and Shueyb Mossa Jokhan. Both pled guilty to conspiring "to attack targets in South Florida for a 'jihad' mission, in which they planned to bomb electrical power stations and a National Guard Armory. These attacks were then to be followed by a list of demands to be placed on the United States government and other governments around the world. The defendants also sought to acquire AK-47 type assault weapons for their jihad training and operations and sought to obtain the release from custody of an individual described as a 'mujahedin' fighter committed to jihad."[105]

Meanwhile, according to Democratic senator Robert Graham of Florida, former chairman of the Senate Intelligence Committee, the Lebanese terrorist group Hezbollah (the Party of Allah), which receives as much as $100 million each year from the Islamic Republic of Iran, "has a significant presence of its trained operatives inside the United States waiting for the call to action.... They are a violent terrorist group. And they have demonstrated throughout their now twenty-five-year history a hatred of the United States and a willingness to kill our people.... There are a number of lessons we should learn from September 11. One of those lessons is that these terrorist groups tend to do what they say they're going to do. If they define the United States as being Satanic—and that therefore they want to kill us—they will find ways to carry out that objective."

Graham asserts that Hezbollah has a core membership in the United States now, and that "in recent years they have been infiltrating into this core in the United States people who have gone through their training camps and have the skills of terrorist activity."[106]

These jihad organizations and activities, operating on four continents and involving thousands of people in their bloody work, are only a fraction of the actual number of groups around the world today that are committing violence in the name of jihad. Most notorious are the Palestinian terrorist groups Hamas and Islamic Jihad, as well as Hezbollah.

The sheer diffusion of the idea of jihad in modern conflicts around the globe reveals as hollow, misleading, and inadequate the blithe dismissals of jihad by American Muslim advocacy groups and scholars as a "spiritual struggle." Jihad has meant many things throughout Islamic history. Its root meaning is struggle, and broadly it refers to the efforts of the believer to conform his life to the will of Allah. Islamic theology allows for a spiritual element of jihad, but also for a martial element. The downplaying of the latter in favor of the former in Muslim apologetic literature today is convincing only to those who haven't studied the issue—Muslims included. Mujahedin worldwide are not reading the Council on American Islamic Relations's (CAIR) fact sheets on Islam and laying down their arms. In fact, there is no indication that groups that position themselves as adhering to moderate Islam, notably CAIR, are making any effort at all within the Muslim community in the United States or abroad to counter extremist understandings of jihad. The London radical Muslim Omar Bakri Muhammad dismisses contemptuously the idea that "Jihad refers to the personal efforts of the individual to become 'a model citizen in whatever society one finds oneself in' "—however much such a construction might warm the heart of American professors who have characterized jihad as a struggle against racism and sexism.

Bakri summed up jihad as "the method adopted by Islam to protect land, honor and life and to save humanity from slavery to man-made regimes."[107]

All over the world today, Muslims are beginning to resist that "slavery." One of the foremost new arenas of this conflict is Europe.

Chapter Two

EUROPE: JIHAD IN THE MAKING?

◼◼◼◼◼◼◼◼◼

"I shot Fortuyn for Dutch Muslims."

The assassination of a liberal: Pim Fortuyn

THIS WAS THE STARTLING CLAIM of Volkert van der Graaf, a thirty-four-year-old non-Muslim Dutchman, as he confessed to the May 2002 murder of "far right" politician Pim Fortuyn.[1] Up until his confession, the international media had reported that van der Graaf was an "animal rights activist" who had killed Fortuyn for his opposition to animal rights.

Probably only in the post-modern, post-Christian Holland of hashish cafes and taxpaying, licensed prostitutes could a "flamboyant," openly homosexual politician like Pim Fortuyn (whose kitchen featured portraits of Marx and Lenin) be described as "far

51

right," but such is the way of the world today. Fortuyn held only one position that earned him that label: the incompatibility of traditional Islamic values with the liberal, secular societies of the West.

Fortuyn's homosexuality led him to this. "I have gay friends," he explained, "who have been beaten up by young Moroccans in Rotterdam."[2] He noted that Muslims had belittled and insulted him, saying that, as a gay man, he was "lower than a pig."[3]

Some of his other statements raised more eyebrows. He called Islam "backward" and asserted that "Christianity and Judaism have gone through the laundromat of humanism and enlightenment, but that isn't the case with Islam." He pointed out that "in Holland homosexuality is treated the same way as heterosexuality. In what Islamic country does that happen?"[4] He proposed curbs on Muslim immigration to Holland and called for the assimilation of the Muslims already in the Netherlands into the secular, multiethnic, multicultural, tolerant framework of modern Dutch society. "We need to integrate these people; they need to accept that, in Holland, gender equality and tolerance of different lifestyles is very, very important to us."[5]

His assassin charged that Fortuyn was making Dutch Muslims into "scapegoats," and that he was exploiting "the weak parts of society to score points."[6] Van der Graaf compared Fortuyn's rise to that of Adolf Hitler, and portrayed the shooting as a noble attempt to save the Netherlands from the far right.[7] He planned his crime carefully and shot Fortuyn six times, for which he received the astonishingly lenient sentence of eighteen years in prison.[8] Perhaps the prevailing sentiment in Europe that Muslims there are an oppressed minority contributed to van der Graaf's light sentencing.

For the European and American press, to characterize someone as "right wing" is to place devil's horns on his head. Yet despite van der Graaf's charge of scapegoating, Fortuyn was not manufacturing the threat he felt as a homosexual man from Holland's rapidly growing Muslim community. Several months after he was murdered, another gay politician, Paris mayor Bertrand Delanoe, was stabbed by a "devout Muslim" who "acted out of opposition to politicians and gays."[9] While Fortuyn still lived, Khalil el-Moumni, a prominent imam in Rotterdam, sparked a national controversy in Holland by calling homosexuality a "sickness" and saying, "Homosexuality does not remain restricted to the people who have this disease. If this disease spreads, everyone could become infected."[10]

Some found offensive the idea that el-Moumni's statement called into question the compatibility of Islam and secularism. Oussama Cherribi, a member of the Dutch Parliament, complained that Christians had made statements similar to el-Moumni's without causing the same firestorm. He recalled a Protestant minister who was fined 300 guilders for comparing homosexuals to thieves, and a Catholic priest who "spoke out against homosexuals in a discriminatory way" in the 1990s—yet neither aroused the public indignation that el-Moumni did.[11]

Maybe the Christians' words were considered less ominous because although the speakers opposed treating homosexuality "the same way as heterosexuality," as Fortuyn put it, they weren't advocating that homosexuals be stoned to death or otherwise physically harmed.

Pundits like to equate Islamic "fundamentalism" with the Christian variety. Critics of Protestant fundamentalists like Jerry Falwell and Pat Robertson quote Old Testament passages prescribing stoning for homosexuality, adultery, and more (Leviticus 20:10,13) without noting that in the New Testament Jesus specifically abrogates this punishment (John 7:53-8:11). Nor has any major Christian group ever tolerated such behavior in two thousand years' worth of history.

The situation in Islam is very different. This punishment still stands in Islamic law. One contemporary Sharia manual mandates stoning for "anyone who fornicates or commits sodomy... no matter whether the person is a Muslim, non-Muslim subject of the Islamic state, or someone who has left Islam."[12] The stoning of adulterers is still practiced in Saudi Arabia, was in Iran and elsewhere until recently, and finds advocates among Muslims worldwide who wish to see full implementation of Islamic law. Several notorious cases in Nigeria recently showed that far from being a medieval relic, the stoning of adulterers is very much on the minds of radical Muslims today.

It is on their minds in Europe as well, where the Sharia is a hot issue. French Muslims agitate on the grounds of pluralism and religious freedom for the right of Muslim women to wear the veil. They have met resistance from secular French officials because both sides know that this is actually only a small element of a much larger issue. Muslims commonly believe that the only legitimate basis for a society is the Sharia. Cherribi himself quotes an imam in Holland: "The Sharia does not have to adapt to the modern world because these are divine laws. People have to bend to the Sharia." Investigating the question of divorce, Cherribi interviewed twelve of the fifteen imams in Amsterdam and found that eleven held to "the most conservative position which give[s] women no rights in the matter of divorce"—in other words, to the Sharia. And defense of the Sharia includes defense of stoning. Hani Ramadan, a prominent Muslim leader in Switzerland, was dismissed from a teaching position in Geneva after publishing an article in the French journal *Le Monde* in September 2002, defending stoning as punishment for adultery.[13]

When the Rotterdam imam el-Moumni condemned homosexuality as a "disease" that could infect everyone, he was accused of hate speech under Dutch law, setting up the confrontation that

Fortuyn envisioned between multiculturalism and tolerance. How could a tolerant society survive the presence of an intolerant minority? In the el-Moumni case, tolerance won: the charges against the imam were dropped in November 2002.[14]

Yet that doesn't end the conflict. While some Muslims in the West inevitably secularize, many others not only reject the idea, but see their goal as nothing less than the establishment of Islamic states in Europe. According to the archbishop of Izmir, Turkey, Giuseppe Bernardini, in Europe "the 'dominion' has already begun." He notes that Saudi "petro-dollars" have been used "not to create work in the poor North African or Middle Eastern countries, but to build mosques and cultural centers in Christian countries with Islamic immigration, including Rome, the center of Christianity.... How can we ignore in all this a program of expansion and reconquest?"

Bernardini recounted a conversation he had with a Muslim leader who said to him: "Thanks to your democratic laws, we will invade you. Thanks to our religious laws, we will dominate you."[15]

The black flag of Islam:
Omar Bakri and Abu Hamza

Maybe Bernardini was just being alarmist. But Muslim radicals have been forthright about their intentions. In England, Sheikh Omar Bakri Muhammad boasts about exploiting the contradiction between freedom of speech and self-preservation. He openly declares his intention to "transform the West into Dar Al-Islam" and establish the Sharia on British soil. "I want to see the black flag of Islam flying over Downing Street," he has said, and his al-Muhajiroun group is dedicated to this goal.[16] That is, in fact, the name of Bakri's daughter: the Black Flag of Islam.[17]

The transformation of Britain into an Islamic state could come about by means of an "invasion [from] without;" in that case, Bakri says, "if an Islamic state arises and invades [the West] we will be its army and its soldiers from within." But if no such Islamic state arises, Bakri says that Muslims will convert the West to Islam "through ideological invasion...without war and killing."

When asked how he could say such things while enjoying the protections of British citizenship, Bakri was sanguine. "As long as my words do not become actions, they do no harm. Here, the law does not punish you for words, as long as there is no proof you have carried out actions. In such a case you are still on the margins of the law, and they cannot punish you. If they want to punish you, they must present evidence against you, otherwise their laws will be in a state of internal contradiction."

If he is punished for things he says, Bakri plans to exploit this contradiction. "We will be able to claim that the capitalist camp has failed in the face of the Islamic camp in actualizing the things in which it believes, like freedom of expression....We must prove that man-made law is a fragile law....Allah said: 'Do not obey the infidels and the hypocrites.'"[18]

Asif Mohammed Hanif, a British citizen who was Bakri's student in England, demonstrated the fragility of man-made law on April 30, 2003, in Tel Aviv. After posing as a peace activist in Israel, he killed three people in a suicide bombing attack at a bar near the American embassy.[19] Hanif's accomplice, Omar Khan Sharif (also one of Bakri's former students), failed to detonate his bomb and escaped, although his body later washed up on a Tel Aviv beach under mysterious circumstances.[20]

Bakri refused to condemn the attack. "There is no way for me to condemn the self-sacrificing operation that took place in Palestine against occupying forces." However, Iqbal Sacranie of the Muslim Council of Britain disagreed. "Let us be absolutely clear, the loss of innocent life is against the laws of humanity."[21]

Some of Sharif's neighbors in Derby wondered at what the *New York Times* described as "the radicalization of the well-educated, thoroughly Westernized Mr. Sharif, 27. Hamida Akhtar, a longtime acquaintance of Sharif, noted a change in the would-be suicide bomber. 'He used to be dressed like this,' Ms. Akhtar said, pointing to her husband, Mohammed, who was wearing a suit and tie. 'Suddenly, he was changed.' He had a new wife, too, named Tahira Tabassum, who wore a traditional Islamic head scarf."

Other Derby Muslims, however, seemed to understand Sharif's actions perfectly. A young man named Basu Hussain said, "What he's done is very good, and they won't ever find him. We should all get together and kill all the Jews." Shaban Yasin, only seventeen years old, agreed, but wasn't sure that suicide bombing was the best means to that end. "We should find out the best way to kill them, and do that." Yasin opined that if he himself became a suicide bomber, "I think my parents would be proud of me."[22]

Another British Muslim, Shakil Muhammad, said that he would be willing to follow in the footsteps of Hanif and Sharif by becoming a suicide bomber as well. "I would volunteer: more and more people will follow him. To be a martyr in our religion is a great honour. It's only a matter of time before somebody blows themselves [sic] up in this country—that will definitely happen. I'm somebody who really believes in this, but the picture is bigger than me. We are going to make a change."[23]

Others admired Hanif and Sharif without committing themselves to imitate them. "Killing people is wrong, obviously, but if he was doing it for God himself—then fair enough. You have to be pretty brave to do something like that, to hold a bomb in your hand and blow yourself up."[24]

It's not surprising that Hanif, Sharif, and these others would think this way. After all, this is what they have been taught. Abu Hamza al-Masri, the forbidding, one-eyed, hook-handed former imam of the notorious Finsbury Park mosque (which shoe bomber Richard Reid, al Qaeda conspirator Zacharias Moussaoui, and other suspected terrorists are said to have frequented), praised the September 11 terrorist attacks. "If it was done because people are desperate and their lives have been threatened, then that is a respectable cause which no one could dare to condemn. Then those people who carried out the attacks would be martyrs. Martyrdom is the highest form of jihad . . . If you do things for the cause of God, losing your life for it is the highest form of pure belief. This is in the Koran. America thinks that it comes first, but Muslims believe that a believer comes first."[25] Abu Hamza has also declared that "bin Laden is a good guy. Everyone likes him in the Muslim world, there is nothing wrong with the man and his beliefs."[26] He praised al Qaeda terrorist attacks on American embassies in Kenya and Tanzania. "If Muslims are having a war against these people, then yes, it is legitimate."

Early in 2003, Scotland Yard raided Abu Hamza's mosque on suspicion that terrorists were operating there. According to police spokesmen, the raid was linked to arrests made several weeks earlier of Muslims who were producing the poison ricin—evidently also "for the cause of God."[27]

Before he was stripped of his British citizenship, Hamza headed up an organization called Supporters of Sharia, which, like al-Muhajiroun, was dedicated to establishing Islamic rule on the sceptered isle. Like other Muslim radicals, he, too, stated that even though he was a British citizen, he was not in fact British, but Muslim. In addresses to his followers, Hamza has said: "If a kafir person (nonbeliever) goes in a Muslim country, he is like a cow. Anybody can take him. That is the Islamic law. . . . If a kafir is walking by and you catch him, he's booty. You can sell him in the market. Most of them are spies. And even if they don't do anything, if Muslims cannot take them and sell them in the market, you just kill them. It's OK."

When challenged about these and other outrageous remarks, Hamza claimed he was quoted out of context and then said, "I say the reality that's in the Muslim books anyway. Whether I say it or not, it's in the books."[28]

Other Muslims, of course, have firmly repudiated the extremism of Bakri and Abu Hamza. But the fact that Hamza can back up his assertion that the roots of his extremism are "in the books" makes for an uncertain future in increasingly Islamic Europe. For his statements are indeed founded on the rules of jihad in Islamic law. If Hamza's unbeliever caught in a Muslim country may be considered a prisoner of war, he could be treated according to the choices delineated by several of the principal schools of Sunni jurisprudence. According to the mainstream Islamic legal tradition known as the Shafi'i school, "the Imam, or his representative for the purposes of jihad, may choose the most expedient from amongst four possibilities—if they remain unbelievers: either to put them to death, or to enslave them, or to exchange them for a ransom or for other captives, or to spare them without ransom. If they surrender, they cannot be put to death, and he can only choose between one of the other three alternatives." Another traditional school of Sharia legal thought, the Maliki, agrees on three of these possibilities but denies that the Muslim can set his captives free without ransom. And a third mainstream tradition, the Hanafi, allows only the choice of death or slavery, denying both ransom and mercy.[29]

The same Islamic legal manual dictates that the caliph, the now-vacant seat of leadership in the *umma* (the Muslim community worldwide), must "make jihad against those who resist Islam after having been called to it until they submit or accept to live as a protected dhimmi-community—so that Allah's rights, may He be exalted, 'be made uppermost above all [other] religion' (Qur'an 9:33)."[30] There has been no caliph since 1924, and Muslim radicals feel his absence keenly—even in Europe. Like Bakri and Al-Muhajiroun in Britain, in Germany Shaker Assem and the Islamic Liberation Party (Hizb ut-Tahrir) work to reestablish the caliphate and institute the Sharia. Noting that Christians are allowed to practice their faith (with restrictions) under Islamic law, Assem says, "People who say there is a conflict between Shari'a and Christianity don't understand Shari'a. But people who say there is a conflict between Shari'a and Western democracy are right."[31]

Is a jihad then on the horizon in Europe? Possibly, but Islamic rule could be established in Holland and other countries of Western Europe without one. The Muslim population of Europe doubled between 1989 and 1998, and if population trends continue, Holland could have a Muslim majority by 2040 or earlier. A Muslim France could emerge by the same year. According to journalist Christopher Caldwell, the French government "now estimates its Muslim population at four to five million. Most social scientists believe this number is too low, speaking of as many as eight million Muslims in France (and twelve to twenty million in the European Union). These numbers underestimate the weight of French Islam, since the population is concentrated and—thanks to a birthrate that, while falling, remains a multiple of the native-French one—extremely young. In parts of Paris, Marseilles, Rhone-Alpes, and Strasbourg, between one-third and one-half of people in their teens and twenties are Muslim."[32] There are significant and growing Muslim populations in other Western European countries as well.

Will these increasingly influential Muslim communities ultimately accept the secular framework developed by the Christians and post-Christians of Europe, or will they adopt a more confrontational course and hold fast to their Muslim traditions?

The utter opposition of these two worlds shows vividly even in their differing ideas of what constitutes acceptable dialogue. Driven by ideas of tolerance that are based in Judeo-Christian and Enlightenment ideas of human dignity, Europeans are trying to stave off a confrontation between Muslims and non-Muslims in Europe. In a spectacular and controversial act, Pope John Paul II even kissed the Qur'an on May 14, 1999, during an audience with Muslim leaders and the Chaldean Catholic Patriarch of Babylon (Baghdad).

For this the Pope was criticized by his Catholic flock and other Christians; yet however ill-advised his kiss might have been, it shows how serious he is about having peaceful relations with Muslims. During his celebrated visit to the Umayyad mosque in Damascus, the Pope said, "It is my ardent hope that Muslim and Christian religious leaders and teachers will present our two great religious communities as communities in respectful dialogue, nevermore as communities in conflict. It is crucial for the young to be taught the ways of respect and understanding, so that they will not be led to misuse religion itself to promote or justify hatred and violence."[33]

Yet while the Pope's words reflect the general sentiments of most in the West, this generosity has not been wholeheartedly reciprocated among Muslims. Radicals in particular have taken umbrage at the very idea of rapprochement between Christians and Muslims; it offends their conviction that Islam embodies the last and greatest revelation from Allah. Accordingly, in a sermon in Mecca, the Saudi Sheikh Adnan Ahmad Siyami denounced the Pope's initiative. "Several years ago, a sinful call arose, which unfortunately garnered support from some clerics and preachers of this religion, Islam . . . [a call] for the unification of the monotheistic religions. . . . This call will lead . . . to presenting the infidels' schools of thought as correct, and to silence regarding them; to permitting conversion to Judaism and Christianity with no shame whatsoever; to the abolition of the vast difference between the Muslims and others—a difference underpinning the conflict between truth and falsehood."

He found this "sinful call" embodied in the Pope's statements in Syria. "The Pope's recent visit to Syria, to the Al-Umawi mosque is, without a doubt, another manifestation of that call. The call by [the Pope]—may Allah punish him as he deserves—to the people of the [different] religions in Syria to live in peaceful coexistence is nothing more than an audacious call for the unification of religions, in accordance with the principle of human religious harmony.... Can we expect compassion from these murderous wolves? What made the Pope go on his visit was his dissatisfaction with the robbing of the Muslims' lands; he wanted also to rob their religion, so that they lose both this world and the Hereafter."[34]

Of course, the Pope was only in a mosque in Syria at the invitation of that country's Grand Mufti, Sheikh Ahmed Kuftaro; but the opinions of the hardliner, not those of Kuftaro, are the sort that are now being disseminated worldwide by Saudi petro-dollars. These opinions find a receptive audience among Muslims in Europe and elsewhere because they are plainly in line with Islamic law, which teaches that "previous revealed religions [that is, Judaism and Christianity] were valid in their own eras, as is attested by many verses of the Holy Koran, but were abrogated by the universal message of Islam, as is equally attested to by many verses of the Koran.... [I]t is unbelief (kufr) to hold that the remnant cults now bearing the names of formerly valid religions, such as "Christianity" or "Judaism," are acceptable to Allah Most High after He has sent the final Messenger [Muhammad] to the entire world."[35]

What then will become of Christian and post-Christian Europe when its Muslim minorities become majorities?

European or Muslim?: Tariq Ramadan

The Muslims of Europe and America are caught between two worlds, and betray a marked ambivalence about which one they will ultimately choose. A crucial element of that choice involves the question of individual identity. Is a European or American Muslim primarily a European or an American, or a Muslim?

Two Americans—Muhammad Junaid and Sergeant Hasan Akbar, the American serviceman who attacked his fellow American soldiers with grenades while shouting about the threat they posed to "our countries"—highlight the difficulty of this choice. Junaid said he was an American computer programmer in New York whose mother had survived the World Trade Center attacks—whereupon Junaid traveled to Afghanistan to fight with the Taliban. Junaid's story could not be verified, and he may have fabricated every bit of it except for his presence in Afghanistan, where he was interviewed; but the one part of it that rings true was his statement that "I may hold an American passport, but I am not an American, I am a Muslim."[36]

Echoes of the same idea, that Islam transcends all nationality, and particularly nationality in a non-Muslim country, abound in the writings of numerous Muslim radicals—notably the influential Egyptian thinker Sayyid Qutb (1906–1966), a key intellectual forerunner of modern-day Muslim terrorists. Qutb revived and insisted upon the sharp division first drawn by medieval Muslim divines between the Muslim world and the world of unbelief. "There is only one place on earth," Qutb argued, "which can be called the home of Islam (Dar-ul-Islam), and it is that place where the Islamic state is established and the Shari'ah is the authority and God's limits are observed, and where all the Muslims administer the affairs of the state with mutual consultation. The rest of the world is the home of hostility (Dar-ul-Harb). A Muslim can have only two possible relations with Dar-ul-Harb: peace with a contractual agreement, or war. A country with which there is a treaty will not be considered the home of Islam."

Consequently, he argued that a Muslim cannot be in the full sense a citizen of a non-Muslim state, and that even his status as a citizen of a Muslim state is secondary to his status as a Muslim. "A Muslim has no country except that part of the earth where the Shari'ah of God is established and human relationships are based on the foundation of relationship with God; a Muslim has no nationality except his belief, which makes him a member of the Muslim community in Dar-ul-Islam; a Muslim has no relatives except those who share the belief in God, and thus a bond is established between him and other Believers through their relationship with God."[37]

While Qutb's ideas have wide currency among Muslims around the world, moderate Muslims, particularly in Europe, have chosen otherwise. One French Muslim, Kamel Hamza, articulates the opposite of Qutb's position, saying, "I'm French first, but also Algerian."[38] Moderate Muslims look to leaders such as Tariq Ramadan for guidance on how to sort out the competing demands of Islam and secularism. Ramadan is the author of a book entitled *To Be a European Muslim*, in which he calls for the discarding of the traditional Islamic division of the world into the *Dar al-Islam* (House of Islam) and the *Dar al-Harb* (House of War). Ramadan instead suggests that Muslims see Europe as *"Dar ash-Shahada"*— House of Testimony.[39] (The Shahada is the Muslim confession of faith: "There is no god but Allah and Muhammad is His Prophet.") This would involve bearing witness to their faith through words and deeds; an essential element of doing this, insists Ramadan, would be to obey the laws of European society in which Muslims find themselves. *"Implementing the Shari'a*, for a Muslim citizen or resident in Europe," he says, "is explicitly to respect the constitutional and legal framework of the country in which he is a citizen."[40] (emphasis his). Very well, but what does this mean for the day when a Western European country has a Muslim majority? Will Ramadan and his followers then call for the implementation of the Sharia in full?

Ramadan has rejected the cardinal principle of Islamic radicalism, which is that the Sharia is the only valid law. "Today," Ramadan stated, "I think that Islam is completely compatible with the separation of the Church and the State."[41]

For thus publicly disputing venerable elements of Islamic tradition and offering a version of Islam that appears to be harmonious with Western secularism, Ramadan has become a media darling. In February 2002, Paul Donnelly of *Salon.com* wondered breathlessly if Ramadan were the "Muslim Martin Luther."[42] A succession of Muslim moderates have enjoyed brief vogues in the American media as allegedly presaging an Islam with a warmer, more Western face. Martin Kramer trenchantly notes in his devastating critique of contemporary Western scholarship on Islam, *Ivory Towers on Sand,* that "the academics were so preoccupied with 'Muslim Martin Luthers' that they never got around to producing a single serious analysis of bin Laden and his indictment of America."[43] Yet none of the Muslims they cast in the Luther role— including the Tunisian Rashid al-Ghannoushi, the Iranian Abdolkarim Soroush, and the Syrian Muhammad Shahrur—actually ever came close to commanding the kind of influence they would have needed to effect a real Islamic reformation.

Ramadan vigilantly guards his reputation as a moderate. When the French magazine *Lyon* suggested that he had secret radical sentiments, calling him "the king of ambiguity," "seemingly inoffensive," and "a veritable time bomb," he sued.[44]

Still, he may not be exactly what his Western boosters would like him to be. Many of his statements seem studiedly ambiguous.

He admits the possibility that "a Muslim is allowed to live in a non-Islamic country" only so long as "he is able to protect his identity and practice his religion"—a caveat that has already become a source of unrest in France and elsewhere over issues, such as the headscarf, that are symbolic of deeper incompatibilities between Islam and secular society.[45] In a 1999 statement that has taken on greater significance since the 2003 Iraq war, Ramadan reminded Muslims that "there exists a general Islamic ruling which forbids a Muslim to fight or kill a fellow Muslim and this ruling should be observed at all times. Therefore, a Muslim citizen of a Western country, in order to avoid placing himself in such a situation, should also plead conscientious objection."[46]

Referring to Islamic law's death sentence for apostates, Ramadan argues that it doesn't apply to "one who would leave the faith for personal conviction without trying to betray Islam and Muslims thereafter, in any way." He adds, "The necessary attitude is therefore a minimal respect for the faith that one leaves and a sensitivity by those that continue to practice it."[47] Ramadan doesn't explain what form this "minimal respect" must take, and since he leaves the death penalty in place for those who do dare to "betray Islam and Muslims" thereafter, one may legitimately wonder just how compatible his self-proclaimed moderate vision of Islam really is with European secularism.

Ramadan is the grandson of Hasan al-Banna (1906–1949), the founder of the pioneering modern Islamic extremist group, Egypt's Muslim Brotherhood. He says that he rejects certain aspects of his radical grandfather's teachings. "Clearly there is a difference," he explains, "between what [al-Banna] said in his day and what I am saying today. I am living and speaking out more than fifty years after he was assassinated, that is, in a different era and in a different historical context. Over the years there have been various developments that I am taking into account in formulating my positions, positions that are congruent with my principles. There are some things of my grandfather's with which I agree and others with which I don't agree."[48]

Nevertheless, Ramadan contributed a foreword to a new edition of Hasan al-Banna's *Risalat al-Ma'thurat,* a collection by al-Banna of key texts from the Qur'an and the Hadith, the traditions of the Prophet Muhammad. Ramadan describes the book as "the core of spiritual education for all members of the Muslim Brotherhood." He writes glowingly of his grandfather, lauding al-Banna for the "quality of his faith and the intensity of his relationship with God. Anyone who had ever been in contact with him perceived and experienced this." He describes al-Banna's teachings as "simple and luminous."[49]

In this document at least, he gives no hint that he rejects any of al-Banna's thoughts. Yet his unreserved praise is hard to reconcile with his carefully cultivated image as a Muslim reformer. Readers of this foreword may be forgiven for getting the impression that Ramadan was labeling "simple and luminous" such aspects of al-Banna's thought as his insistence that Muslims must make war against Jews and Christians. "In [Muslim] Tradition," al-Banna writes, "there is a clear indication of the obligation to fight the People of the Book [that is, Jews and Christians], and of the fact that God doubles the reward of those who fight them. Jihad is not against polytheists alone, but against all who do not embrace Islam."

In his depiction of a downtrodden Muslim world invaded by the West and with jihad as its only recourse, al-Banna sounds like many of today's Muslim leaders calling for a jihad in Iraq. "Today the Muslims, as you know, are compelled to humble themselves before non-Muslims, and are ruled by unbelievers. Their lands have been trampled over, and their honor besmirched. Their adversaries are in charge of their affairs, and the rites of their religion have fallen into abeyance within their own domains, to say nothing of their impotence to broadcast the summons [to embrace Islam]. Hence it has become an individual obligation, which there is no evading, on every Muslim to prepare his equipment, to make up his mind to engage in jihad, and to get ready for it until the opportunity is ripe and God decrees a matter which is sure to be accomplished."

Does he mean a military jihad? Most certainly. "Know then that death is inevitable, and that it can only happen once. If you suffer it in the way of God, it will be your profit in this world, and your reward in the next."[50]

Al-Banna is not Ramadan's only familial connection to the Islamic hardline. He is the brother of Hani Ramadan, the Swiss Muslim leader mentioned earlier who was recently fired from a teaching position in Geneva for defending stoning for adultery in the French journal *Le Monde*.[51] Tariq Ramadan affirmed his disapproval of the stoning punishment while objecting to Hani's firing.[52]

Most telling of all may be the fact that Tariq Ramadan, by his own account, based his famous objection to the Dar al-Harb designation on the grounds that it "does not derive from the Quur'ân, and is not part of the Prophetic tradition."[53] Ramadan declares that "Muslims must take from the West those values that do not contradict Islam," but he never directly calls upon Muslims to discard elements of the Qur'an and Islamic law that contradict the principles of secular society. A citizen of Switzerland, he warns, "Don't ask me to be a less Muslim to be a good Swiss."[54]

Consequently, it's hard to see how any reform Ramadan's teachings might inspire can escape the assessment of the Muslim writer A. L. Tibawi. "Perceptible 'reform' cannot be affected in the doctrines of the faith without diminishing or cancelling their validity."[55] Yet among the doctrines of the faith are teachings about armed jihad and the subjugation of non-Muslims—teachings that are strongly reaffirmed by Muslim radicals such as Ramadan's grandfather.

Al-Banna's teachings, whatever Ramadan really thinks of them, are still influential enough among Muslims in Europe and elsewhere to be reprinted in handsome new editions complete with words of praise from the author's famous grandson. As long as Muslims in Europe and around the world continue to value these writings, the specter of jihad and Islamic radicalism is not likely to disappear from Europe or anywhere else anytime soon. Another Muslim moderate, the Tunisian Abdelwahab Meddeb, has written a book entitled *La Maladie de l'Islam* (*The Malady of Islam*). In it, he takes Wahhabi extremism to task and invokes medieval Islam as a model of tolerance and a model for a modern secular Islam. "He notes," according to Christopher Caldwell, "that in the Mutazilite era of the ninth century, when the caliphate was controlled by rationalists who believed the Koran was created rather than eternal, Islam was open to every sort of liberal possibility." Similarly the Grand Mufti of Marseilles, Soheib Bencheikh, has advocated a return to these glory days.

But, as Caldwell points out, that rationalistic period "lasted all of a couple of decades, never to recur." The expansive Islam envisioned by Meddeb and Bencheikh suffers from being ahistorical, wishing as it does to reverse or simply ignore the dominant tendencies of Islamic theological and historical development. The extremist version of Islam that Meddeb excoriates, on the other hand, is firmly grounded in the Qur'an, the example of Muhammad, Islamic law, and the history of Islam. As such, it's not enough simply to say that extremists like al-Banna and Qutb are misusing those sources. Even if they are, their interpretation is amply supported and compelling enough to win adherents worldwide.[56] Tariq Ramadan, despite his reputation as a moderate, sidesteps the extremists only by taking refuge in ambiguity.

In light of this, Europe cannot look forward to a relaxation of tensions between the Muslim minority and the established culture anytime soon.

Rising tensions: Dyab Abou Jahjah

The Arab European League (AEL), a Muslim advocacy organization in Belgium and the Netherlands, displays the same ambiguity that plagues the statements of Tariq Ramadan. Founded by a Lebanese Muslim immigrant named Dyab Abou Jahjah, whom the *New York Times* has dubbed "Belgium's Malcolm X," the AEL has gone on record saying that it opposes the imposition of the Sharia in Holland.[57] With magnificent contempt, Jahjah has said, "We're not folkloristic clowns who want to force Islamic law on other people."[58] As part of its "vision and philosophy," the AEL states, "We believe in a multicultural society as a social and political model where different cultures coexist with equal rights under the law." So far so good, as far as the Netherlands is concerned.

The league operates as an advocacy group for Muslims against the backdrop of increasing tensions between Muslims and non-Muslims in Europe. A poll taken in 2000 has 63 percent of the French population thinking that the country is now home to "too many Arabs."[59] Racism? Maybe, but the French also generally regard Muslims as victims. In early 2003, the National Consultative Committee on Human Rights found "that thirty-nine percent of French people thought that Arabs were the main victims of racism in France." Dyab Abou Jahjah opines that conditions for European Muslims have gotten even worse since September 11, 2001. "Eleven September also meant a new era for many Arabs and Muslims living abroad. It meant that the anti-Islamic sentiment which is inherent in European culture, but that had been marginalized by the politically correct mainstream, could now manifest itself again."[60]

The AEL, which originated in Belgium and now operates in the Netherlands as well, positions itself as the defender of these Muslims. "Only strong communities are treated as equal," it asserts. "Therefore we must work within the boundaries of the law towards eliminating social-economic problems and creating the necessary organizational structures and tools in order to achieve a more dignified and empowered position as a community."

Muslims in France, as well as in other European countries, have indeed experienced discrimination and worse. European Muslims worry about the precedent set by both the murder of the Muslim teenager Rachid Ardjouni and the injustice of its aftermath. In May 1997, Ardjouni was killed by a drunk policeman while lying face down on the ground; his killer was suspended from the police force for eighteen months. However, no criminal offense was put on his record, so to the dismay of French Muslims, he was able to return to work as a policeman after his suspension.[61] There have been other incidents of police brutality and harassment all over France.

Yet more disquieting was the AEL's proclamation that Muslims in Europe "do not want to assimilate"—just as Pim Fortuyn had pointed out. It continues, "We want to foster our own identity and culture while being law-abiding and worthy citizens of the countries where we live. In order to achieve that it is imperative for us to teach our children the Arabic language and history and the Islamic faith. We will resist any attempt to strip us of our right to our own cultural and religious identity, as we believe it is one of the most fundamental human rights."[62] Jahjah, displaying a master politician's talent for the memorable phrase, declared, "Assimilation is cultural rape. It means renouncing your identity, becoming like the others."[63]

Jahjah says that he wants to "work within the boundaries of the law" and even bid unsuccessfully for a seat in the Belgian Parliament in May 2003 (he called the results "a positive signal for

2006".)[64] But when Jahjah arrived in Belgium in 1991, he identified himself as a member of the Shi'ite terrorist group Hezbollah. He explained his desire to enter Belgium as part of his flight from the Hezbollah leadership after a dispute.

Jahjah now denies having been a member of Hezbollah. For good reason: the group has been linked to a number of kidnappings of Westerners in the 1980s, the suicide attack that killed over two hundred Marines in Beirut in 1983, the bombing of a Jewish community center in Argentina in 1994 (in which ninety-five people were killed), and many other terrorist attacks. To be sure, over the years Hezbollah has evolved into much more than just a terrorist group, and is now a significant force in Lebanese politics; however, it is still designated a "foreign terrorist organization" by the U.S. State Department.[65]

Jahjah now explains his 1991 claim of Hezbollah membership this way. "That was a lie. I was a nineteen-year-old boy and I had to make up a story so I could get asylum. I emigrated because I wanted a better life."[66]

Maybe it was a lie. Nonetheless, when Jahjah was arrested last November and charged with inciting Muslims in Antwerp to riot, his rhetoric sounded much like that of Hezbollah (which refers to Israel as the "Zionist enemy"). He charged that "he was being demonized by manipulators in the Belgian government and the 'Zionist lobby.'" Belgian Prime Minister Guy Verhofstadt wasn't buying; he declared that the Arab European League was "trying to terrorize the city." Jews were favored targets. According to the English journalist Ambrose Evans-Pritchard, in Antwerp "Arab gangs have been preying on Hassidic children as they walk to school, forcing those identifiable as Jewish to move around with escorts."[67]

This problem is not restricted to Belgium. Despite the popular perception in France that Muslims are the most frequent victims of racism, the most common victims of racist attacks in that country have not been Muslims, but Jews. The National Consultative Committee on Human Rights discovered that in 2002, "there had been a sixfold increase over 2001 in acts of violence against Jewish property and persons. Of 313 acts of racist violence documented in 2002, 193 were anti-Semitic."[68] The popular perception that Muslims are the primary victims of racist attacks is, quite simply, wrong.

Moreover, the attackers are often Muslims, although at this, Mouloud Aounit, leader of France's Movement Against Racism and for the Friendship of Peoples (MRAP), cries foul. He has complained that, "since September 11, the taboo against Islamophobia has been broken. Certain people are jumping to conclusions, as when they designate young Arab-Muslims as a potentially anti-Semitic group."[69] Yet is this really such an outlandish idea? According to Omer Taspinar, a visiting fellow at the Brookings Institution, "The perpetrators of anti-Semitic incidents in France are not right-wing extremists protecting the 'French race' from Jewish contamination: The four hundred or so anti-Semitic incidents documented in the country during 2001 have mostly been attributed to Muslim youth of North African origin."[70]

Some of these attacks have been particularly damaging. On March 30, 2002, "masked assailants smashed stolen cars into a synagogue in Lyon before setting them ablaze. A witness said a group of approximately fifteen youths stormed the building. No one was injured in the incident, but the synagogue was destroyed."[71] A synagogue in Marseille was burned the same weekend, after surviving a Molotov cocktail attack the previous fall.

In May 2002, Mohamed Latreche, the founder of the French Muslims' Party (PMF), "held a rally in Strasbourg with Hamas and Hezbollah representatives, at which flyers were handed out calling for boycotts of Israeli, American, and British products. Those with Jewish owners were marked with the Nazi yellow star and the

German word Jude."[72] Early in 2003, a Paris rabbi was stabbed in the stomach not long after receiving "a threatening letter referring to Jihad—the Muslim holy war—against enemies of the Palestinians."[73]

Another victim was a fifteen-year-old named Jérémy Bismuth, who "was attacked by a group of other children, mostly Muslim, at the private Catholic school he then attended. They dragged him into the school's locker room showers, shouting that they were going to gas him as the Nazis had gassed Jews. He was beaten and flogged with a pair of trousers... [a] zipper scratched one of his corneas."[74]

What does the AEL think of all this? Navma Elmaslouhi, press officer for AEL's new branch in Holland, was quoted as telling the *Handelsblad* newspaper that "she didn't disapprove of Moroccan youngsters chanting 'Hamas, Hamas, gas the Jews,' as happened during a protest march in Amsterdam in 2002."[75]

Demonizing the opposition: Ayaan Hirsi Ali

Muslims in Europe have other targets too. One recent example is a young Somali immigrant to the Netherlands named Ayaan Hirsi Ali, who describes herself as an "ex-Muslim." Her experiences reveal a great deal about the tensions between Islam and European secularism. Hirsi Ali, who was elected to the Dutch Parliament in January 2003, has assailed Islam from the standpoint of women's rights. "At the very least Islam is facing backward and it has failed to provide a moral framework for our time. If the West wants to help modernize Islam, it should invest in women because they educate the children."[76]

Hirsi Ali charges that Islam at its core is oppressive to women. "The most important verse, which I still refer to, is in the Koran and it is the verse which says women should obey the male members of their families—their fathers and their husbands—and if they do not do that then the husband may beat his wife. That's also a side of Islam and I've pointed to it and I've said there are millions of people who carry out just that simple verse. Millions of Muslim women all around the world are oppressed in the name [of] Islam. And as a woman who was brought up with the tradition of Islam, I think it's not just my right but also my obligation to call these things by name."[77]

In this she was referring to Sura 4:34 of the Qur'an:

> Men are in charge of women, because Allah hath made the one of them to excel the other, and because they spend of their property (for the support of women). So good women are the obedient, guarding in secret that which Allah hath guarded. As for those from whom ye fear rebellion, admonish them and banish them to beds apart, and scourge them. Then if they obey you, seek not a way against them. Lo! Allah is ever High, Exalted, Great.

Most provocatively, Hirsi Ali said that the Muslim Prophet Muhammad, "measured by our Western standards, is a perverse man, a tyrant. If you don't do what he says, then it's going to end badly for you. It reminds me of all the megalomaniac leaders in the Middle East: Bin Laden, Khomeini, Saddam."[78] *IslamOnline* reported that she also charged that "the Prophet (peace be upon him) was against the freedom of women, since, she claimed, he ordered them not to leave their houses, [to] wear the veil, and denied them the right to work and inheritance, not to mention a number of other calumnies mouthed frequently by some venomous orientalists."

Muslim groups in the Netherlands charged Hirsi Ali, who was raised a Muslim, with ignorance of Islam. According to the *IslamOnline* story, "Amr Riyad, an Egyptian researcher at Leiden University, said Ayaan is ignorant about the fact that there is a whole sura (chapter) in the Glorious Qur'an entitled Al-Nissa (women), which spelled out women's rights enshrined by Islam some fourteen centuries ago, when the West was viewing women as a devil and animal incarnate."

But had Hirsi Ali really been listening to "venomous orientalists"? In light of what is at stake not only in the Netherlands but in all of Western Europe, it's important to examine in detail her charges about women's rights in Islam. Riyad's observation that there is a chapter of the Qur'an entitled "Women" establishes nothing. There are also chapters of the Qur'an entitled "Spoils of War" (Sura 8), "Haggling" (Sura 64), "Divorce" (Sura 65), "Soul-Snatchers" (Sura 79), "The Cheats" (Sura 83), "The Earthquake" (Sura 99), "The Calamity" (Sura 101), "The Traducer" (Sura 104), and "The Disbelievers" (Sura 109). That's not to say that the Qur'an regards women on the level of a calamity or an earthquake, but only that to bear the name of a sura of the Qur'an is not automatically a sign of approval.

But Riyad is correct that the Qur'an's Sura An-Nisa ("Women") contains the foundation of Islamic feminism in the verse that says that Allah "created you from a single soul and from it created its mate and from them twain hath spread abroad a multitude of men and women" (Sura 4:1). If Allah created men and women from a single soul, goes the argument, they are equal in dignity. The same sura, however, almost immediately places men and women on an unequal footing by giving Muslim men permission to practice polygamy and concubinage: "Marry women of your choice, two or three or four; but if ye fear that ye shall not be able to deal justly (with them), then only one, or (a captive) that your right hands possess, that will be more suitable, to prevent you from doing injustice" (Sura 4:3).

The same Sura also contains the verse to which Hirsi Ali alluded, which says that women must be obedient and gives husbands permission to beat those that are disobedient: Sura 4:34.

Hirsi Ali also charged, according to *IslamOnline*, that Muhammad "ordered [women] not to leave their houses." According to the renowned medieval Muslim philosopher Abu Hamid al-Ghazali (1058–1111) in *The Revival of the Religious Sciences*, the Prophet Muhammad said, "The right a husband acquires over the wife is that she should not keep herself away from him [even] if they were on the back of a camel and he desired her and tried to take her. . . . If she goes out from his house without his permission, the angels curse her till she comes back to his house or repents."[79]

This is no medieval artifact. The Islamic legal manual *'Umdat al-Salik* (published in English translation as *Reliance of the Traveller*), endorsed by Al-Azhar in 1991 as conforming "to the practice and faith of the orthodox Sunni community," and also carries endorsements from Muslim authorities in Jordan, Syria, and Saudi Arabia, stipulates that "the husband may forbid his wife to leave the home." It cites in support a saying of the Prophet: "It is not permissible for a woman who believes in Allah and the Last Day to allow someone into her husband's house if he is opposed, or to go out if he is averse."[80] Muslims take such laws seriously. In her searing account of the honor killing of her childhood friend, the Jordanian writer Norma Khouri notes that life in her friend's house "was basically like life in all Muslim homes in Amman, regardless of class, money, or neighborhood. . . . She was not allowed to leave her home unless she was accompanied by one of the men in her family."[81]

Muhammad, according to Hirsi Ali, commanded Muslim women to "wear the veil." This stems also from the Qur'an, in Sura 24:31:

And say to the believing women that they should lower their gaze and guard their modesty; that they should not display their beauty and ornaments except what (must ordinarily) appear thereof; that they should draw their veils over their bosoms and not display their beauty except to their husbands, their fathers, their husband's fathers, their sons, their husbands' sons, their brothers or their brothers' sons, or their sisters' sons, or their women, or the slaves whom their right hands possess, or male servants free of physical needs, or small children who have no sense of the shame of sex."

This drawing "the veil over their bosoms" is also justified by several Muslim traditions (*ahadith*). According to the most beloved of Muhammad's wives, Aisha, "The Prophet said: Allah does not accept the prayer of a woman who has reached puberty unless she wears a veil."[82] Also, when the Prophet took a woman, Safiyya, from among the captives of Khaibar after his victorious battle with the Jews there, his followers speculated over whether he was taking her as a wife or a slave. "Some of them said, 'If the Prophet makes her observe the veil, then she will be one of the Mothers of the believers [that is, one of the wives of the Prophet], and if he does not make her observe the veil, then she will be his lady-slave.' "[83] She—and by extension all respectable women in the Muslim world—was given the veil.

Finally, Hirsi Ali charged that Muhammad "denied them the right to…inheritance." The Qur'an does not exactly deny women inheritance, but it awards sisters only half of what their brothers receive: "Allah (thus) directs you as regards your children's (inheritance): to the male, a portion equal to that of two females" (Sura 4:11).

It's hard to see, in light of all this, how Hirsi Ali's charges can validly be termed "calumnies mouthed frequently by some venomous orientalists."

Yet will criticism of Islam be allowed in this free society, the secular Netherlands, which has tolerated criticism of Christianity for hundreds of years?

Ayaan Hirsi Ali risked falling victim to more than the harsh rhetoric of her Islamic critics. The *IslamOnline* story added, "Riyad also said that Ayaan wanted to be famous by following the footsteps of the notorious Soleiman Rushdi [Salman Rushdie] and Taslima Nisreen (both of whom were sentenced to death by Islamic authorities for statements they considered derogatory to Islam). Dr. Ali Juma'ah, professor of Principles of Islamic Jurisprudence, states that such insults against the Prophet stress his high status and noble character. In Islam, it is well known that the punishment for the one who insults the Prophet is to be killed because it constitutes an attack against the Seal of the Prophets and the symbol of Monotheism. However, we Muslims are ordered to be forgiving and pardoning, Dr. Juma'ah said."

Despite Juma'ah's call for pardon, Hirsi Ali says she did receive death threats. In November 2002 she was "forced to flee her adopted country under threat of death. Now she is becoming known as a latter-day Salman Rushdie."[84]

Muslim groups both condemned the threats and denied that they had been made. Yassin Hartog, a spokesman for Islam and Citizenship, the Netherlands' main Muslim lobby group, says he believes the death threats against Hirsi Ali may have been fabricated to blacken the Muslim community. "We're getting more and more signs that these death threats are bogus," he told *The Observer*. In an effort to distance themselves from the affair, seventeen Muslim organizations have signed a declaration condemning the death threats. However, this is not the first time anti-Islamic rhetoric has attracted death threats in the Netherlands and else-where."[85]

Death threats to Hirsi Ali or others who left Islam could find justification in traditional Islamic law: "When a person who has reached puberty and is sane voluntarily apostasizes from Islam, he deserves to be killed."[86]

Dutch Muslim groups tried to deny Hirsi Ali the seat in Parlia-ment to which she had been elected because of her "hate speech." Said the Arab European League's Jahjah, "She would better have shut her mouth about Islam, because she has become a politi-cian."[87]

But she wasn't backing down. Hirsi Ali said that some Muslims supported her stance. "Well, among some Muslims who are not willing to come to [the] foreground because they do not want to face the same dangers, I am welcome. But there is also a small group who are so enraged that they're willing to do something ter-rible to me. And I think that is also another horrible side of Islam—the fact that there is absolutely no toleration."

The fate of Europe

French authorities have been reluctant to antagonize their growing and restive Muslim minority. The multiculturalism that has utterly taken over the Western intelligentsia has made it difficult for authorities to take action against Muslim jihadist doctrines even when those doctrines threaten the stability of the secular society. According to Michel Zaoui of the Representative Council of Jew-ish Institutions in France (CRIF), "The previous leftist government didn't do anything to discourage anti-Israel and anti-Semitic propo-sitions by militant Islamic preachers, in part because their philoso-phy was to show sympathy to the 'damned' and poor. Now, the rightist government would like to act but is afraid of antagonizing Muslims."[88]

Indeed, when the popular French writer Michel Houellebecq called Islam "the stupidest religion" and "a dangerous religion right from the start," he was hauled into court on charges of inciting racial hatred—though, of course, Muslims are of all races. The rector of the Grand Mosque of Paris, Dalil Boubakeur, who is generally regarded as supportive of the French secular regime, cried, "Islam has been reviled, attacked with hateful words. My community has been humiliated."

Houellebecq faced a 70,000-euro fine and eighteen months in prison, but he was ultimately cleared of the charges. The Italian journalist Oriana Fallaci, author of a rhetorical attack on Islam entitled *The Rage and the Pride*, faced unsuccessful attempts by French Muslims to get the book banned.[89] Even the venerable siren Brigitte Bardot ran afoul of French political correctness when she said of Muslim immigration, "For twenty years we have submitted to a dangerous and uncontrolled underground infiltration. Not only does it fail to give way to our laws and customs. Quite the contrary, as time goes by it tries to impose its own laws on us."[90] For this statement Bardot is also being prosecuted for "racism."

Though the charges against Houllebecq and Fallaci didn't stick, these trials set a dangerous precedent. While one can say anything one desires about Christianity without facing criminal charges, Islam is regarded as a protected minority religion—and perhaps, covertly, as being too volatile to criticize without risk of violence.

Islam is on the march in France, as has been seen with the electoral success of the Union of French Islamic Organizations (UOIF), which represents most of the 1,500 mosques in France. The UOIF is linked both with the Saudi Wahhabis and the radical Egyptian Muslim Brotherhood.[91] During the 2003 Iraq war, the Brotherhood recruited several thousand Egyptians to fight in Iraq in the name of jihad.[92] In France the UOIF is a voice of Islamic reaction—at its conventions (which are attended by upwards of 100,000 people) it sponsors workshops with titles like "Liberated Women, De-Natured Women."[93] UOIF secretary-general Fouad Alaoui, after negotiations with the government on the status of Muslims in France, announced that he rejected a "definition of secularism that seals off religion in the private sphere." UOIF president Thami Breze declared his support for a "modification of secularism, in order to respect certain specificities of Islam."[94]

In the face of this, the French government has attempted to create an Islamic Council to ease the integration of Muslims into French society as a whole. This backfired in April 2003, when the UOIF won nineteen of fifty-eight seats on the Council, compared to only fifteen for the group favored by the government, the moderate Mosque of Paris.[95] Also, some twenty percent of French mosques refused to have anything at all to do with the Council, which was formed with the express purpose of creating an "official Islam for France."[96]

Why would the French government want to create an "official Islam for France"? Perhaps it is because the French government recognizes Islam as a looming threat to France's identity and sovereignty. Journalist Christopher Caldwell notes:

> ... practically all of France's 1,200 mosques are funded by foreign governments. Of the country's 230 major imams, none is French. In fact, imams are often chosen by foreign governments for loyalty to their ideological priorities. These priorities are decidedly not those of France. One imam in Roubaix met Lille mayor Martine Aubry on the edge of the Muslim-majority neighborhood where he preaches, declaring it Islamic territory into which Mme. Aubry—the most important minister of labor in modern French history, the early favorite to win France's presidential elections in 2007, and the daughter of former prime minister Jacques Delors—had no authority to venture."[97]

And according to Antoine Sfeir of Paris's Middle East Studies Center, "For a long time the UOIF has been trying to infiltrate the cogs of state and assume control of the Muslim community by marginalizing secular Muslims."[98] But French secularism is fighting back. After the union's electoral victory, French interior minister Nicolas Sarkozy warned Islamic extremists: "We want to say very simply: imams who propagate views that run counter to French values will be expelled."[99] He simultaneously affirmed that Muslims had a place in France. "It is precisely because we recognize the right of Islam to sit at the table of the republic that we will not accept any deviation. . . . Any prayer leader whose views run contrary to the values of the republic will be expelled."

And the Sharia? "Islamic law will not apply anywhere, because it is not the law of the French republic."[100]

Yet the day before in Holland, a young attendee at a seminar on Islamic law stated, "I don't want a separation of state and religion. I want Shariah here and now."[101]

Which road will European Muslims ultimately take? "If Islam evolves in the direction of greater religious openness, then there is the possibility of dialogue," said the Archbishop of Lublin, Poland, Józef Miroslaw Zycinski, about the Muslims in Europe. "But if a fundamentalist version dominates in which religion is mixed with politics, then optimism will not be justified."[102] That's an understatement.

Chapter Three

THE JIHAD WAY
OF WAR

J IHAD THROWS OUT THE WINDOW conventional Western ideas of limited warfare between nation states with surrenders and peace treaties. Jihad internationalizes war and makes it perpetual. With jihad there is no peace.

Flashpoints around the world that otherwise might have been pacified remain flashpoints because of jihad and mujahedin. Long after the Taliban has been driven from power and a pro-American government installed in Kabul, the anti-terror war in Afghanistan continues to flare. In April 2003, seventeen months after the Karzai government took power, supporters of the Taliban and al Qaeda were still fighting. Maintaining their taste for terror, they have targeted such noncombatants as Red Cross workers and United Nations mine-clearing personnel.[1] "Nearly every day," according to the *New York Times*, "there are killings, explosions, shootings and targeted attacks on foreign aid workers, Afghan officials, and American forces."[2] One radical Muslim predicted that "the war in Afghanistan is the beginning of a long war that will last several years, perhaps decades and eventually end with victory for the believers and a good outcome for the Muslim Ummah [community]."[3]

After World War II in Japan, the emperor told his subjects that, contrary to what they had been taught all their lives, he was not divine. He formally renounced the religious justifications that had fueled the drive to war. But as long as the religious leaders (*ulema*) of Muslim countries around the world do not renounce jihad and its attendant doctrines, conflicts with Islamic extremists will have no end.

Israel and Palestine

The foremost example of this is Israel and Palestine. To be sure, injustices have been committed on both sides, but what has undone every attempt at a negotiated settlement and peace is the trafficking in jihad rhetoric by the Palestinians and their supporters. If Israel occupies part of the Dar al-Islam—the House of Islam—then it cannot by rights house a non-Muslim majority. It is not enough for Israel to set aside land for a Palestinian state; in the radical view, Israel must be subsumed within—and the Jews subjugated to—an Islamic state.

The different stated aspirations of the forerunner to the Palestinian Authority, the Palestine Liberation Organization (PLO), and the group that has emerged as the chief obstacle to the latest peace initiatives, Hamas (*Harakat Muqawama Islamiyya*—the Islamic Resistance Movement) epitomize the impact of jihad rhetoric on the situation in Israel. The chief difference between the two groups is not their attitudes toward terror, as both groups have abundant ties to terrorism. Rather, their fundamental difference lies in their public positions (which, of course, may differ from their genuine views) on the possibility and efficacy of negotiations with Israel—a question with long-term implications for the region. According to Dr. Raphael Israeli, a professor of Islamic History at Hebrew University, "while the PLO charter is a political document which can be amended, the Hamas charter is presented as a religious document, based on the Koran and with many references to sacred texts, which cannot be changed once it has been published."[4]

The problem is not just that it can't be changed, but that it presents a vastly different vision of the nature of the conflict and its resolution from that of the PLO. Yasir Arafat, although he himself has called for jihad on many occasions and is notorious for appearing to say one thing to the West and something very different to the Muslim world, still keeps a cross on his desk and is careful, especially when speaking on the international stage, to call for "one democratic state where Christian, Jew, and Muslim live in justice, equality, fraternity, and progress."[5] Of course, this statement (from his 1974 UN speech) doesn't amount to as much as it seems to, for Arafat was calling for "one state" under PLO rule, which would have had a strong Sharia influence militating against "justice, equality, fraternity, and progress." But, in any case, Arafat was on record calling for a secular state, calculating that in the West his aspirations would be understood as identical to the preferred option of many American analysts of the Middle East.

Hamas, on the other hand, was founded in 1988 in direct opposition to secularism, however watered-down Arafat's version was in the first place. The Hamas charter confronts this problem directly, describing the idea of a secular state as a Western colonial imposition upon the Muslim world. "Under the influence of the circumstances which surrounded the founding of the PLO, and the ideological confusion which prevails in the Arab world as a result of the ideological invasion which has swept the Arab world since the rout of the Crusades, and which has been reinforced by Orientalism and the Christian Mission, the PLO has adopted the idea of a Secular State."

Such a state, in Hamas's view, must be rejected. "Secular thought is diametrically opposed to religious thought. Thought is the basis for positions, for modes of conduct, and for resolutions. Therefore, in spite of our appreciation for the PLO and its possible transformation in the future, and despite the fact that we do not denigrate its role in the Arab-Israeli conflict, we cannot substitute it for the Islamic nature of Palestine by adopting secular thought. For the Islamic nature of Palestine is part of our religion, and anyone who neglects his religion is bound to lose." The charter follows this with a quotation from the Qur'an: "And who forsakes the religion of Abraham, save him who befools himself?" (Sura 2:130).

But Hamas holds out hope for future accord with the PLO. "When the PLO adopts Islam as the guideline for life, then we shall become its soldiers, the fuel of its fire which will burn the enemies."

Hamas identifies itself in the charter as "one of the wings of the Muslim Brothers in Palestine. The Muslim Brotherhood Movement is a world organization, the largest Islamic Movement in the modern era. It is characterized by a profound understanding, by precise notions and by a complete comprehensiveness of all concepts of Islam in all domains of life: views and beliefs, politics and economics, education and society, jurisprudence and rule, indoctrination and teaching, the arts and publications, the hidden and the evident, and all the other domains of life."

The Muslim Brotherhood, of course, is the Egyptian radical movement founded by Hasan al-Banna, who is quoted in the Hamas charter as saying, "Israel will rise and will remain erect until Islam eliminates it as it had eliminated its predecessors." In keeping with this guiding idea that Islam must be and will be the force that ultimately eliminates Israel, and that Islamic principles must rule all aspects of life, Hamas describes its membership and its mission in the broadest possible terms, complete with copious quotes from the Qur'an:

> The Islamic Resistance Movement consists of Muslims who are devoted to Allah and worship Him verily [as it is written]: 'I have created Man and Devil for the purpose of their worship' [of Allah].... They have raised the banner of Jihad in the face of the oppressors in order to extricate the country and the people from the [oppressors'] desecration, filth and evil. 'Nay, but we hurl the true against the false; and it does break its head and lo! it vanishes' Sura 21 (the Prophets), verse 18."

In contrast to Yasir Arafat's frequent public overtures to Christian Arabs (which are not necessarily matched by his less-publicized behavior), Hamas is an exclusively Muslim movement. "The Movement welcomes all Muslims who share its beliefs and thinking, commit themselves to its course of action, keep its secrets, and aspire to join its ranks in order to carry out their duty. Allah will reward them."

Hamas's goal is likewise religious. "As the Movement adopts Islam as its way of life, its time dimension extends back as far as the birth of the Islamic Message and of the Righteous Ancestor. Its ultimate goal is Islam, the Prophet its model, the Quran its Constitution." Nor is its mission restricted to Israel only. Like Ibn Khaldun and other Muslim thinkers, and in accord with the Prophet

Muhammad's vision for Islam as recorded in the Hadith, wherein he delineates the triple choice for unbelievers, Hamas sees its Islamic mission as universal. "Its spatial dimension extends wherever on earth there are Muslims, who adopt Islam as their way of life; thus, it penetrates to the deepest reaches of the land and to the highest spheres of Heavens. . . . By virtue of the distribution of Muslims, who pursue the cause of the Hamas, all over the globe, and strive for its victory, for the reinforcement of its positions and for the encouragement of its Jihad, the Movement is a universal one."

Also in contrast to Arafat's taste for negotiations, feigned as it may be, is Hamas's disdain for peace talks. "[Peace] initiatives, the so-called peaceful solutions, and the international conferences to resolve the Palestinian problem, are all contrary to the beliefs of the Islamic Resistance Movement. For renouncing any part of Palestine means renouncing part of the religion; the nationalism of the Islamic Resistance Movement is part of its faith, the movement educates its members to adhere to its principles and to raise the banner of Allah over their homeland as they fight their Jihad: 'Allah is the all-powerful, but most people are not aware.' "[6]

In laying out its aims in this way, Hamas and similar groups such as Islamic Jihad have painted themselves—and the Middle East—into a corner. The Muslim militants who see their struggle against Israel as part of their religious responsibility cannot recognize Israel's right to exist, or reach any kind of negotiated settlement with "the Zionist entity," without denying what it has identified as "part of its faith." After all, the Prophet Muhammad himself warned Muslims that "the last hour would not come unless the Muslims will fight against the Jews and the Muslims would kill them until the Jews would hide themselves behind a stone or a tree and a stone or a tree would say: Muslim, or the servant of Allah, there is a Jew behind me; come and kill him."[7]

This tradition is repeated, with small variations, numerous times in the Hadith, and is well known among Palestinian Muslims. On April 12, 2002, an employee of the Palestinian Authority, Sheikh Ibrahim Madhi, preached in a sermon carried on Palestinian Authority television. "A reliable Hadith [tradition] says: 'The Jews will fight you, but you will be set to rule over them.' What could be more beautiful than this tradition? 'The Jews will fight you'— that is, the Jews have begun to fight us. 'You will be set to rule over them'—Who will set the Muslim to rule over the Jew? Allah.... Until the Jew hides behind the rock and the tree. But the rock and tree will say: "'Oh Muslim, oh servant of Allah, a Jew hides behind me, come and kill him." Except for the Gharqad tree, which is the tree of the Jews.' We believe in this Hadith. We are convinced also that this Hadith heralds the spread of Islam and its rule over all the land."

Sheikh Madhi continued, "We are convinced of the [future] victory of Allah; we believe that one of these days, we will enter Jerusalem as conquerors, enter Jaffa as conquerors, enter Haifa as conquerors, enter Ramle and Lod as conquerors, the [villages of] Hirbiya and Dir Jerjis and all of Palestine as conquerors, as Allah has decreed.... Anyone who does not attain martyrdom in these days should wake in the middle of the night and say: 'My God, why have you deprived me of martyrdom for your sake? For the martyr lives next to Allah.'...Our enemies suffer now more than we do. Why? Because we are convinced that our dead go to Paradise, while the dead of the Jews go to Hell, to a cruel fate. So we stand firm and steadfast, in obedience to Allah."

Like Hamas, Sheikh Madhi also predicted the ultimate worldwide supremacy of Islam, in accordance with the ultimate goal of all jihads. "Oh beloved, look to the East of the earth, find Japan and the ocean; look to the West of the earth, find [some] country and the ocean. Be assured that these will be owned by the Muslim nation, as the Hadith says...'from the ocean to the ocean.'...Oh Allah, accept our martyrs in the highest heavens....Oh Allah, show the Jews a black day....Oh Allah, annihilate the Jews and their supporters....Oh Allah, raise the flag of Jihad across the land."[8]

For anyone who believes all this, the only prospect for peace is the death of Israel.

Hamas announces its intention to fight "until the Decree of Allah is fulfilled, the ranks are over-swollen, Jihad fighters join other Jihad fighters, and all this accumulation sets out from everywhere in the Islamic world, obeying the call of duty, and intoning 'Come on, join Jihad!' This call will tear apart the clouds in the skies and it will continue to ring until liberation is completed, the invaders are vanquished and Allah's victory sets in. 'Verily Allah helps one who helps Him. Lo! Allah is strong, Almighty.' Sura XXII (Pilgrimage), verse 40."

Is all this merely religious window dressing for Hamas's political goals? The charter itself rules out that interpretation in the course of a fervently pious reading of history. "The greedy," it asserts, "have coveted Palestine more than once and they raided it with armies in order to fulfill their covetousness. Multitudes of Crusades descended on it, carrying their faith with them and waving their Cross." While the Crusaders met with some success, they weren't able to withstand the Muslims once they returned to the full practice of their religion. "They were able to defeat the Muslims for a long time, and the Muslims were not able to redeem it until they sought the protection of their religious banner; then, they unified their forces, sang the praise of their God and set out for Jihad under the Command of Saladin al-Ayyubi, for the duration of nearly two decades, and then the obvious conquest took place when the Crusaders were defeated and Palestine was liberated."

Against Palestinians and others who may place their hope in socialism, or democracy, or the United Nations, or some other imported Western utopia, the charter asserts that Islam and jihad represent "the only way to liberation, there is no doubt in the testimony of history. That is one of the rules of the universe and one of the laws of existence. Only iron can blunt iron, only the true faith of Islam can vanquish their false and falsified faith. Faith can only be fought by faith. Ultimately victory is reserved to the truth, and truth is victorious."

Not that Hamas doesn't offer its own vision of peace. "Under the shadow of Islam," its charter asserts, "it is possible for the members of the three religions: Islam, Christianity, and Judaism to coexist in safety and security. Safety and security can only prevail under the shadow of Islam, and recent and ancient history is the best witness to that effect.... Islam accords his rights to everyone who has rights and averts aggression against the rights of others."[9]

In this the charter is referring to the laws that designate Jews and Christians as *dhimmis*, protected people who are accorded certain rights and restrictions in Islamic society. This means that the peace that Hamas offers "under the shadow of Islam" is unlikely to be identical with the unfettered tolerance of secular society. For the laws of dhimmitude only allow Jews and Christians to "coexist in safety and security" with Muslims under conditions that relegate them to second-class status. "The subject peoples," according to a manual of Islamic law, must "pay the non-Muslim poll tax (jizya)" and "are distinguished from Muslims in dress, wearing a wide cloth belt (zunnar); are not greeted with 'as-Salamu 'alaykum' [the traditional Muslim greeting, "Peace be with you"]; must keep to the side of the street; may not build higher than or as high as the Muslims' buildings, though if they acquire a tall house, it is not razed; are forbidden to openly display wine or pork ... recite the Torah or Evangel aloud, or make public display of their funerals or feastdays;

and are forbidden to build new churches."[10] If they violate these terms, the law further stipulates that they can be killed or sold into slavery at the discretion of the Muslim leader.

In line with the graffiti seen frequently in the Palestinian Authority, "First the Saturday people, then the Sunday people," these laws would be applied to Christian Arabs as well as to Jews.[11]

The Hamas charter is very carefully worded when it announces that "Islam accords his rights to everyone who has rights." Who does *not* have rights? Under traditional Islamic law, the answer would be someone who was at war with Islam, or a dhimmi who has violated the terms of "safety and security" specified for Muslims under Islamic law. Such would be life for Jews and Christians "under the shadow of Islam."

Hamas continues to hold to all this. In a 1998 statement delivered to Yasir Arafat, the organization reaffirmed its "militant Jihad for the implementation of our national project for liberation, in the shadow of the escalation of the malicious Zionist settlement attack on our land, our sanctuaries and on our people."[12]

Consistent with its stance against any and all negotiations with Israel, Hamas has rejected Arafat's offer of cabinet posts in the government of the Palestinian Authority, for if it were part of the authority it would be involved in Arafat's talks with Israel. Standing outside of the government of the Palestinian Authority, Hamas has nevertheless been able to exercise a good deal of influence—and throw roadblocks in the way of any potential new peace accord—by waving the banner of jihad. When a new Palestinian cabinet was formed in April 2003, Hamas leader Abdel Aziz Rantissi said, "Hamas will support the new government if it fights the Zionist occupation, but if the government thinks of declaring war on the Jihad warriors, Hamas will fight it."[13] Along with Islamic Jihad, Hamas defiantly rejected calls from the new Palestinian Authority Prime Minister Mahmoud Abbas (that is, Abu Mazen, himself "a Holocaust revisionist, a conspiracy theorist, and a promoter of terrorism") to lay down arms.[14]

Other radical Muslims share the views of Hamas. On May 13, 2003, "police arrested the leader and fourteen members of Islamic Movement, the largest Arab political group in Israel, on suspicion they funneled millions of dollars to Hamas."[15]

Support from other Muslims is long-standing. As long ago as 1968, General Mahmud Shit Khattab of Iraq declared, "The return to Islam will entail the proclamation of Islamic jihad. In that case, there will be 75 million Moslem fighters on the battlefields facing Israel. They will be able to eliminate Israel even without weapons."[16] More recently, in a sermon broadcast on official Palestinian Authority television in 2000, Dr. Ahmad Abu Halabiya, a member of the Palestinian Authority's Fatwa Council, declared, "Allah the almighty has called upon us not to ally with the Jews or the Christians, not to like them, not to become their partners, not to support them, and not to sign agreements with them. And he who does that is one of them, as Allah said: 'O you who believe, do not take the Jews and the Christians as allies, for they are allies of one another. Who from among you takes them as allies will indeed be one of them.'...Have no mercy on the Jews, no matter where they are, in any country. Fight them, wherever you are. Wherever you meet them, kill them."

In this Abu Halabiya recalled the words of the Qur'an: "...slay the idolaters wherever ye find them, and take them (captive), and besiege them, and prepare for them each ambush" (Sura 9:5). He applied these words to the contemporary political situation: "Wherever you are, kill those Jews and those Americans who are like them—and those who stand by them—they are all in one trench, against the Arabs and the Muslims—because they established Israel here, in the beating heart of the Arab world, in Palestine. They created it to be the outpost of their civilization—and the vanguard of their army, and to be the sword of the West and the crusaders, hanging over the necks of the monotheists, the Muslims in these lands."

The remedy, once again, is jihad. "Let us put our trust in Allah, close ranks, and unite our words, and the slogan of us all should be, 'Jihad! Jihad!'...Allah, deal with the Jews, your enemies and the enemies of Islam. Deal with the crusaders, and America, and Europe behind them, O Lord of the worlds."[17]

Several Wahhabi sheikhs, in speaking of the Israeli-Palestinian conflict, likewise ruled out the idea that it is a political problem that can be solved at the negotiating table. Preaching in 2000 in the Saudi city of al-Khobar's al-Nour mosque, Sheikh Nasser Muhammad Al-Ahmad assailed the Israeli-Palestinian peace initiatives of the 1990s. "There is no doubt that the [Muslim] nation is today reaping the fruit of agony because of its renunciation of its honor on the day it begged [peace] at the negotiating tables, chasing after a false peace that could never be. Because, in all honesty, these are people with whom no agreement or pact can be made.... These crimes [against the Palestinians and the Muslims] will be stopped only by Jihad. The sites holy to Muslims will be regained only by Jihad for the sake of Allah.... When true Islamic Jihad is declared, the balance of power will shift. What frightens the West more than anything else is the word Jihad, because they understand what it means.... There is no solution to this problem, and to any problem to which the infidel enemy is party, except by waving the banner of Jihad."

Sheikh Sultan Al-'Uweid, in a sermon in the Prince Tareq mosque in Al-Damam, Saudi Arabia, lamented that Israel, although greatly outnumbered, was able to survive in the Middle East: "Who would have believed it?!...A handful of brothers of apes and pigs torments a billion [Muslims].... There is no other way, oh Muslims, but restoring the missing precept—Jihad for the sake of Allah.... There is no other way but educating to Jihad."

Others agreed. According to Sheikh 'Abd Al-'Aziz Qari at a recent sermon in the Qabaa mosque in Islam's second holiest city, Medina, "the war between us and the Jews is, in truth, a religious war, and only Islam can wage it in the path of truth.... It is a divine decree, a military-political decree, a religious decree, but it is not directed at those who still fight in the name of the olives, the oranges, and the watermelon. It is a divine decree directed at the nation of Jihad, the Islamic nation, the Muslims."

The sheikh was saying that those who considered the Israeli-Palestinian conflict to be a simple dispute over land (olives, oranges, and watermelon) were missing the point. It was not, in fact, a conflict over politics or land—it was a religious war. In the words of Sheikh Muhammad Saleh Al-Munajjid at a mosque in Al-Damam, Saudi Arabia, "The [Palestinian] cause is exploited by hypocrites, the secular, polytheists, and pan-Arabs.... They must be silenced, disregarded. We must unite around those who talk of the Islamization of the cause.... If we say that the cause is an Arab cause, there are among us Christian Arabs, and infidels... and Socialists. What do all these have to do with Al-Aqsa Mosque?!"

In the Suleiman Bin Muqiran mosque in Riyadh, the Saudi capital, Sheikh Majed 'Abd Al-Rahman Al-Firian also rejected the idea that the Israeli-Palestinian issue was a local or even a pan-Arab issue. "This is a deep-rooted solution to the conflict: Intifada and Jihad for the sake of Allah, not for the sake of pan-Arabism, and not for the sake of protecting the homeland and the soil. Today, the Islamic nation already knows that the Holy Land will not be liberated by dallying at vacation sites or sitting around the negotiating table with infidels. The solution is to do what the Prophet did to the Jews when they violated the agreements.... The solution regarding the Jews is as the Prophet Muhammad said: 'I have brought slaughter upon you.'...Yes, the solution for these is not peace and harmony.... Jihad, not peace, is the solution."[18]

Sheikh Mustafa Bin Said Aytim pointed a finger at "globalization" during a sermon in Mecca. "The Jews, Christians, and the hypocrites gnaw away at the body of the nation and then carry out raids on it with the knights of the destructive media and with the deadly weapon of globalization."

During an April 2002 telethon to raise money for the Palestinians, a Wahhabi Muslim cleric employed by the Saudi government, Sheikh Saad Al-Buraik, said, "Oh Believer, it's a wish, as much as it is pains, but we have hopes that the situation in Palestine will explode. No one dies before their day. How many Muslims have died in Chechnya, Bosnia, Kashmir, and Kosovo!! Is it too dear to us that among our honorable beloved [we] die as martyrs?...Which is better, to suffer a slow death, or die as a martyr in your way to heaven? A death that you will be forgiven on the first drop of your blood."

Then he addressed the Palestinians directly and criticized peace efforts in the name of jihad. "Oh Palestinian Authority, don't you see that you are tested once or twice a year?...Isn't [it] time yet to wage jihad, and call for holy war? Isn't [it] time that Muslim countries which normalized relations with the Jews to cancel everything that happened from Madrid to Oslo, and [Wye] River, which forbids the supplying of weapons to Muslims in Palestine? The agreements which canceled jihad, and disassociation from non-Muslims, should all be demolished. It's a call to close all embassies opened for the Jews in the land of Islam; it is a call to end normalization with Israel."

This sheikh, who has accompanied Crown Prince Abdullah as a member of Saudi government delegations, described the conflict between Israelis and Palestinians as a religious war and a larger conflict than one simply over disputed land. "People should know that

Jews are backed by the Christians, and the battle that we are going through is not with Jews only, but also with those who believe that Allah is a third in a Trinity, and those who said that Jesus is the son of Allah, and Allah is Jesus, the son of Mary." His language here was derived from the Qur'an. "They do blaspheme who say: Allah is one of three in a Trinity: for there is no god except One Allah" (Sura 5:73). "In blasphemy indeed are those that say that Allah is Christ the son of Mary" (Sura 5:17).

However much the ACLU may protest, when Sheikh Saad says that the war is against Christians, he is saying that it is against America. This official of our friend and ally Saudi Arabia declared, "I am against America until this life ends, until the Day of Judgment; I am against America even if the stone liquefies. My hatred of America, if part of it was contained in the universe, it would collapse. She is the root of all evils, and wickedness on earth. Who else implanted the tyrants in our land, who else nurtured oppression? Oh Muslim Ummah [community], don't take the Jews and Christians as allies." This was also a reference to the Qur'an: "O ye who believe! take not the Jews and the Christians for your friends and protectors" (Sura 5:51).

In accordance with Qur'anic directions to be "harsh" or "ruthless" to unbelievers (Sura 48:29), particularly those who war against Muslims, he concluded with a ringing peroration. "Muslim Brothers in Palestine, do not have any mercy neither compassion on the Jews, their blood, their money, their flesh. Their women are yours to take, legitimately. God made them yours. Why don't you enslave their women? Why don't you wage jihad? Why don't you pillage them?"[19]

As outrageous as all this sounds, it is perfectly justifiable according to the Sharia. Traditional Islamic law dictates that women and children captured in jihad "become slaves by the fact of capture, and the woman's previous marriage is immediately annulled."[20]

Israelis and Palestinians alike can count on more bloodshed, for even the goal of the conflict for Palestinians has been obscured by jihad ideology. On Palestinian Authority television in June 2002, two eleven-year-old girls who had been thoroughly indoctrinated by the warriors of jihad went so far as to exclaim that they would prefer death by suicide bombing to justice and peace for the Palestinian people. When asked by the show's host, "What is better, peace and full rights for the Palestinian people, or Shahada [martyrdom]?" one replied readily, "Shahada. I will achieve my rights after becoming a Shahida [martyr]." Her companion added: "Of course Shahada is a good thing. We don't want this world, we want the Afterlife. We benefit not from this life, but from the Afterlife.... The children of Palestine have accepted the concept that this is Shahada, and that death by Shahada is very good. Every Palestinian child aged, say twelve, says 'Oh Lord, I would like to become a Shahid.' "[21]

The Balkans

The conflict between Israel and Palestine is just one of many in the world today exacerbated by the doctrine of jihad. The Balkans were the fault line between the Eastern and Western branches of Christianity even before the Muslim invasions of the Middle Ages. Islam added to the conflict by introducing not only jihad but the stipulations of dhimmitude.

Historian Bat Ye'or points out that "in the 1830s, forced by the European powers, the Ottomans adopted a series of reforms aiming at ending the oppression of the Christians." The fiercest opponents of these reforms were the Muslims of Bosnia. "They fought against the Christian right to possess lands and, in legal matters, to have equal rights as themselves."[22]

Nevertheless, by 1860 the British consul J. E. Blunt could write that conditions for Christians were improving in Macedonia.

"Christian churches and monasteries, towns and inhabitants, are not now pillaged, massacred, and burnt by Albanian hordes as used to be done ten years ago." He reported that Islamic laws subjugating non-Muslim minorities were no longer rigorously enforced. "Ten years ago...Churches were not allowed to be built; and one can judge of the measure of Turkish toleration practiced at that time by having had to creep under doors scarcely four feet high. It was an offense to smoke and ride before a Turk; to cross his path, or not stand up before him, was equally wrong...." Blunt notes that Christian testimony was not admissible in Muslim courts, such that a Muslim who murdered a fellow Muslim in Skopje was allowed to go free for lack of witnesses; two Christians who saw the deed were not allowed to testify. Blunt attributes "the uncivil conduct and contemptuous conduct" of the Muslim authorities toward Christians to "the difference of religion."[23]

Relaxations of Islamic law were slow, irregular, and hard to count on. The consul William R. Holmes wrote from Bosnia in 1861 that "the promise of permission to build churches as other Christian subjects of the Porte seems delusive, when it is known here that one of the Christian communities—the Orthodox Greeks—have collected money to build a church, but are prevented from doing so on the frivolous pretext of its being near a mosque, the said mosque being more than 150 yards from the site proposed for the church, and hardly visible from it."[24]

The seeds of later conflicts between Christians and Muslims in Bosnia can be seen in a letter also written in 1860 by acting consul James Zohrab. "The hatred of the Christians toward the Bosniak Mussulmans is intense. During a period of nearly three hundred years they were subjected to much oppression and cruelty. For them no other law but the caprice of their masters existed."[25]

There were at least three distinct conflicts in the Balkans in the 1990s. Jihad initially had little, if anything, to do with them. The conflicts originated in Serbian/Croatian squabbles encouraged by governments in Belgrade and Zagreb. But when jihad entered the fight, attracting mujahedin from all over the world, it made a peaceful resolution incalculably more difficult.

A sizable proportion of Balkan Muslims were Europeans who had, over the centuries, converted to Islam to escape their second-class status. They practiced a Europeanized and relatively benign form of the religion. But with the collapse of communism in Yugoslavia and the resurgence of Islamic radicalism, the tenor of Islam in the Balkans changed, especially as the Balkans became a crucible of war. At a conference of the Islamic group Al-Jama'ah al-Islamiyyah in Pakistan in October 1998, "the convention determined the struggle against India, Israel, Serbia, and Eritrea as a *Jihad.* This means that the Islamic movements should not only support the Muslims that are oppressed there, but 'Press to the world community to exert all possible political, economic and diplomatic pressures against these nations.'"[26]

The Balkans had, in fact, become a favored destination for mujahedin several years before the Al-Jama'ah al-Islamiyyah conference, when veterans of the wars in Afghanistan and Chechnya against the Soviets made their way to Europe to fight the next jihad. The flamboyant commander Abu Abdel Aziz described a meeting he had with prominent Muslim scholars regarding the conflict in Bosnia. "I—alhamdulillah [thanks be to Allah]—met several prominent Ulema [Muslim religious authorities], among them Sheikh Nasir ad-Din al-Albani, Sheikh Abdel Aziz Bin Baz, and Sheikh Muhammad Bin Otheimin, and others in the Gulf area. Alhamdulillah, all grace be to Allah, they all support the religious dictum that 'the fighting in Bosnia is a fight to make the word of Allah supreme and protect the chastity of Muslims.' It is because Allah said (in his holy book), 'Yet, if they ask you for succor against religious persecution, it is your duty to give [them] this succor.'

[Literally, 'to succor them in religion', Qur'an, al-Anfal, 8:72]. It is then our [religious] duty to defend our Muslim brethren wherever they are, as long as they are persecuted because they are Muslims and not for any other reason."[27]

It's interesting to note that one of the clerics mentioned— Sheikh Abdel Aziz Bin Baz—was the late Grand Mufti of Saudi Arabia who may be most famous for coming out in favor of a peace accord between Israel and the Palestinians, "only on condition that it is a temporary peace, until the Muslims build up the strength needed to expel the Jews."[28]

Also active in the Balkans was the hidden hand of Osama bin Laden. According to Marcia Christoff Kurop, a former editor of *Defense News*, the Balkans served in the 1990s as "a major recruiting and training center of Osama bin Laden's al Qaeda network." Bin Laden himself visited the area three times in the mid-1990s, and even investigated the possibility of settling there when the United States put increased pressure on Afghanistan's Taliban to surrender him in 1999.[29]

Money and weapons flowed into the Balkans to support the mujahedin. The Clinton Administration turned a blind eye. The now-disbanded Kosovo Liberation Army "continued to receive official NATO/U.S. arms and training support and, at the talks in Rambouillet, France, then-Secretary of State Madeleine Albright shook hands with 'freedom fighter' Hashim Thaci, a KLA leader. As this was taking place, Europol [the European Police Organization based in The Hague] was preparing a scathing report on the connection between the KLA and international drug gangs. Even Robert Gelbard, America's special envoy to Bosnia, officially described the KLA as Islamic terrorists."[30]

Although it has receded from the international headlines, this conflict still simmers. In March 2002, the Macedonian government arrested two Jordanians and two Bosnians and turned them over to

American authorities on suspicions that they were planning terrorist activity. According to a news report, "One senior official, who asked not to be identified, said the men arrived in Macedonia shortly before their arrest and were recorded speaking of plans to 'destroy the devil'"—that is, the United States. Macedonian Interior Minister Ljube Boskovski acknowledged that "there was a continuing terrorist threat in Macedonia.... Boskovski has said repeatedly that mujahedin were fighting alongside ethnic Albanians in Macedonia."[31] There is evidence that the warriors of jihad are trying to use Macedonia as their European base; meanwhile, in Bosnia, hundreds of them "became Bosnian citizens after battling Serbian and Croatian forces." Now they "present a potential terrorist threat to Europe and the United States, according to a classified U.S. State Department report and interviews with international military and intelligence sources."[32]

According to Yossef Bodansky, Osama bin Laden's biographer and the director of the United States Congress's Task Force on Terrorism and Unconventional Warfare, these mujahedin stayed in Bosnia in full accordance with the will of the Muslim government of Alija Izetbegovic. "Sarajevo's willingness and determination to continue the Islamist jihad in Bosnia-Herzegovina has been clearly demonstrated. The latter activities are most significant, for they are in flagrant contradiction with Sarajevo's promise to Washington that it would evict all the mujahedin by mid-January 1996."[33]

It was no surprise that Izetbegovic would find the company of the mujahedin congenial. He was, after all, the author of *The Islamic Declaration*, which got him jailed by the Communists in 1970. In it he declares that the only path to "dignity and enlightenment" for Muslims is "the implementation of Islam in all fields of individuals' personal lives, in family and in society, by renewal of the Islamic religious thought and creating a uniform Muslim community from Morocco to Indonesia." He advocates "a struggle for creating a great Islamic federation from Morocco to Indonesia, from the tropical Africa to the Central Asia."

There is little, if any, difference between this and the calls of Muslim radicals for the restoration of the caliphate and the unification of Muslim political power.

Ominously for a political figure in a multireligious, multiethnic society, Izetbegovic heaped disdain on other models for political and social unity. "Islam is not a nationality, it is above nationalities. . . . A nation, and an individual, who has accepted Islam is incapable of living and dying for another ideal after that fact. It is unthinkable for a Muslim to sacrifice himself for any tzar or ruler, no matter what his name may be, or for the glory of any nation, party, or some such, because acting on the strongest Muslim instinct he recognizes in this a certain type of godlessness and idolatry. A Muslim can die only with the name of Allah on his lips and for the glory of Islam, or he may run away from the battlefield."

Consequently, "Muslim nations will never accept anything that is explicitly against Islam, because Islam here is not merely a faith and the law, Islam has become love and compassion. He who rises against Islam will reap nothing but hate and resistance."

What, then, about one's non-Muslim neighbors, who don't live by Islamic law? They must live under Islamic rule. "An Islamic society without Islamic power is incomplete and weak; Islamic power without an Islamic society is either a utopia or violence. . . . History knows of no true Islamic movement which was not at the same time a political movement as well. This is because Islam is a faith, but also a philosophy, a set of moral codes, an order of things, a style, an atmosphere—in a nutshell, an integral way of life."

Elaborating on these assertions, Izetbegovic emphasizes "the incompatibility of Islam and non-Islamic systems. There can be no peace or coexistence between the 'Islamic faith' and non- Islamic societies and political institutions. . . . Islam clearly excludes the right and possibility of activity of any strange ideology on its own turf. Therefore, there is no question of any laicistic principles, and the state should be an expression and should support the moral concepts of the religion.... Islamic renewal cannot be initiated without a religious [revolution], and cannot be successfully continued and concluded without a political revolution."

In accordance with Islamic law, he notes, "Islamic order may be implemented only in countries where Muslims represent the majority of the population.... The Islamic movement should and must start taking over the power as soon as it is morally and numerically strong enough to not only overthrow the existing non-Islamic, but also to build up a new Islamic authority."

But surely he is just cloaking his nationalism in religious dress, no? He takes pains to rule out this possibility. "Panislamism always came from the very heart of the Muslim peoples, nationalism was always imported stuff."[34]

Izetbegovic wrote this more than thirty years ago, but has never renounced it.

As in Israel, the mujahedin in Bosnia, Macedonia, Kosovo, and elsewhere are unlikely to regard a negotiated settlement as final, short of the attainment of their Islamic goals. Already in connection with the Dayton Accords, Muslim spokesmen have characterized the settlement as part of the West's struggle against Islam. According to Bodansky, "pro-Islamist circles in Tehran stressed the anti-Islamic character of the Dayton accords. 'The West only thinks of... stopping an Islamic state from taking root in Bosnia,' they argued. The all-out support from the entire Muslim world should ensure that this design did not materialize."[35]

"Western security officials," according to a news report about jihadist activity in Macedonia, "believe there are serious concerns about the Pakistani, Jordanian, Bosnian, and other Muslim fighters operating alongside and independently of rebel groups such as the self-styled National Liberation Army and the Albanian National Army. 'These fighters are those who have been least amenable to the idea of disarming and participating in Macedonia's ongoing peace process,' said one European security official. 'They want to keep on fighting, whether it's the Macedonian government or western embassies who may be the target.' "[36]

Saudi Arabia

Islamic doctrines—and not only Osama bin Laden's calls to jihad—are also responsible, at least in part, for the attacks on the World Trade Center and the Pentagon on September 11, 2001. While in the wake of the attacks an avalanche of analyses attempted to answer the question "Why do they hate us?" few paid much attention to the reasons actually stated by bin Laden himself.

After retailing a laundry list of political grievances against the U.S., in his declaration of jihad against the United States in 1996, bin Laden adds, "The latest and the greatest of these aggressions... is the occupation of the land of the two Holy Places [i.e., Saudi Arabia]—the foundation of the house of Islam, the place of the revelation, the source of the message and the place of the noble Ka'ba, the Qiblah of all Muslims—by the armies of the American Crusaders and their allies. (We bemoan this and can only say: 'No power and power acquiring except through Allah')."[37]

He reiterated this in 1998. "For over seven years the United States has been occupying the lands of Islam in the holiest of places, the Arabian Peninsula, plundering its riches, dictating to its rulers, humiliating its people, terrorizing its neighbors, and turning its bases in the Peninsula into a spearhead through which to fight the neighboring Muslim peoples."[38]

These reasons are deeply rooted in the teachings and traditions of Islam. The same sourcebook of Islamic law that contains these regulations for Jews and Christians also stipulates that adherents of these religions "are forbidden to reside in the Hijaz, meaning the area and towns around Mecca, Medina, and Yamama, for more than three days (when the caliph allows them to enter there for something they need)."[39]

This prohibition is founded on the Prophet Muhammad's famous deathbed statement that "no two religions are allowed in Arabia."[40] Muhammad also said, "I will expel the Jews and Christians from the Arabian Peninsula and will not leave any but Muslims."[41]

These sayings of Muhammad are also the basis for the modern-day draconian Saudi laws prohibiting any non-Muslim religious practice in the kingdom, so that even American soldiers on duty defending the House of Saud from its predatory neighbors are not allowed to observe the rites of their religions unless they are Muslim. According to the Foundation for the Defense of Democracies, "In Saudi Arabia, Islam is the state religion and all citizens must be Muslims. It is illegal to import, print, or own Christian or non-Muslim religious materials, and Christians have been jailed and deported."[42]

In light of the origin of these laws, it's hard to see how journalist Stephen Schwartz, author of a critique of Wahhabism and Saudi Arabia entitled *The Two Faces of Islam*, can assert that "Saudis claim falsely that exclusion of non-Muslim religious rituals in the Arabian Peninsula reflects Islamic tradition."[43]

How can something founded on two widely known statements of Muhammad not reflect Islamic tradition? Not only is it founded on the words of the Prophet, but this prohibition has been enforced throughout history, first by the early Islamic empires, then by the Ottomans, and finally by the Saudi Wahhabis. Indeed, Muslims have jealously guarded this restriction for centuries. Its breach has never been a light or trivial matter. In 1853, the English adventurer Sir Richard Francis Burton posed as Mirza Abdullah, a Persian Muslim, to make the pilgrimage to Mecca and Medina. When some Turks told a British associate of Burton that however accomplished the British were, they could not make the pilgrimage, the official "promised himself a laugh at the Turks' beards" over Burton's deed. But "the subject made [the Turks] look so serious, that he did not like recurring to it."[44]

The words of Muhammad made this humiliation more than simply political. According to journalist Michael Dobbs, to bin Laden and other Muslim radicals "the presence of foreign forces was an intolerable affront to 1,400 years of Islamic tradition, dating back to an injunction from the prophet Muhammad that there 'not be two religions in Arabia.' "[45]

While people in other countries have had their pride hurt by the presence of foreign forces sent there to "assist" them, radical Islam adds fires of fanaticism to that pride. And it's not just Osama bin Laden who expresses it. On July 10, 2002, the former imam of the Great Mosque of Riyadh's King Saud University, Sheikh Mohsin Al-'Awaji, told al-Jazeera television, "Americans are in three American bases... that are there because of a decision by the Gulf rulers, and the [Islamic] nation knows that they violate the words of the Prophet, who ordered the banishment of the Jews and Christians from the Arabian peninsula."

Another Wahhabi sheikh, Dr. Safar Al-Hawali, added, "America and its supporters must know that if it extends its hand to attack the land of the two holy places [Saudi Arabia], it will have no protection from the cruelty of God and the vengeance of the soldiers of Allah, the mujahiddeen. It will have no protection, even if it digs a hole in the earth or seeks refuge in space."[46]

On May 12, 2003, suicide attackers struck American military targets in Riyadh, killing at least twenty-nine people and wounding almost two hundred others.[47] The day before the attack, an al Qaeda member calling himself Abu Mohammed al-Ablaj emailed a London magazine to warn of impending "martyrdom" operations in Saudi Arabia—the beginning of what he called a "guerrilla war" against the House of Saud and the United States.[48] Although in theory American officials had a chance in this case to track a major al Qaeda cell with the full cooperation of local authorities, the Prophet's commands may have gotten in the way. News reports noted laconically that "the size of the FBI contingent headed to Saudi Arabia to investigate the deadly bombings was scaled back amid concern about Saudi sensitivity to a large U.S. law enforcement presence."[49]

Turkey

Similarly, Islamic doctrine played a role in Turkey's recent reluctance to fight alongside its American ally in Iraq. Turkey, of course, prides itself on being the first secular democracy in the Muslim world. Its present system was established in the 1920s by Kemal Ataturk after the downfall of the Ottoman empire. However, according to analyst John Eibner, "the Islamic tradition of the caliphate also permeates Turkey's political culture. The election of two Islamist governments within the past ten years—including that of the current prime minister, Recep Tayyip Erdogan—points to a dangerous revival of Sharia-inspired political Islam."[50]

Turkey had abundant pragmatic reasons to aid America in the war in Iraq. It could have supported its most important ally, America, while simultaneously moving to ensure that the restive Kurds in northern Iraq didn't join forces with their separatist brothers in southeastern Turkey. But "never should a believer kill a believer... If a man kills a believer intentionally, his recompense is Hell" (Sura 4:92–93). If the Erdogan government had fought on the side of the United States against Iraq, it risked not only the ire of the rest of the Islamic world, but retaliation from the Islamic radicals who put Erdogan in power in the first place. According to Paul Berman, an analyst of Islamic radicalism, "From their point of view, to see the Turks line up with the U.S. now must be enraging. And the fact that Turkey is led by an Islamist party which appears to have become a liberal party in its principal instincts, this fact must be enraging beyond words."[51]

Turkey's alliance (and, arguably, its self-interest), were on one side, and Islam on the other. Islam won.

Of course, there is no reason why Turkey or any other state with a Muslim majority shouldn't take Islamic teachings and sensibilities into account when deciding policy. Islam has always been a political religion, and it still wields tremendous influence even in states in the Islamic world that have secular governments—Egypt is a particularly notable example. But Westerners should understand that when an Islamic state acts in accordance with Islamic law, the specter of armed jihad is ever-present, for it is still very much a part of that law. Underscoring this is the fact that by choosing its ties to the Islamic world over its alliance with the United States, Turkey has implicitly endorsed a fundamental principle of jihad ideology: the idea that religion transcends nationality, and that the needs of the Muslim *umma* come before those of any nation state.

As the great scholar of the Muslim world Bernard Lewis puts it, "In the modern world, the political role of Islam, internationally as well as domestically, differs significantly from that of its peer and rival, Christianity. The heads of state or ministers of foreign affairs of the Scandinavian countries and Germany do not from time to time foregather in a Lutheran summit conference. Nor was it customary, when the Soviet Union still existed, for its rulers to join with those of Greece and Yugoslavia, and, temporarily forgetting their political and ideological differences, to hold regular meetings on the basis of their current or previous adherence to the Orthodox Church. . . . The very idea of such a grouping, based on religious identity, might seem to many modern Western observers absurd or even comic. But it is neither absurd nor comic in relation to Islam."[52]

Such beliefs are rooted in the teachings of the Qur'an itself, and, as we'll see, have played themselves out throughout the entirety of Islamic history.

Part Two

JIHAD THEN

⊠

Chapter Four

JIHAD IN THE QUR'AN

Is War the Will of Allah?

Terrorists: misusing the Qur'an?

ACCORDING TO ROHAN GUNARATNA, author of *Inside Al-Qaeda*, terrorists recruit new members to the cause of jihad by using "selected verses in the Koran."[1] However, he articulated the prevailing view of the terrorists' Qur'anic exegesis when writing about the Asian Islamic terrorist group Jemaah Islamiah (JI). "Like al Qaeda, JI misinterprets and misrepresents the Koran to advance its own objectives."[2]

In a profile of the mother of accused "twentieth hijacker" Zacarias Moussaoui, journalist Susan Dominus refers to "inflammatory religious texts" that terrorists give to "young, foundering

Muslim men," but she gives no indication of what those inflammatory texts might contain.[3] Indeed, few have attempted to study exactly how terrorists use the Qur'an to recruit young men, or why their exegesis is convincing.

But if terrorism is going to be cut off at its root, this must be examined. If Gunaratna is right that terrorists "misinterpret" and "misrepresent" the Qur'an, the long-term prospects of the terrorist threat worldwide immediately contract. As their arguments become better known, terrorists' appeals to the Qur'an will be refuted by more level-headed Muslim voices. Lacking religious justification, the terrorists' rage will melt away in the warmth of massive infusions of American cash in Afghanistan, Iraq, and around the world.

This is what those who dismiss religion as a true motivation for terrorism imagine will be the ultimate outcome of the war on terror. It is strange to secular Westerners that the interpretation of an ancient holy book could have important policy implications; hence the many efforts by American and European analysts to reduce the stated Islamic motives of Osama bin Laden, Hamas, the Bali bomber, and all the rest to more familiar categories of economic, political, and social grievances. But this reductionism is not only redolent of the patronizing ethnocentrism that multiculturalists ostensibly eschew—it also risks severely misreading the dimensions of the terrorist threat.

One pro-Osama website put it this way: "The truth is that a Muslim who reads the Qur'an with devotion is determined to reach the battlefield in order to attain the reality of Jihad. It is solely for this reason that the Kufaar [unbelievers] conspire to keep the Muslims far away from understanding the Qur'an, knowing that Muslims who understand the Qur'an will not distance themselves from Jihad."[4]

The question is: is this true?

One Qur'an, two readings

The renowned ex-Muslim Ibn Warraq, author of *Why I Am Not a Muslim* and editor of several collections of scholarly essays on the Qur'an and Muhammad, calls the Qur'an the most "gnomic, elusive, and allusive of holy scriptures"—not least because people seem to be able to read it and come to diametrically opposite conclusions about what it says.[5]

Some of these conclusions may have had motivations other than the purely theological. In the wake of the September 11 attacks, the *Detroit Free Press* told readers that "the Quran teaches nonviolence" and the president of the United States proclaimed that "Islam is peace." Only a few dared to sound any sour notes.[6] Christian Broadcasting Network spokesman and former presidential candidate Pat Robertson drew vehement and indignant criticism when he declared, "I'm very familiar with what goes on in the Islamic world, where our reporters are all over that area, and it's clear from the teachings of the Koran and also from the history of Islam that it's anything but peaceful."[7] Jerry Falwell and Billy Graham's son Franklin also drew fire—as well as bloody riots in India and a call for their deaths from a Muslim official in Iran[8]—for similar remarks.

Tolerance in the Qur'an

Within the Qur'an itself one finds abundant verses devoted to peace and tolerance—and abundant verses devoted to violent intolerance.

Live-and-let-live tolerance appears in the Qur'an in Sura 109: "Say: O disbelievers! I worship not that which ye worship; Nor worship ye that which I worship. And I shall not worship that which ye worship. Nor will ye worship that which I worship. Unto you your religion, and unto me my religion."

Other verses link this seeming indifference to the fact that Allah will ultimately judge the unbelievers and cast them into hell. Allah tells Muhammad in the Qur'an not to waste his time arguing with those who reject his message, but to leave them in peace until that terrible day: "So leave them alone until they encounter that Day of theirs, wherein they shall (perforce) swoon (with terror)" (Sura 52:45-47).

This counsel is repeated in Sura 73:10-11: "And have patience with what they say, and leave them with noble (dignity). And leave Me (alone to deal with) those in possession of the good things of life, who (yet) deny the Truth; and bear with them for a little while."

Likewise, Allah admonishes his prophet not to argue with the Jews and Christians of Arabia, who are called "the People of the Book" in the Qur'an. Instead, he is to emphasize that he believes in the same God they do: "And dispute ye not with the People of the Book, except with means better (than mere disputation), unless it be with those of them who inflict wrong (and injury): but say, 'We believe in the revelation which has come down to us and in that which came down to you; Our Allah and your Allah is one; and it is to Him we bow (in Islam)'" (Sura 29:46).

Muhammad is to present his message in an attractive manner and preach it with patience: "Invite (all) to the Way of thy Lord with wisdom and beautiful preaching; and argue with them in ways that are best and most gracious: for thy Lord knoweth best, who have strayed from His Path, and who receive guidance. And if ye do catch them out, catch them out no worse than they catch you out: But if ye show patience, that is indeed the best (course) for those who are patient" (Sura 16:125-126).

Above all, no Muslim should forcibly convert an unbeliever: "Let there be no compulsion in religion: Truth stands out clear from Error: whoever rejects evil and believes in Allah hath grasped the most trustworthy hand-hold, that never breaks. And Allah heareth and knoweth all things" (Sura 2:256). Following this celebrated verse comes another threat of hell: "Allah is the Protector of those who have faith: from the depths of darkness He will lead them forth into light. Of those who reject faith the patrons are the evil ones: from light they will lead them forth into the depths of darkness. They will be companions of the fire, to dwell therein (for ever)" (Sura 2:257).

Fighting in self-defense

The threats of hellfire accompanying the above verses counseling Muhammad to leave the unbelievers alone are combined with the necessity of self-defense in the eighth Sura, *Al-Anfal* ("The Spoils of War"):

> Remember thy Lord inspired the angels (with the message): 'I am with you: give firmness to the Believers: I will instill terror into the hearts of the Unbelievers: smite ye above their necks and smite all their finger-tips off them.' This is because they contended against Allah and His Messenger: If any contend against Allah and His Messenger, Allah is strict in punishment. Thus (will it be said): 'Taste ye then of the (punishment): for those who resist Allah, is the penalty of the Fire.' O ye who believe! when ye meet the Unbelievers in hostile array, never turn your backs to them. If any do turn his back to them on such a day—unless it be in a stratagem of war, or to retreat to a troop (of his own)—he draws on himself the wrath of Allah, and his abode is Hell, an evil refuge (indeed)!
>
> *(Sura 8:12-16)*

Another verse commands the Muslim community to defend not only itself but also houses of worship—not just mosques, but all kinds:

> Sanction is given unto those who fight because they have been wronged; and Allah is indeed able to give them victory; Those who have been driven from their homes unjustly only because they said: Our Lord is Allah—for had it not been for Allah's repelling some men by means of others, cloisters and churches and oratories and mosques, wherein the name of Allah is oft mentioned, would assuredly have been pulled down. Verily Allah helpeth one who helpeth Him. Lo! Allah is Strong, Almighty.
>
> *(Sura 22:39-40)*

The Qur'an returns elsewhere to this theme of self-defense.

> Fight in the cause of Allah those who fight you, but do not transgress limits; for Allah loveth not transgressors. [Another prominent Muslim translation renders this as "begin not hostilities. Lo! Allah loveth not aggressors."] And slay them wherever ye catch them, and turn them out from where they have turned you out; for tumult and oppression are worse than slaughter; but fight them not at the Sacred Mosque, unless they (first) fight you there; but if they fight you, slay them. Such is the reward of those who suppress faith. But if they cease, Allah is Oft-forgiving, Most Merciful. And fight them on until there is no more tumult or oppression, and there prevail justice and faith in Allah; but if they cease, Let there be no hostility except to those who practice oppression.
>
> *(Sura 2:190-193)*

Significant also for the understanding of jihad as self-defense is the following verse, which Abdullah Yusuf 'Ali's translation of the Qur'an renders in part: "If then any one transgresses the prohibition against you, transgress ye likewise against him" (Sura 2:194). Another Muslim translator, Mohammed Marmaduke Pickthall, translates this more explicitly: "And one who attacketh you, attack him in like manner as he attacked you." This is a foundation for the revenge culture that dominates so much of the Islamic world.

Fight is defensive, but not optional: "Fighting is prescribed for you, and ye dislike it. But it is possible that ye dislike a thing which is good for you, and that ye love a thing which is bad for you. But Allah knoweth, and ye know not" (Sura 2:216).

Nor should this defensive struggle be limited in scope. Allah even tells Muhammad to take no prisoners: "It is not fitting for a prophet that he should have prisoners of war until he hath thoroughly subdued the land." This verse comes in the context of warning the Muslims not to fight simply for booty: "Ye look for the temporal goods of this world; but Allah looketh to the Hereafter: And Allah is Exalted in might, Wise" (Sura 8:67). At the battle of Uhud against the pagan Quraysh tribe of Mecca, the Muslims failed to destroy their enemies utterly because of their lust for the spoils of war: "Allah did indeed fulfil His promise to you when ye with His permission were about to annihilate your enemy, until ye flinched and fell to disputing about the order, and disobeyed it after He brought you in sight (of the booty) which ye covet. Among you are some that hanker after this world and some that desire the Hereafter. Then did He divert you from your foes in order to test you but He forgave you: For Allah is full of grace to those who believe" (Sura 3:152).

However, the prohibition against taking prisoners doesn't seem to be absolute, since Allah also gives the Muslims permission to take the wives of those they have slain in battle as concubines: "O

Prophet! We have made lawful to thee thy wives to whom thou hast paid their dowers; and those whom thy right hand possesses [i.e., slaves] out of the prisoners of war whom Allah has assigned to thee" (Sura 33:50).

However, warfare in this context still must be limited. One verse particularly favored by Muslim moderates since the September 11 attacks forbids the taking of innocent life: "Whosoever killeth a human being for other than manslaughter or corruption in the earth, it shall be as if he had killed all mankind, and whoso saveth the life of one, it shall be as if he had saved the life of all mankind" (Sura 5:32).

Muslims are also able to enter into treaties with unbelievers. In one Qur'anic passage Allah says of the "hypocrites":

> If they turn renegades, seize them and slay them wherever ye find them; and (in any case) take no friends or helpers from their ranks; except those who join a group between whom and you there is a treaty (of peace), or those who approach you with hearts restraining them from fighting you as well as fighting their own people. If Allah had pleased, He could have given them power over you, and they would have fought you: therefore if they withdraw from you but fight you not, and (instead) send you (guarantees of) peace, then Allah hath opened no way for you (to war against them).
>
> *(Sura 4:89-90)*

The rewards of fighting

Those who fight are more pleasing to Allah than those who do not: "Not equal are those believers who sit (at home) and receive no hurt, and those who strive and fight in the cause of Allah with their goods and their persons. Allah hath granted a grade higher to those who strive and fight with their goods and persons than to those who sit (at home). Unto all (in Faith) Hath Allah promised good: But those who strive and fight hath He distinguished above those who sit (at home) by a special reward" (Sura 4:95).

Allah calls his people to be fearless in the face of death in view of the rewards he offers afterward: "And if ye are slain, or die, in the way of Allah, forgiveness and mercy from Allah are far better than all they could amass. And if ye die, or are slain, Lo! It is unto Allah that ye are brought together" (Sura 3:157-158).

This reward is guaranteed to those who sacrifice for Allah: "He who forsakes his home in the cause of Allah, finds in the earth many a refuge, wide and spacious: should he die as a refugee from home for Allah and His Messenger, His reward becomes due and sure with Allah: and Allah is Oft-forgiving, Most Merciful" (Sura 4:100).

For warriors this is especially true: "No blame is there on the blind, nor is there blame on the lame, nor on one ill (if he joins not the war): but he that obeys Allah and his Messenger, (Allah) will admit him to Gardens beneath which rivers flow; and he who turns back, (Allah) will punish him with a grievous Penalty" (Sura 48:17). The obedience in question here is not general religious obedience, but that of obeying the call to go to war for the sake of Allah.

Indeed, those who wage jihad rank highest among the believers: "Do ye make the giving of drink to pilgrims, or the maintenance of the Sacred Mosque, equal to (the pious service of) those who believe in Allah and the Last Day, and strive with might and main in the cause of Allah [*jihad fi sabil Allah*]? They are not comparable in the sight of Allah: and Allah guides not those who do wrong. Those who believe, and suffer exile and strive with might and main, in Allah's cause [*jihad fi sabil Allah*], with their goods and their persons, have the highest rank in the sight of Allah: they are the people who will achieve (salvation)" (Sura 9:19-20). *Jihad fi sabil Allah* refers in Islamic theology to taking up arms for the Muslim cause.

Finally there is a cluster of verses containing general and open-ended commands to fight: "O ye who believe! Fight the unbelievers who gird you about, and let them find firmness in you: and know that Allah is with those who fear Him" (Sura 9:123).

"O Prophet! Strive hard against the unbelievers and the hypocrites, and be firm against them. Their abode is Hell, an evil refuge indeed" (Sura 9:73). The Arabic word translated here as "strive hard" is *jahidi*, a verbal form of the noun *jihad*.

The command applies first to fighting those who worship other gods besides Allah: "Then, when the sacred months have passed, slay the idolaters wherever ye find them, and take them (captive), and besiege them, and prepare for them each ambush. But if they repent and establish worship and pay the poor-due, then leave their way free. Lo! Allah is Forgiving, Merciful" (Sura 9:5).

However, Muslims must fight Jews and Christians as well, although the Qur'an recognizes that as "People of the Book" they have received genuine revelations from Allah: "Fight those who believe not in Allah nor the Last Day, nor hold that forbidden which hath been forbidden by Allah and His Messenger, nor acknowledge the religion of Truth, (even if they are) of the People of the Book, until they pay the Jizya [the special tax on non-Muslims] with willing submission, and feel themselves subdued" (Sura 9:29).

Tolerance or war?

So, in the final analysis, we must ask ourselves: Ultimately, does the Qur'an preach tolerance or war?

The answer depends on who's doing the explaining. Spokesmen for the Council on American Islamic Relations and other American Muslim advocacy groups tend to gloss over the violent verses and construct a vision of Islam out of the tolerant passages. Yet the Qur'an's violent verses have to be accounted for somehow. Many Muslims have offered a simple explanation: Pat Robertson and the other preachers were quoting the Qur'an out of context. "After all," notes Javeed Akhter, a Muslim intellectual and biographer of Muhammad, "studying the Qur'an is not exactly like reading Harry Potter. Like any other scripture there are rules that may be followed for a proper understanding of the text."[9] Fedwa Wazwaz of the Minnesota-based Islamic Resource Group says that "any allegation that the Qur'an teaches violence and religious hatred is totally unfounded and violate [sic] the textual, historical, linguistic and broader context of the Qur'anic teachings and amounts to serious distortions of its teachings."[10]

Understandably, many find this assertion wanting. Claiming to have been quoted out of context is the first, easiest, and emptiest refuge nowadays for anyone caught saying something embarrassing. Ibn Warraq calls this claim "that old standby of crooked, lying politicians."[11] And uncomfortably for Wazwaz, saying that the Qur'an justifies terrorism is not a sin restricted to Protestant preachers; even Muslims do it. Examples abound: the "Letter to the American People" that appeared in November 2002 purporting to be a message from Osama bin Laden quotes eight passages from the Qur'an. Osama's 1996 declaration of jihad against the United States refers to sixteen Qur'an passages.[12] Each of the communiqués from the Qassam Brigades of Hamas begins with a quotation from the book of Allah.[13]

Finding the Qur'an's context

The context of Qur'anic passages can moreover backfire on those who use this argument today to claim that Islam is essentially identical in its moral teachings to Christianity and Judaism. A notorious example is the context of the gracious and much-quoted words of Sura 5:32, which I reproduced above: "Whosoever killeth a human being for other than manslaughter or corruption in the earth, it shall be as if he had killed all mankind, and whoso saveth the life of one, it shall be as if he had saved the life of all mankind" (Sura 5:32).

The full Qur'anic text gives a very different picture. The verse comes after a sketchy retelling of the story of Cain and Abel. Cain murdered his brother and "became full of regrets."

> On that account We ordained for the Children of Israel that if any one slew a person—unless it be for murder or for spreading mischief in the land—it would be as if he slew the whole people: and if any one saved a life, it would be as if he saved the life of the whole people. Then although there came to them Our messengers with clear signs, yet, even after that, many of them continued to commit excesses in the land. The punishment of those who wage war against Allah and His Messenger, and strive with might and main for mischief through the land is: execution, or crucifixion, or the cutting off of hands and feet from opposite sides, or exile from the land: that is their disgrace in this world, and a heavy punishment is theirs in the Hereafter.
>
> *(Sura 5:31-33)*

Ibn Warraq sums it up: "The supposedly noble sentiments are in fact a warning to Jews. 'Behave, or else' is the message. Far from abjuring violence, these verses aggressively point out that anyone opposing the Prophet will be killed, crucified, mutilated, and banished!"[14]

The Qur'anic context is not usually that revealing. For a book that provokes so many charges that readers are taking it out of context, the Qur'an is remarkably decontextualized. Although it retells many biblical stories (usually in slightly altered form), in its overall form it lacks the chronological arrangement of the Old Testament historical books or even the rough temporal movement of the Gospels. Instead, its 114 chapters (*suras*) are arranged by length from the longest to the shortest; the biblical stories and other narratives are distributed haphazardly throughout the book. Also, when Muslims say that the Qur'an is the Word of Allah, they don't mean the same thing that Christians and Jews mean when they say that the Bible is the Word of God. The traditional (and still nearly universal) Muslim understanding of the Qur'an is far beyond the biblical idea that God inspired human authors. Allah dictated every word of the Qur'an to the Prophet Muhammad through the Angel Gabriel. Allah Himself is the only speaker throughout the Qur'an, and most often he addresses Muhammad, frequently telling him what to say to various adversaries.

Consequently, reading the Qur'an is often like walking in on a conversation between two people with whom one is only slightly acquainted. Frequently they make reference to people and events without bothering to explain what's going on. In other words, the context is often not supplied. Wishing, perhaps, to fill this gap, early in Islamic history Muslims elaborated two principal sources for that context: *tafsir* (commentary on the Qur'an) and *hadith*, traditions of the Prophet Muhammad.

These sources cannot establish a "correct" or "orthodox" understanding of jihad and label others as wrong or heterodox, but they do provide clues as to how jihad was understood in Islam's founding period, which has enormous influence on how it has been understood throughout history. They will also shed light on how closely the modern terrorist understanding of the Qur'an and jihad gibes with the traditional ways the term has been used.

According to the German Muslim scholar Ahmad von Denffer, exegesis of the Qur'an (*tafsir*) is "the most important science for Muslims. . . . Without *tafsir* there would be no right understanding of various passages of the Qur'an." But a lone believer reading the Qur'an and trying to understand its teachings on his own is not proceeding properly: "The best *tafsir*," Von Denffer advises, "is the explanation of the Qur'an by the Qur'an." After that, one should look to the example of the Prophet Muhammad, who always "acted according to what he understood from the Qur'an." After that, one turns to the examples of the Prophet's Companions.[15]

All this ground has been covered long ago, such that today Muslims can consult various venerable books of *tafsir* that carry enormous weight in the Islamic world. A useful starting point is the work of Ibn Kathir.

Isma'il bin 'Amr bin Kathir al Dimashqi (1301–1372), known popularly as Ibn Kathir, is not the only eminent commentator on the Qur'an, but he does represent a broad mainstream in Islamic tradition. Von Denffer calls his Qur'an commentary one of the "better-known" and "more valuable books of *tafsir*," and notes that it is "of greatest importance to Muslims."[16] The Muslim publisher of an English translation and abridgement of this massive work (which is over three thousand pages long in the Arabic original) says that it is "the most popular interpretation of the Qur'an in the Arabic language, and the majority of the Muslims consider it to be the best source based on the Qur'an and Sunnah" for understanding the Qur'anic text.[17]

Ibn Kathir relies extensively upon various collections of *hadith* (the Arabic plural is *ahadith*) or traditions about the Prophet Muhammad's words and deeds. These collections largely comprise the *Sunna*, the extra-Qur'anic material about Muhammad that Muslims read to this day as a guide to human behavior. Many ahadith directly explain the circumstances in which a certain book was revealed.

One hadith, for example, recounts the occasion on which Muhammad was reciting a verse that scolds Muslims who take no part in jihad: "Those of the believers who sit still...are not on an equality with those who strive in the way of Allah with their wealth and lives. Allah hath conferred on those who strive with their wealth and lives a rank above the sedentary. Unto each Allah hath promised good, but He hath bestowed on those who strive a great reward above the sedentary" (Sura 4:95).

At that point, a blind man spoke up: "O Allah's Messenger! If I had power, I would surely take part in Jihad." Whereupon "Allah sent down the revelation to His Messenger" of another segment of the verse, removing the Prophet's blind friend from this condemnation: "...other than those who have a (disabling) hurt."[18]

The hadith is so important in Islamic thought that, according to Von Denffer, "there is agreement among Muslim scholars that the contents of the *sunna* are [in addition to the Qur'an] also from Allah. Hence they have described it as also being the result of some form of inspiration."[19]

The authority of the hadith is complicated, however, by the fact that in the early years of Islam a huge number of words and deeds of Muhammad were forged. In the ninth century, several Islamic scholars ranged through the Muslim world collecting traditions about Muhammad and then attempting to winnow the true ones from the false. The imam Muhammad Ibn Ismail al-Bukhari (810–870), who compiled the most respected and authoritative hadith collection (known as *Sahih Bukhari*), is said to have gathered 300,000 ahadith. These he examined carefully, trying to trace each back through a discernible chain of transmission (*isnad*) to the Prophet himself. Ultimately he chose and published around two thousand separate ahadith as authentic; repetitions bring the number of ahadith in his collection to over seven thousand.

Sahih Bukhari alone fills nine volumes in a deluxe English-Arabic edition published in Saudi Arabia. Besides the context of an enormous number of verses of the Qur'an, it gives the reader

Muhammad's wisdom and example on a huge range of topics, including ablutions, characteristics of prayer and actions while praying, funerals, the obligatory charity tax (*zakat*), the obligatory pilgrimage to Mecca (*hajj*), fasting, sales and trade, loans, mortgaging, wills and testaments, jihad, marriage, divorce, good manners, laws of inheritance, punishment of unbelievers, blood money, interpretation of dreams, and much more.

Sahih Bukhari is just one of six collections, all lengthy, that Muslims generally regard as trustworthy. Among these *sahih sittah*, or "reliable collections," is another that bears the designation *sahih*—meaning "sound" or "reliable." This is *Sahih Muslim*, which was compiled by Muslim ibn al-Hajjaj al-Qushayri (821–875). The others are considered lesser authorities after Bukhari and Muslim, but still enjoy great respect: *Sunan Abu-Dawud* by Abu Dawud as-Sijistani (d. 888); *Sunan Ibn Majah* by Muhammad ibn Majah (d. 896), *Sunan At-Tirmidhi* by Abi 'Eesaa Muhammad At-Tirmidhi (824–893), and *Sunan An-Nasai* by Ahmad ibn Shu'ayb an-Nasai (d. 915).

Also highly regarded, although not numbered among the *Sahih Sittah*, are several other collections, notably one known as *Muwatta Imam Malik* (or simply *Muwatta Malik*). Malik bin Anas bin Malik bin Abu Amir Al-Asbahi (715–801), or Imam Malik, lived closest in time to the life of Muhammad of all the collectors of ahadith— and he was born over eighty years after the death of the Prophet.

In Islam the study of ahadith is a complex and absorbing science. Scholars grade individual traditions according to such designations as "sound," "good," "weak," "forged," and many others. If a tradition appears in Bukhari or Muslim, it has a great presumption of reliability, and if it's in both, its authenticity is virtually assured—at least from a traditional Muslim perspective. This is not just the view of Muslim scholars. Bukhari and Muslim are highly regarded in the popular mind as well: one Islamic Internet resource, while assuring readers that "nothing on this site violates the fixed principles of Islamic law," sums up the prevailing opinion of Muslims succinctly: "Sahih Bukhari is distinguished with it's [sic] strong reliability;" regarding *Sahih Muslim,* it adds: "Out of 300,000 Hadiths which were evaluated by Muslim, only four thousand approximately—divided into forty-two books—were extracted for inclusion into his collection based on stringent acceptance criteria."[20]

Many Western scholars are more hesitant. The great scholar of Islam Ignaz Goldhizer and others have done ground-breaking work in researching which ahadith reflect what Muhammad really said and did, and which are pious legend.[21] As important as these researches are, they do not concern us here: it is more important for us to examine the ahadith that are generally taken as authentic within the Islamic world, because these are the ahadith that sway peoples and lead to action.

The Verse of the Sword in context

A cornerstone of the Qur'an's teaching about jihad is "the Verse of the Sword," Sura 9:5: "So when the Sacred Months have passed, then fight the Mushrikin [unbelievers] wherever you find them, and capture them and besiege them, and lie in wait for them in each and every ambush. But if they repent and perform the Salah [Islamic prayers five times daily], and give the Zakah [alms as required by Islamic law], then leave their way free. Verily, Allah is Oft-Forgiving, Most Merciful."

Osama bin Laden, or another radical Muslim speaking in his name, made clear the importance of this verse in a sermon broadcast by the Qatari al-Jazeera TV network on the first day of the Muslim holy day Eid al-Adha, the Feast of Sacrifice. The sermon began, "Praise be to Allah who revealed the verse of the Sword to his servant and messenger [the Prophet Muhammad], in order to establish truth and abolish falsehood."[22]

Sura 9 also contains many other verses that rank among the Qur'an's most ferocious. According to Ibn Kathir, "the first part of this honorable Surah was revealed to the Messenger of Allah when he returned from the battle of Tabuk."[23] This expedition against the Eastern Roman Empire took place late in Muhammad's life—in fact, it was his last military adventure, undertaken within a year or so of his death in 632 A.D.

Sahih Muslim gives this reason for the foray: "Ibn Shihab reported that Allah's Messenger made an expedition to Tabuk and he (the Holy Prophet) had in his mind (the idea of threatening the) Christians of Arabia in Syria and those of Rome."[24] In doing this the Prophet was in line with Ibn Kathir's gloss on Sura 9:5's *slay them wherever you find them*: "Do not wait until you find them. Rather, seek and besiege them in their areas and forts, gather intelligence about them in the various roads and fairways so that what is made wide looks ever smaller to them. This way, they will have no choice, but to die or embrace Islam."[25]

According to Hazrat Moulana Sayyed Abul Hassan Ali Nadwi, a Muslim scholar and biographer of Muhammad, the Prophet had decided on a strategy that will be familiar to modern readers, a preemptive strike: "the Messenger of Allah decided to lead a Muslim army into Roman territory before the Roman armies crossed the Arab borders and threatened the heart of Islam."[26] By the time the Muslim armies had made their way through the scorching desert heat to the frontier, the Byzantine armies had withdrawn—a show of weakness, indifference, or both that set the stage for the warriors of jihad to conquer Syria within five years.

It was not the most propitious time for a military adventure. Ibn Kathir says that "some people from Al-Madinah [Medina] and some hypocrites, in and around it, lagged behind" Muhammad's expedition, "for that year was a year of drought and intense heat. . . . it was a hard year and the people were weak."[27] In the Qur'an, Allah scolds those who chose not to accompany the Prophet to Tabuk: "Those who were left behind (in the Tabuk expedition) rejoiced in their inaction behind the back of the Messenger of Allah: they hated to strive and fight, with their goods and their persons, in the cause of Allah: they said, 'Go not forth in the heat.' Say, 'The fire of Hell is fiercer in heat.' If only they could understand!" (Sura 9:81).

Sura 9 has two titles: it is known as *Sura At-Taubah* ("repentance") or *Sura Bara'ah* ("release"). Referring as it does to Muhammad's last military expedition, it is also "the last Sura which was revealed in full."[28] It is the only one of the Qur'an's 114 suras that doesn't begin with the classic Muslim invocation *Bismillah ar-Rahman ar-Rahim*: In the Name of Allah, the Compassionate, the Merciful. Opinions differ as to why this is so: a renowned ancient commentator on the Qur'an, Fakhr al-Din al-Razi (1149–1209), articulated the still-popular view that this was because the Prophet himself didn't begin recitation of this sura with the *Bismillah*, and later Muslims, scrupulous to adhere to the Qur'an as it was transmitted by Muhammad in even the smallest detail, have followed suit.

But why didn't Muhammad begin this sura with the customary invocation? An intriguing answer comes from another commentary that is still highly valued today in the Islamic world, *Tafsir al-Jalalayn*, a fifteenth-century work by the renowned imams Jalal al-Din Muhammad ibn Ahmad al-Mahalli (1389–1459) and Jalal al-Din 'Abd al-Rahman ibn Abi Bakr al-Suyuti (1445–1505). The invocation, suggests this *tafsir*, "is security, and [Sura 9] was sent down when security was removed by the sword."[29]

Security's removal by the sword meant specifically the end of many treaties the Muslims had made with non-Muslims. To the distress of those who claim that while Muhammad may have fought these particular infidels, he didn't actually mean to leave his followers with a universal command to fight *all* infidels, Ibn Kathir quotes an earlier authority, Ad-Dahhak bin Muzahim, to establish that the Verse of the Sword "abrogated every agreement of peace between the Prophet and any idolater, every treaty, and every term." He adds from another authority: "No idolater had any more treaty or promise of safety ever since Surah Bara'ah was revealed."[30] Another early commentator, Ibn Juzayy (d. 1340), agrees that one of this verse's functions is "abrogating every peace treaty in the Qur'an."[31]

In other words, the Muslim community is indeed commanded to fight against any and all unbelievers, not just against those Muhammad was facing when the Verse of the Sword was revealed.

This is underscored by the fact that Sura 9 is a Medinan Sura. Islamic theologians classify the 114 suras of the Qur'an as either "Meccan" or "Medinan." The Meccan suras date from the early period of the Prophet's career, when he concentrated on calling people to accept his new faith. In the year 622, Muhammad fled from Mecca to Medina to escape the growing hostility of the pagans in his native city; this was the *Hegira*, the event that marks the beginning of the Muslim calendar. In Medina, he became a head of state and a military leader for the first time.

There is general agreement among Muslim authorities about which suras come from Mecca and which from Medina, although a few are disputed (including the opening sura of the Qur'an, the *fatiha*, which has a status among Muslims akin to that of the Lord's Prayer among Christians). Most Muslim scholars estimate that slightly less than two-thirds of the Qur'an comes from Medina. Meccan suras tend to be shorter than their Medinan counterparts, as well as less preoccupied with matters of law and ritual for the new community. The verses that form the foundation of the celebrated Islamic principles of tolerance also generally come from Mecca, when Muhammad nurtured hopes that the Jews and Christians of the area would accept his claim to be a prophet. The verses with a more violent and intolerant edge generally date from Medina, when the Jews' and Christians' rejection of the Prophet of Islam was clear, and Muhammad was in no mood to be conciliatory.

The distinction between Meccan and Medinan suras becomes important because of the Muslim doctrine of abrogation (*naskh*), to which Ibn Juzayy referred when he said that the Verse of the Sword abrogated the Qur'an's peace treaties. Abrogation is the Islamic doctrine that Allah modifies and even cancels certain directives, replacing them with others. It is based on the Qur'an: "None of Our revelations do We abrogate or cause to be forgotten, but We substitute something better or similar: Knowest thou not that Allah Hath power over all things?" (Sura 2:106).

Allah complains to Muhammad in the Qur'an about how the Prophet's opponents use this idea to cast aspersions on him: "When We substitute one revelation for another,—and Allah knows best what He reveals (in stages),—they say, 'Thou art but a forger': but most of them understand not" (Sura 16:101; the parenthetical phrase is not in the Arabic original, but was added for clarity by the translator). Still, Muslim theologians use it to explain away difficulties in the Qur'an, such as that in one place the holy book says that wine has "some profit" (Sura 2:219) for mankind, but elsewhere declares it an "abomination, of Satan's handwork" (Sura 5:90).

The wine verses are a relatively clear instance of abrogation. Beyond that, there is wide disagreement among Muslim theologians as to precisely which verses have been abrogated and which others have replaced them. Still, Von Denffer says that a working knowledge of the idea of abrogation is "one of the important preconditions for explanation (*tafsir*) of the Qur'an."[32] And generally, if a verse revealed at Mecca contradicts another revealed later at Medina, Muslim theologians will give great weight to the idea that the Meccan verse has been abrogated and replaced by the verse from Medina.

This idea is crucial as a guide to the relationship of the Qur'an's peaceful passages to its violent ones. Suras 16, 29, 52, 73, and 109—the sources of most of the verses of peace and tolerance above—are all Meccan.[33] That means that anything they teach must be considered in light of what was revealed later in Medina. (The sole exception to this is the "no compulsion in religion" verse from the Medinan Sura 2, discussed below.) On the other hand, the last sura revealed, Sura 9, is Medinan. Thus it is in effect the Qur'an's last word on jihad, and all the rest of the book—including the "tolerance verses"—must be read in its light.

Ibn Kathir states this explicitly in his commentary on another "tolerance verse": "And he [Muhammad] saith: O my Lord! Lo! these are a folk who believe not. Then bear with them (O Muhammad) and say: Peace. But they will come to know" (Sura 43:88-89). The commentator explains that "say Salam (peace!) means, 'do not respond to them in the same evil manner in which they address you; but try to soften their hearts and forgive them in word and deed.'"

That, however, is not the last word on the subject. As Ibn Kathir notes, "But they will come to know. This is a warning from Allah for them. His punishment, which cannot be warded off, struck them, and His religion and His word was supreme. Subsequently Jihad and striving were prescribed until the people entered the religion of Allah in crowds, and Islam spread throughout the east and the west."[34]

In other words, Muhammad gave peace a chance with the pacific suras, and then understood that jihad was the more expedient course.

Three stages and two enemies

By examining contexts, comparing different (and differing) Qur'anic verses, and studying the circumstances of their revelation and other factors, Muslim theologians have distinguished three stages in the evolution of the Qur'an's understanding of jihad. According to the Chief Justice of Saudi Arabia, Sheikh 'Abdullah bin Muhammad bin Humaid, "at first 'the fighting' was forbidden, then it was permitted and after that it was made obligatory." He also distinguishes two groups Muslims must fight: "(1) against them who start 'the fighting' against you (Muslims) and (2) against all those who worship others along with Allah . . . as mentioned in *Surat Al-Baqarah* (II), *Al-Imran* (III) and *At-Taubah* (IX)...and other Surahs (Chapters of the Qur'an)."[35] (The Roman numerals after the names of the chapters of the Qur'an are the numbers of the Suras: Sheikh 'Abdullah is referring to verses quoted above such as Suras 2:216, 3:157-158, 9:5, and 9:29.)

This understanding of the Qur'an isn't limited to the ultra-strict Wahhabi sect of Saudi Arabia, to which Sheikh 'Abdullah belongs. The Pakistani Brigadier S. K. Malik's 1979 book *The Qur'anic Concept of War* (which made its way to the American mujahedin Jeffrey Leon Battle and October Martinique Lewis, and which carried a glowing endorsement from Pakistan's then-future President Muhammad Zia-ul-Haq, who said that it explained "the only pattern of war" that a Muslim country could legitimately wage) delineates the same stages in the Qur'anic teaching about jihad: "The Muslim migration to Medina brought in its wake events and decisions of far-reaching significance and consequence for them. While in Mecca, they had neither been proclaimed an Ummah [community] nor were they granted the permission to take up arms against their oppressors. In Medina, a divine revelation proclaimed them an 'Ummah' and granted them the permission to take up arms against their oppressors. The permission was soon afterwards converted into a divine command making war a religious obligation for the faithful."[36]

No compulsion . . . but no tolerance

Does that mean that Sura 2:256, "Let there be no compulsion in religion," is abrogated? Not necessarily. While Ibn Kathir quotes an early Muslim to say that the Verse of the Sword abrogated all of Muhammad's peace treaties, it doesn't follow that Muslims were now allowed to force unbelievers into the faith. As we have seen, Ibn Kathir states the two choices left open to unbelievers: "to die or embrace Islam."[37] But non-Muslims were also given a third choice: second-class status within the Islamic state. Islamic law has forbidden forced conversions since the beginnings of Islam—although this law has often been more honored in the breach than the observance.

This is made clear by another passage from the Sura that gives the Qur'an's last word on jihad: "Fight those who believe not in Allah nor the Last Day, nor hold that forbidden which hath been forbidden by Allah and His Messenger, nor acknowledge the religion of Truth, (even if they are) of the People of the Book, until they pay the Jizya with willing submission, and feel themselves subdued" (Sura 9:29). As for the context, Ibn Kathir explains that "this honorable *Ayah* [verse] was revealed with the order to fight the People of the Book . . . Allah commanded His Messenger to fight the People of the Scriptures, Jews and Christians, on the ninth year of Hijrah, and he prepared his army to fight the Romans and called the people to Jihad announcing his intent and destination."[38]

This verse doesn't say that Muslims are not to fight against Christians, Jews, and unbelievers until they are all Muslim or dead, but only until they pay the *jizya*, the non-Muslim protection tax, and are humbled under Islamic rule.

Modern Islamic apologists frequently reference Islamic tolerance, pointing to the Qur'an's recognition that Jews and Christians have received legitimate revelations from Allah. They point out also that Jews and Christians were granted the right to practice their religions in Islamic states. However, it is a grave anachronism, not to mention a gross factual error, to equate the stipulations of Islamic law with modern-day notions of freedom of thought and tolerance. This hadith attests to the decidedly second-class status to which non-Muslims were relegated: "As for Sura Tauba [Sura 9], it is meant to humiliate (the non-believers and the hypocrites)."[39]

Ibn Kathir elaborates on this in his commentary on Sura 9:29. That verse says that the People of the Book should "feel themselves subdued;" he glosses "subdued" as "disgraced, humiliated and belittled. Therefore, Muslims are not allowed to honor the people of *Dhimmah* or elevate them above Muslims, for they are miserable, disgraced and humiliated."[40] He quotes a hadith recorded by Imam Muslim, in which Muhammad says: "Do not greet the Jews and the Christians before they greet you and when you meet any one of them on the roads force him to go to the narrowest part of it."[41]

He quotes at length from an agreement made with a group of Christians by the second caliph, Umar ibn al-Khattab, who led the Muslims from 634 to 644 (Muhammad died in 632). The stipulations in this agreement formed the foundation for the Sharia's rules regarding the dhimmis; although various specific regulations were relaxed or ignored outright in various times and places throughout Islamic history, generally they remain part of the Sharia for anyone with the will and power to enforce them. According to Ibn Kathir, the Christians making this pact with Umar say:

We made a condition on ourselves that we will neither erect in our areas a monastery, church, or a sanctuary for a monk, nor restore any place of worship that needs restoration nor use any of them for the purpose of enmity against Muslims.[42]

This, of course, allowed Islamic rulers great and small to take possession of churches whenever they so desired. Since the testimony of Christians was discounted and in many cases disallowed, often a simple charge by a Muslim that a church was being used to foment "enmity against Muslims" was sufficient for that church to be seized.

The great historian of jihad and dhimmitude, Bat Ye'or, notes that "the refusal to accept the testimony of the dhimmi was based on the belief in the perverse and mendacious character of infidels since they stubbornly persisted in denying the superiority of Islam."[43] Ibn Kathir states this plainly. "Had they been true believers in their religions, that faith would have directed them to believe in Muhammad ... Therefore, they do not follow the religion of the earlier Prophets because these religions came from Allah, but because these suit their desires and lusts."[44]

As a result, Jews and Christians had no recourse. "Churches and synagogues were rarely respected. Regarded as places of perversion, they were often burned or demolished in the course of reprisals against infidels found guilty of overstepping their rights."[45]

The Christians' agreement with the caliph Umar continues. "We will not prevent any Muslim from resting in our churches whether they come by day or night. . . . Those Muslims who come as guests, will enjoy boarding and food for three days."[46] It should be obvious to any impartial observer how far this is from modern-day Western ideas of tolerance. Just how far is made clearer by the fact that this charity was not returned. A traveler to Famagusta in North Cyprus in 1651, when laws regarding dhimmitude were still very much in effect in the Ottoman Empire, "recounts that all the churches there had been converted into mosques and that Christians did not have the right to spend the night there."[47]

The more things change, the more they stay the same: Famagusta was overrun by Turkish troops in 1974. The Greek population was forced to evacuate and the city was sealed off; no one was allowed to enter. Now the city's many churches are marketed to international tourists as "icon museums," while the mosques (many of them converted churches) are still in active use. Tourists to the former St. Nicholas Cathedral, now the Lala Mustafa Pasha Mosque, are advised by one tour guide that "the interior is of course a Muslim prayer hall, the floor being covered with carpets, and all visitors must go round with the Imam."[48]

Umar's agreement with the Christians also mandates a number of humiliating regulations to make sure that the dhimmis "feel themselves subdued." The Christians concede:

> We will not... prevent any of our fellows from embracing Islam, if they choose to do so. We will respect Muslims, move from the places we sit in if they choose to sit in them. We will not imitate their clothing, caps, turbans, sandals, hairstyles, speech, nicknames and title names, or ride on saddles, hang swords on the shoulders, collect weapons of any kind or carry these weapons.

The regulations about different clothing and hairstyle, of course, made it easier to spot a dhimmi in a crowd and to make sure that he had paid the jizya and submitted to other legal requirements. The prohibition against weapons made it less likely that such investigations would meet with resistance.

> We will not encrypt our stamps in Arabic, or sell liquor. We will have the front of our hair cut, wear our customary clothes wherever we are, wear belts around our waist, refrain from erecting

crosses on the outside of our churches and demonstrating them and our books in public in Muslim fairways and markets. We will not sound the bells in our churches, except discreetly, or raise our voices while reciting our holy books inside our churches in the presence of Muslims.

After these and other rules are fully laid out, the agreement concludes:

These are the conditions that we set against ourselves and followers of our religion in return for safety and protection. If we break any of these promises that we set for your benefit against ourselves, then our *Dhimmah* (promise of protection) is broken and you are allowed to do with us what you are allowed of people of defiance and rebellion.[49]

Ibn Kathir also explains that the *jizya* was designed to offer financial compensation to Muslims who suffered losses by breaking all commercial ties with the early Muslim community's polytheistic neighbors. "Allah compensated them for the losses they incurred because they severed ties with idolaters, by the *Jizyah* they earned from the People of the Book."[50]

The Verse of the Sword, in sum, is still in effect, and various other passages of Sura 9 clarify its precise meaning and applicability. While the regulations of dhimmitude are not enforced in countries where the Sharia is not the law of the land, and is ignored in whole or part in many places that do hold to the Sharia, they are still a part of Islamic law—as a Saudi preacher recently emphasized. In a Friday sermon at a mosque in Mecca, Sheikh Marzouq Salem Al-Ghamdi echoed Ibn Kathir. "The Jews and Christians are infidels, enemies of Allah, his Messenger, and the believers. They deny and curse Allah and his Messenger. . . . How can we draw near to these infidels?...They deny even the messengers sent to them. They do not believe in Moses, they do not believe in Jesus— because if they really believed in them, they would join Islam, because every prophet heralded to his nation the coming of the Prophet Muhammad and the need to believe in him." He also repeated the Sharia's classic injunctions on dhimmitude:

> If the infidels live among the Muslims, in accordance with the conditions set out by the Prophet—there is nothing wrong with it provided they pay *Jizya* to the Islamic treasury. Other conditions are...that they do not renovate a church or a monastery, do not rebuild ones that were destroyed, that they feed for three days any Muslim who passes by their homes...that they rise when a Muslim wishes to sit, that they do not imitate Muslims in dress and speech, nor ride horses, nor own swords, nor arm themselves with any kind of weapon; that they do not sell wine, do not show the cross, do not ring church bells, do not raise their voices during prayer, that they shave their hair in front so as to make them easily identifiable, do not incite anyone against the Muslims, and do not strike a Muslim...If they violate these conditions, they have no protection.[51]

Even in Saddam Hussein's relatively secular Iraq, Christians had a hard time. The Reverend Said Bello, a Chaldean Catholic who left Iraq for Canada in 1990 but has maintained close ties with the Christian community there, reports that Christians in Iraq are "living like slaves. . . . The Christians have no work, and no revenue. The powerful are taking advantage of the weak. In some cases, young mothers whose husbands were killed in war have been obliged to become Muslims to feed their children."[52]

While the interpretation of Ibn Kathir and the others isn't the last word on the Qur'an, or the only way to look at it, it is a traditional and common view in Islam. Ibn Kathir, Imam Bukhari, Imam Muslim, and the other authorities I have cited are not marginal figures in the Islamic world. Radical Muslims are able to appeal to a firmly traditional and well-known understanding of the Qur'an to justify their concept of jihad. A Muslim who attends a *madrassa*, an Islamic religious school, will study these texts as he attempts to become proficient in understanding the Qur'an.

No doubt these texts were carefully taught in the Malaysian Luqmanul Hakiem madrassa, where three Muslims named Amrozi, Imam Samudra, and Idris studied Islam. In the name of Islam, these three men on October 12, 2002, set off explosions that killed 202 people in Bali.[53] They were certainly studied in Sheikh Omar Abdel Rahman's classes at the prestigious and venerable Al-Azhar University of Cairo, Egypt. Sheikh Omar, who is now in federal prison in the United States for conspiring to blow up the World Trade Center in 1993, was once approached by a Muslim student at Al-Azhar who asked him why he never taught about love and forgiveness, but only about "jihad and killing." Sheikh Omar responded: "Listen, my brother, there is a whole Sura called Al-Anfal ["Spoils of War," Sura 8]; there is no Sura of Peace. Jihad and killing is the head of Islam. If you take it out, you cut off the head of Islam."[54] Saddam Hussein took the name of this Sura for his genocide against the Kurds in 1988: Operation al-Anfal.

It should be clear by now that these men are anything but marginalized eccentrics preaching a twisted minority version of Islam. On the contrary, the ideas of jihad and dhimmitude are widespread in the Muslim world today—as they always have been.

The Carolina Qur'an controversy

That's the main reason why the 2002 controversy over the University of North Carolina's assignment of a translation of a part of the Qur'an to all incoming freshmen was a cause for genuine concern. The assigned book was *Approaching the Qur'an: The Early Revelations*, translated by Michael Sells. The "early revelations" of the subtitle are the Meccan suras examined above, which preach tolerance and mutual coexistence without a hint of the doctrines of jihad and dhimmitude that unfold in later Qur'anic revelations.

The question springs to mind: what was such a misleading presentation designed to accomplish, especially in light of continuing threats from terrorists? Sells has defended his decision to translate only early Meccan Suras on the grounds that they are the most accessible introduction to the Qur'an and Islamic study as a whole. That may be true, but taken in isolation as the only book a young non-Muslim would read about Islam, *Approaching the Qur'an* could be severely misleading about the nature of the religion as a whole and about the intentions and motives of Islamic terrorists, the very people who have made Islam such a "hot topic" for students.

Most Americans are uneasy about the idea that terrorism might be rooted in the Qur'an, because religious toleration is such a fundamental American belief. Sells himself has summed up the prevailing view. "If you look at history, you'll find that every religion is both a religion of peace and a religion of violence, depending on who is interpreting it, which passages they foreground, and how they interpret those passages. To say that any religion is either peaceful or violent is a useless simplification, really."[55]

Similarly, many are quick to say that the Qur'an is not alone; the Bible—or the Old Testament in particular—contains exhortations to violence. But even if this were true, it is beside the point, because it does nothing to explain why the world today is filled with Muslim terrorist groups, not Christian ones.

The important difference is this: certainly people of all religions have committed horrific acts of violence in the name of their religion. But Islam has a long-established tradition of interpreting the Qur'an in a way that allows Muslims to justify such violence, and indeed even to think that it might be required of them. Christianity—with its emphasis on turning the other cheek, redemptive suffering, loving one's neighbor—and other religions have no comparable tradition. Christian martyrs meet their end by being persecuted unto death, while Islamic martyrs are suicide killers. That's a big difference.

Chapter Five

MUHAMMAD IN THE FIELD

The Wars of the Prophet

S ECOND IN AUTHORITY ONLY to the Qur'an itself is the
example and teaching of the Prophet Muhammad. Also, his
career provides the first and best example of how Muslims
understood the Qur'an. It would add considerable weight to claims
that "the Qur'an teaches nonviolence" if Muhammad himself con-
fronted his enemies in a nonviolent manner. Conversely, if Muhammad took seriously the Qur'an's verses on jihad, it becomes
exponentially more difficult for moderate Muslims to advise their
coreligionists not to do so today.

Muhammad's teachings

Modern Muslims, particularly in America and Western Europe, never tire of quoting a remark made by the Prophet Muhammad upon his return from a battle: "We are returning from the lesser jihad to the greater one."[1] When his followers asked him what constituted the greater jihad, he replied that it was the struggle to bring the soul into conformity with Allah's will. The lesser jihad includes, but is not limited to, struggle on the battlefield for the sake of truth and justice—and who can object to that, particularly the post-Christian West, with its "just war" theory? Muslims also point to long-established elaborations of the meaning of jihad as a spiritual struggle within the soul of the believer.

While these traditions provide some comfort for non-Muslims with its suggestion that Muslims would do better to tend to their own souls rather than to wage war against their neighbors, they actually don't establish what both Muslims and non-Muslims seem to wish they did. On one hand, the traditional pedigree of the spiritual jihad is not as firm as it is often advertised to be; on the other, like it or not, military jihad has much greater support in Islamic scripture, tradition, and actual practice. Some Muslim scholars and, more ominously, some leading radical Muslim theorists, including Hasan al-Banna, the founder of the Muslim Brotherhood, and Abdullah Azzam, Osama bin Laden's friend and intellectual mentor, even deny the authenticity of the saying in which Muhammad makes a distinction between "greater jihad" and "lesser jihad."[2]

I am not suggesting that the radicals are right and that the moderates are wrong; only that their extremist followers are teaching and convincing young men all over the world today that they are right and that the moderates are wrong. To do so, they invoke the teaching and example of the Prophet.

The Prophet spoke clearly about his own responsibility to wage war for the religion he had founded. "I have been ordered (by Allah) to fight against the people until they testify that none has the right to be worshipped but Allah and that Muhammad is the Messenger of Allah, and perform *As-Salat* (prayers) and give *Zakat* [obligatory charity], so if they perform all that, then they save their lives and properties from me except for Islamic laws, and their reckoning (accounts) will be with (done by) Allah."[3]

This is one of the best attested statements in the Hadith. Bukhari repeats it five times; it also appears three times in *Sahih Muslim* and once in *Sunan Abu Dawud*.[4] Muslims who study Hadith give a statement a presumption of authenticity if it appears even once in *Bukhari* or *Muslim*; the repetitions and its presence in a third respected Hadith collection make its authenticity virtually certain. The repetitions are attested by different chains of transmission, suggesting that Muhammad said this on numerous occasions, or to many different people, or both.

Muhammad was firm about the necessity of jihad not only for himself personally, but for every Muslim. He warned believers that "he who does not join the warlike expedition (jihad), or equip, or looks well after a warrior's family when he is away, will be smitten by Allah with a sudden calamity."[5]

But the incentives weren't all negative. When one of his followers asked him what was the "best deed" after belief in Allah and the prophethood of Muhammad, the Prophet answered, "To participate in Jihad (holy fighting) in Allah's Cause."[6] Elsewhere Muhammad names jihad as the third best deed, after regular daily prayer and obedience to one's parents.[7] Yet another Hadith has the Prophet asserting that "no good deeds done on other days are superior to those done on these (first ten days of Dhul Hijja)"—that is, the days of the great Muslim pilgrimage to Mecca, the Hajj. But when some of his companions ask, "Not even jihad?" Muhammad adds: "Not even Jihad, except that of a man who does it by putting himself and his property in danger (for Allah's sake) and does not return with any of those things (i.e., is martyred)."[8]

"Paradise," said Muhammad, "is under the shades of swords."[9] The Prophet also told believers that jihad guarantees the warrior a place in Paradise—unless he fights out of a desire for worldly gain or some other impure motive. "Allah assigns for a person who participates in (holy battles) in Allah's cause and nothing causes him to do so except belief in Allah and His Messengers, that he will be recompensed by Allah either with a reward, or booty (if he survives) or will be admitted to Paradise (if he is killed in the battle as a martyr)."[10] But if he fights in jihad "desiring some worldly advantage," then "there is no reward for him."[11]

Muhammad explained the tripartite offer that Muslims are to make to non-Muslims: convert to Islam, submit to Islamic rule, or face war. "When you meet your enemies who are polytheists," the Prophet directed his followers, "invite them to three courses of action. If they respond to any one of these you also accept it and withhold yourself from doing them any harm. Invite them to (accept) Islam; if they respond to you, accept it from them and desist from fighting against them. . . . If they refuse to accept Islam, demand from them the Jizya. If they agree to pay, accept it from them and hold off your hands. If they refuse to pay the tax, seek Allah's help and fight them."[12]

How long will jihad last? Muhammad envisioned it not as a limited defensive action to establish his religious community in the face of its enemies, as some Muslim and non-Muslim Islamic apologists claim today. On the contrary, he saw it continuing far beyond his lifetime. "Jihad will be performed continuously since the day Allah sent me as a prophet until the day the last member of my community will fight with the Dajjal (Antichrist)." Nor can the call for jihad be altered by unjust rulers—or just ones, for that matter.

"The tyranny of any tyrant and the justice of any just (ruler) will not invalidate it. One must have faith in Divine decree."[13] That was one reason why Saddam Hussein, as detested as he was by pious Muslims, was able to get a hearing for his calls to jihad: the Muslim media broadcast and promoted his claim that the very survival of Islam itself was at stake. Against that, his being a tyrant mattered not a whit.

Muhammad's actions

Muhammad didn't just teach about jihad. He led Muslim armies in battle against non-Muslim foes, such that by the end of his life Islam was virtually the sole religion in Arabia and Muslim armies were in a position to threaten the great empires of Byzantium and Persia.

It's no surprise that Muhammad's battles are a hotly contested issue these days. Sources disagree about whether these battles were offensive or defensive, and to what extent Muhammad was justified in his actions; the number of battles and the casualty rates vary widely as well.

However, no one disputes that the Prophet of Islam did actually fight battles, and that he did so in the name of jihad. I limit my discussion here to purely Islamic sources, including Hadith collections accepted as reliable by Muslims. What follows is not a comprehensive report of Muhammad's military campaigns (*maghazi*), but merely an examination of some details that have bearing on the modern-day Muslim understanding of jihad.

Bukhari records a hadith saying that Muhammad took part in nineteen battles.[14] According to the Prophet's biographer Ibn Ishaq (Muhammad Ibn Ishaq Ibn Yasar, 704–773), Muhammad participated in twenty-seven raids and battles, ordering and directing all of them and actually fighting in nine. Ibn Ishaq records this information in his book *Sirat Rasul Allah (Biography of the Prophet of Allah)*, the first biography of Muhammad.

Unfortunately, this book in its original form is lost to history. It exists only in a later revised and shortened version by Ibn Hisham, who died sixty years after Ibn Ishaq, and in fragments quoted by other early Muslim writers. Ibn Hisham explains that in his version he omits, among other material from Ibn Ishaq's biography, "things which it is disgraceful to discuss; matters which would distress certain people; and such reports as al-Bakka'i told me he could not accept as trustworthy."[15] Some of these "disgraceful" matters may have induced Malik ibn Anas (715–801), himself the compiler of a respected Hadith collection, *Muwatta*, to call Ibn Ishaq "an antichrist" and to complain that the biographer "reports traditions on the authority of the Jews."[16] However, Malik and Ibn Ishaq later reconciled, and numerous other early Muslim authorities attest to the biographer's reliability. One Muslim who knew him for many years stated that "none of the Medinans suspected him or spoke disparagingly of him"; another contemporary called him "truthful in tradition."[17]

In favor of Ibn Ishaq's trustworthiness as a historical source is the fact that the distaste that some early Muslims felt for him stemmed from his writings on Islamic law, not his historical writings. He was suspected of quoting legal traditions with incomplete or inadequate chains of transmitters establishing their authority (although he scrupulously includes such chains for most of his historical accounts). He was further accused of Shi'ite tendencies and other deviations from orthodoxy. But the great Islamic jurist Ahmed ibn Hanbal (780–855) summed up the prevailing view: "in *maghazi* [Muhammad's military campaigns] and such matters what Ibn Ishaq said could be written down; but in legal matters further confirmation was necessary."[18]

Ibn Ishaq's biography of the Prophet is, in any case, by far the earliest source extant on the life of Muhammad, and its contents have over the centuries passed into the general consciousness of Muslims. Many incidents in the Prophet's life, including ones that became influential in Islamic history, have no other source; later Muslim historians' accounts often depend solely on Ibn Ishaq. He is read and respected by Muslims today; Muslim bookstores still stock copies of his biography among more modern lives of the Prophet.[19]

The main thing that makes Ibn Ishaq's life of Muhammad questionable as history is that it has the air more of pious hagiography than of a sober historical study. Ibn Ishaq was a believing Muslim with an obviously deep faith. He was anxious to portray Muhammad as a larger-than-life figure, as in an incident in which the captive wife of a man he had ordered killed poisons the Prophet's dinner. According to Ibn Ishaq, the Prophet had some preternatural awareness of the woman's deed; he spat out the poisoned meat, exclaiming, "This bone tells me that it is poisoned."[20] On another occasion his men were digging a large trench for a battle and came upon a huge rock that no one could move. The Prophet spat in some water and sprinkled it on the rock, whereupon the obstacle became "pulverized as though it were soft sand so that it could not resist axe or shovel."[21]

But for our present purposes it is less important what really happened in Muhammad's life than what Muslims have generally accepted as having happened, for the latter has formed the foundation of Muslim belief, practice, and law throughout the centuries. And for that, Ibn Ishaq is an entirely adequate source.

The first great battle Muhammad fought was the battle of Badr, where a vastly outnumbered Muslim force defeated an army of the pagan Quraysh, Muhammad's own people from Mecca who had rejected his prophetic status. The battle began over a raid by the

Muslims on a Quraysh caravan. According to Ibn Ishaq, Muhammad discovered that Abu Sufyan, a Quraysh leader and determined enemy of the Prophet, "was coming from Syria with a large caravan of Quraysh, containing their money and merchandise." Muhammad called together his followers and said, "This is the Quraysh caravan containing their property. Go out and attack it, perhaps God will give it as a prey." Ibn Ishaq adds, "The people answered his summons, some eagerly, others reluctantly because they had not thought that the apostle would go to war."[22]

The planned raid escalated into a full-scale battle, during which Muhammad exhorted his troops with the promise of Heaven. "By God in whose hand is the soul of Muhammad, no man will be slain this day fighting against them with steadfast courage advancing not retreating but God will cause him to enter Paradise." One who heard his words then exclaimed, "Fine, Fine! Is there nothing between me and my entering Paradise save to be killed by these men?" He flung away some dates that he had been eating, rushed into the thick of the battle, and fought until he was killed.[23]

Such accounts still resonate today among mujahedin around the world, including suicide bombers. Nor did Muhammad hesitate to repeat this promise on numerous occasions. One of his companions once asked him, "Is it not true that our men who are killed (in Jihad in Allah's cause) will go to Paradise and theirs (i.e., those of Al-Mushrikun [the unbelievers]) will go to the (Hell) fire?" The Prophet answered simply, "Yes."[24] According to Muhammad, "Leaving (for Jihad) in the way of Allah in the morning or in the evening (will merit a reward) better than the world and all that is in it."[25]

Fighting in jihad will also gain the warrior a higher level of Paradise. The Prophet spoke of an act "which elevates the position of a man in Paradise to a grade one hundred (higher), and the elevation between one grade and the other is equal to the height of the heaven from the earth." That act? "Jihad in the way of Allah! Jihad in the way of Allah [*jihad fi sabil Allah*]!"[26]

Another tradition has a Muslim asking Muhammad, "Messenger of Allah, do you think that if I am killed in the way of Allah, my sins will be blotted out from me?" Muhammad replied, "Yes, if you were patient and sincere and always fought facing the enemy and never turning your back upon him, (all your lapses would be forgiven) except debt. Gabriel has told me this."[27]

A later engagement with the Quraysh, the battle of Uhud, didn't go as well for the Muslims. But in the wake of the defeat Allah promised them that "soon shall We cast terror into the hearts of the unbelievers, for that they joined companions with Allah, for which He had sent no authority: their abode will be the fire: and evil is the home of the wrong-doers!" (Sura 3:151). This terror from Allah, an image that recurs in the Qur'an and other Muslim sources, has become a favorite rejoinder of contemporary Islamic radicals when charged with terrorism or sympathy with terrorists. As the Saudi Sheikh Wajdi Hamza Al-Ghazawi put it in a sermon, "The meaning of the term 'terror' used by the media . . . is Jihad for the sake of Allah."[28]

The turn of the Quraysh would come in time, but presently Muhammad dealt with the Banu Nadir, a Jewish tribe of Medina. One of Muhammad's followers had murdered two men with whom Muhammad had a friendship agreement. Muhammad thus, according to the customs of the day, owed blood money; he went to the men of the Banu Nadir to ask them for help in raising the necessary funds. They agreed to help but secretly plotted to drop a stone on Muhammad's head from a rooftop as he left the area. The Prophet got wind of the plot (from Allah, according to Ibn Ishaq) and secretly returned to his headquarters in Medina, whence he ordered an attack on the Banu Nadir.

When the men of the tribe saw Muhammad's army approaching, they sued for peace. Muhammad gave praise to Allah, who had, in accordance with his promise after the battle of Uhud, "cast terror into their hearts" (Sura 59:2). The Banu Nadir were deported from Medina; they were allowed to take only as much of their belongings as they could carry on their camels' backs. Ibn Ishaq records that only two members of this tribe accepted Islam, and they only did so "in order to retain their property."[29]

But other Jews in Arabia were still opposed to Muhammad, and now they joined with the Quraysh to attack the Muslims in Medina. The Prophet set his followers to digging a large trench around the city "and worked at it himself encouraging the Muslims with the hope of reward in heaven." One worker recounted:

> I was working with a pick in the trench where a rock gave me much trouble. The apostle [Muhammad] who was near at hand saw me hacking and saw how difficult the place was. He dropped down into the trench and took the pick from my hand and gave such a blow that lightning showed beneath the pick. This happened a second and a third time. I said, "O you, dearer than father or mother, what is the meaning of this light beneath your pick as you strike?" He said, "Did you really see that, Salman? The first means that God has opened up to me the Yaman [Yemen]; the second Syria and the west; and the third the east."...Abu Hurayra used to say when these countries were conquered in the time of 'Umar and 'Uthman and after, "Conquer where you will, by God, you have not conquered and to the resurrection day you will not conquer a city whose keys God had not given beforehand to Muhammad."[30]

Everyone in this story—Muhammad, Salman, Abu Hurayra, and evidently Ibn Ishaq himself—seem to assume that Allah will "open up" Yemen, Syria, and other territories to the Muslims not by the word, but by the sword: not by preaching, but by conquest. And that is how it happened.

Doubtless the people of those regions were invited to accept Islam before the fight was engaged. In line with Muhammad's instructions quoted above, that is what Islamic law dictates. The Battle of the Trench (as it came to be known among Muslims) was one of the occasions in which these principles were forged. One warrior of the Quraysh, Amr, challenged the Muslims to send out one man for hand-to-hand combat and taunted them about Muhammad's promises of Paradise. "Where is your garden of which you say that those you lose in battle will enter it? Can't you send a man to fight me?" As might be expected, since Muhammad was himself from Mecca, the home of the Quraysh, Amr had relatives among the Muslims. His nephew Ali, who was also Muhammad's cousin and son-in-law (and later the great revered figure of Shi'a Islam), took up his challenge. To his uncle he said, "I invite you to God and His apostle and to Islam."

Amr rebuffed the overture and refused to dismount. But he added, "O son of my brother, I do not want to kill you."

Ali was less sentimental. He replied to his uncle: "But I want to kill you," and he did.[31]

After the Battle of the Trench, which was another victory for the Muslims, the Angel Gabriel himself made sure that Muhammad continued fighting and pressed his advantage against his enemies. According to a hadith transmitted by his favorite wife, Aisha, "When Allah's Messenger returned on the day (of the battle) of *Al-Khandaq* (i.e., the Trench), he put down his arms and took a bath. Then Jibril (Gabriel), whose head was covered with dust, came to him saying, 'You have put down your arms! By Allah, I have not put down my arms yet.' Allah's Messenger said, 'Where (to go now)?' Jibril said, 'This way,' pointing towards the tribe of Bani Quraiza. So Allah's Messenger went out towards them."[32]

Gabriel was determined that the Prophet should deal with the Banu Qurayza, another Jewish tribe of Arabia, because they had treacherously broken an agreement with the Muslims not to aid their enemies. As his armies approached their fortifications, Muhammad addressed them in terms that have become familiar usage for Muslim radicals speaking of Jews today—language that, as we have seen, also made its way into the Qur'an. "You brothers of monkeys, has God disgraced you and brought His vengeance upon you?"[33]

According to Ibn Ishaq, they replied to this, "O Abu'l-Qasim [Muhammad], you are not a barbarous person." If they were trying to soften his wrath, they failed. Muhammad even told his followers that a warrior who passed by on a white mule was actually Gabriel, "who has been sent to Banu Qurayza to shake their castles and strike terror to their hearts." The Muslims "besieged them for twenty-five nights until," says Ibn Ishaq, "they were sore pressed" and, as Muhammad had warned, "God cast terror into their hearts."[34]

Also, casting terror into their hearts may have been the choices offered them by their own chief, Ka'b ibn Asad, who had made and broken the treaty with Muhammad. The first was to accept Muhammad and Islam, "for by God it has become plain to you that he is a prophet who has been sent and that it is he that you find mentioned in your scripture; and then your lives, your property, your women and children will be saved."[35] The second choice was to kill their wives and children, "leaving no encumbrances behind us," and go fight Muhammad. The third choice was to ambush the Prophet on the Sabbath. The Banu Qurayza rejected all three, but chose to surrender to the Muslims.

After some deliberation, Muhammad decided to put the fate of the tribe into the hands of a man named Sa'd ibn Mu'adh. A hadith tells what happens next. "When the tribe of Bani Quraiza was ready to accept Sa'd's judgment, Allah's Messenger sent for Sa'd who was near to him. Sa'd came, riding a donkey, and when he came near, Allah's Messenger said (to the *Ansar*), 'Stand up for your leader.' Then Sa'd came and sat beside Allah's Messenger who said to him, 'These people are ready to accept your judgment.' Sa'd said, 'I give the judgment that their warriors should be killed and their children and women should be taken as captives.'"

The Prophet was pleased. "O Sa'd! You have judged amongst them with (or similar to) the judgment of the King (Allah)."[36] Ibn Ishaq reports this, carefully noting a chain of transmitters back to Muhammad, "You have given the judgment of Allah above the seven heavens."[37] (Later, when Sa'd died, Ibn Ishaq records several early Muslim traditions asserting that the very throne of Allah shook.[38])

Sa'd's sentence was duly carried out. "The apostle went out to the market of Medina (which is still its market today) and dug trenches in it. Then he sent for [the men of Banu Qurayza] and struck off their heads in those trenches as they were brought out to him in batches." One of the Prophet's fiercest enemies among the Banu Qurayza, Huyayy, proclaimed, "God's command is right. A book and a decree, and massacre have been written against the Sons of Israel." Then Muhammad struck off his head.

Sa'd's judgment had been to kill the men and enslave the women and children; one of the captives, Attiyah al-Qurazi, explained how the Muslims determined who was a man and who wasn't: "I was among the captives of Banu Qurayzah. They (the Companions) examined us, and those who had begun to grow hair (pubes) were killed, and those who had not were not killed. I was among those who had not grown hair."[39]

Ibn Ishaq puts the number of those massacred at "six or seven hundred in all, though some put the figure as high as eight or nine hundred."[40]

This incident has been understandably a source of embarrassment to Muslims, particularly in the modern period. Various Muslim apologists have attempted to deny the incident altogether or to minimize the number of casualties. Others point to the treachery of the Banu Qurayza as justifying Sa'd's sentence and Muhammad's approval of it.

The incident is amply attested in various ahadith. One summarizes Muhammad's dealings with several groups of Arabian Jews. "Bani An-Nadir and Bani Quraiza fought (against the Prophet violating their peace treaty), so the Prophet exiled Bani An-Nadir and allowed Bani Quraiza to remain at their places (in Medina) taking nothing from them till they fought against the Prophet again. He then killed their men and distributed their women, children and property among the Muslims, but some of them came to the Prophet and he granted them safety, and they embraced Islam. He exiled all the Jews from Medina. They were the Jews of Bani Qainuqa', the tribe of 'Abdullah bin Salam and the Jews of Bani Haritha and all the other Jews of Medina."[41]

Ibn Ishaq also notes that the Qur'an speaks about the event in Sura 33. Referring to the Quraysh and the Banu Qurayza who helped them instead of Muhammad, it says: "And those of the People of the Book who aided them—Allah did take them down from their strongholds and cast terror into their hearts. (So that) some ye slew, and some ye made prisoners" (Sura 33:26).

Ultimately it is not so important for considerations of the present-day scene how many of the Banu Qurayza were killed by Muhammad, or other aspects of this horrifying event. The important thing is that it established a precedent that was enshrined in Islamic law. The Sharia gives Muslim captors the right to kill or enslave their non-Muslim prisoners as they deem expedient. According to the renowned jurist of the Hanafi school, Ya'qub Abu Yusuf (731–798), "There is no objection to the use of any kind of arms against the polytheists... one can even pursue those that run away, finish off the wounded, kill prisoners who might prove dangerous to the Muslims." No doubt Muhammad considered the Banu Qurayza to be possibly "dangerous to the Muslims."

In line with the Muslims' distinction (as recounted by Attiyah al-Qurazi) between men and boys among the Banu Qurayza, Abu Yusuf further directs that what he has outlined about prisoners "is only applicable to those on the chin of whom a razor has passed, for the others are children and are not to be executed."

The ultimate decision is up to the imam. "As for the prisoners who are led before the imam, the latter has the choice, as he pleases, of executing them or making them pay a ransom, opting for the most advantageous choice for the Muslims and the wisest for Islam."[42]

A Sharia manual from the Shafi'i jurisprudential school agrees. "When an adult male is taken captive, the caliph considers the interests (O: of Islam and the Muslims) and decides between the prisoner's death, slavery, release without paying anything, or ransoming himself in exchange for money or for a Muslim captive held by the enemy. If the prisoner becomes a Muslim (O: before the caliph chooses any of the four alternatives) then he may not be killed, and one of the other three alternatives is chosen."[43] (The parenthetical phrases marked "O" refer to commentary by an Islamic jurist, Sheikh 'Umar Barakat.)

These old laws have never been repudiated or abrogated. Their non-enforcement in many Muslim countries today is due to their partial or complete disregard of the Sharia, not because the content of the Sharia has been fundamentally altered. But when Iraqi Foreign Minister Naji Sabri Ahmad al-Hadithi said in March 2003 that American prisoners would "be treated according to the principles of Islam," he could only have been referring to principles such as those outlined above.[44]

After the Banu Qurayza incident, Muhammad "went out against Banu Lihyan to avenge his men killed at al-Raji.... He made as though he was going to Syria in order to take the people by surprise."[45] But the men of the Banu Lihyan learned of the surprise attack and took up fortified positions in the mountains. The Prophet thus contented himself with curses. During prayers "the Prophet invoked evil on the infidels every morning for thirty days. He invoked evil upon the (tribes of) Ri'l, Dhakwan, Bani Lihyan and Usaiyya, who disobeyed Allah and His Messenger."[46]

He had better luck at al-Hudaybiya, ten miles north of Mecca, where he went on a pilgrimage and ended up concluding a ten-year treaty with the Quraysh allowing the Muslims access to the holy sites of Mecca. This too has passed into Islamic law. A truce, according to the Shafi'i school, "is a matter of the gravest consequence because it entails the nonperformance of jihad, whether globally or in a given locality." Nonetheless, "if the Muslims are weak, a truce may be made for ten years if necessary, for the Prophet made a truce with Quraysh for that long."[47]

This pact with the Quraysh effectively ended that tribe's alliance with the remaining Arabian Jews in Khaybar, whom the Muslims proceeded to attack. Among these Jews of the Khaybar were the Banu Nadir, who had fled there after Muhammad had exiled them from Medina. Muhammad now summoned Kinana ibn al-Rabi, the keeper of the Banu Nadir's treasury, and asked him where the wealth of the Banu Nadir was kept. Kinana denied knowing where it was, whereupon Muhammad asked, "Do you know that if we find you have it I shall kill you?" He ordered Kinana tortured and then beheaded.[48]

Then "the apostle besieged the people of Khaybar in their two forts al-Watih and al-Sulalim until when they could hold out no longer they asked him to let them go, and spare their lives, and he did so." He agreed to let the Jews of Khaybar continue to work the land and give the Muslims half of the produce, with the under-standing that, in Muhammad's words, "if we wish to expel you we will expel you."[49] It was a foundation of the dhimmi status later elaborated in Islamic law: the Jews would live as virtual slaves, turning over a large portion of their substance to the Muslims, all the while knowing that if they violated the terms of their agreement, they would be driven from their homes.

Finally there came the conquest of Muhammad's home city of Mecca and the ultimate reconciliation of the Quraysh to the new religion. The Quraysh had attacked a tribe allied with the Muslims, effectively ending the treaty of al-Hudaybiya. Facing an over-whelming Muslim force, the Quraysh commander Abu Sufyan, heretofore "the enemy of God," paid a visit to the Prophet. Abbas, one of Muhammad's companions, told Abu Sufyan, "Submit and testify that there is no God but Allah and that Muhammad is the apostle of God before you lose your head." Abu Sufyan complied, and directed the Meccans not to resist the Muslim army.[50] Muhammad entered the ancient Meccan shrine, the Ka'ba, and removed the idols; he also removed them from surrounding areas. As Islamic law later stipulated in regard to the dhimmis, no one would be forced to accept Islam; however, the old pagan religions of Mecca were driven underground, and those who converted to Islam were given superior status.

Muhammad consolidated his victory with a successful expedi-tion against the pagan Hawazin and the Thaqif tribes, whom he defeated at Hunayn, a valley near Mecca. Finally, he moved against the Byzantines in Tabuk. He also contacted the Byzantine emperor, Heraclius, and other rulers in the region, sending them letters: "the Prophet of Allah wrote to Chosroes (King of Persia), Caesar (Emperor of Rome) [that is, Heraclius], Negus (King of Abyssinia) and every (other) despot inviting them to Allah, the Exalted."[51]

Abu Sufyan, the former bitter foe of the Prophet, delivered Muhammad's letter to Heraclius when the Byzantine emperor was visiting Jerusalem. Bukhari reproduces the letter:

> In the name of Allah the Most Gracious, the Merciful (This letter is) from Muhammad, the slave of Allah and His Messenger to Heraclius the ruler of the Byzantines. Peace be upon him who follows the right path. Then after: I invite you to Islam, and if you become a Muslim you will be safe, and Allah will double your reward, and if you reject this invitation of Islam you will be committing a sin by misguiding your *Arisiyin* (peasants). (And I recite to you Allah's Statement:) "O people of the Scripture (Jews and Christians)! Come to a word that is between us and you, that we worship none but Allah and that we associate no partners with Him, and that none of us shall take others as lords beside Allah. Then, if they turn away, say: Bear witness that we are Muslims." (V.3:64).[52]

Again, the Prophet offers the triple choice: conversion, death, or submission under Islamic rule.

Although he "invites" Heraclius to embrace Islam, there is a threat in this: the emperor would not be "safe" if he refused. And sure enough, not long after Muhammad's death, the Muslims invaded the Byzantine Empire, certain they were fighting in the service of Allah, and certain that they would be richly rewarded whether they died or lived.

They gained this certainty from the words of Muhammad himself, who made his intentions absolutely clear. He promised, "The first army amongst my followers who will invade Caesar's city [Constantinople] will be forgiven their sins."[53]

And in Islamic history, the mujahedin would have plenty of other chances to prove their mettle.

Chapter Six

IN THE PROPHET'S FOOTSTEPS

Jihad and Dhimmitude in
Early and Modern Islam

Arab expansion or Islamic jihad?

WHEN MUHAMMAD DIED in 632, his followers understood that he had left them with a religion that was at once both missionary and martial. Almost immediately, the Muslims showed that they considered it a fundamental part of their duties before Allah to invite their neighbors to accept Islam and to make war upon them if they refused. In one of the most impressive records of conquest by any people anywhere at any time, Muslim armies swept out of Arabia and established a vast Islamic empire in an astonishingly brief period. Caesar's city, the object of Muhammad's promise of forgiveness of sins, very quickly had good reason to feel threatened.

The rapid expansion of the Islamic empire is a historical fact. Its significance in illuminating what jihad really means and how it is practiced cannot be minimized. If the Qur'an and the Prophet taught that jihad was solely or primarily a spiritual struggle, or one of self-defense, why did Muhammad's own followers get it all so drastically wrong? How could such a titanic figure have failed so utterly to instruct his followers properly? Whatever the murkiness of the details surrounding the life of the Prophet, there is no doubt that the early Muslims revered him as the best of men and the enduring example for all mankind. It strains credulity to believe that they completely misunderstood his teachings about jihad, as central as these teachings were to early Islam. Clearly the words and actions of those who knew and loved the Prophet are the best indication of what Muhammad actually meant by jihad and a great deal else. Now these too, of course, are almost as shrouded in legend and special pleading as are the teachings and deeds of Muhammad himself, but about one thing there is no doubt: in the years immediately following Muhammad's death, the Muslims carried out a series of raids and invasions against their non-Muslim neighbors, and these had a new religious dimension that previous raids by Arabian tribes had never had. Jihad had begun, and the world would never be the same.

American Muslim advocacy groups and scholarly apologists try to explain away (with varying degrees of success) the Prophet Muhammad's battlefield career as a matter of defending the infant *umma* against enemies bent on destroying it, but the history of Islam under the early caliphates is tougher to explain. Nevertheless, academics have attempted numerous explanations. The great historian Bernard Lewis brushes aside the idea that these wars were examples of jihad. "Initially, the great conquests were an expansion not of Islam but of the Arab nation, driven by the pressure of over-population in its native peninsula to seek an outlet in the neighboring countries."[1] Islamic scholar John Esposito even asserts that "many early Muslims regarded Islam solely as an Arab religion," although he immediately acknowledges the contrary fact that Muslim invaders offered the triple choice of conversion, submission, or death to non-Muslims in the lands they conquered. "As Islam penetrated new areas, people were offered three options: (1) conversion, that is, full membership in the Muslim community, with its rights and duties; (2) acceptance of Muslim rule as 'protected' people and payment of a poll tax; (3) battle or the sword if neither the first nor the second option was accepted."[2]

However, another popular historian of the Arab world, Philip K. Hitti, explicitly rejects the idea that the conquests were fueled by religion. "Not fanaticism but economic necessity drove the Bedouin hordes (and most of the armies of conquest were recruited from the Bedouins) beyond the confines of their arid abode to the fair lands of the north. The dream of heaven in the next life may have influenced some, but desire for the comforts and luxuries of the civilized regions of the Fertile Crescent was just as strong in the case of many."[3]

These desires may have made up part of a complex of motives for the Muslims, but the historical record simply doesn't allow for the motive of jihad to be set aside entirely. The chance for economic gain doesn't mean that religious motives are not present, especially in an Islamic context, where warfare and booty are legislated by divinities as religious matters. In the seventh century, as in the present day, a variety of motivations coalesced in the hearts and minds of a large number of men; it would be condescending and ethnocentric to discount their explicit avowals of religious motives as a mere cover for what was more important to them. Then, as now, religion was more important to a great many people outside the West than to postmodern, secular Americans and Europeans. The motivations of Islamic warriors changed the entire nature of what one might very imperfectly call East-West conflict in the seventh century, just as it does today. If the early Muslims were really impelled by a desire for *lebensraum* and economic gain, why did they continue to fight non-Muslims when the Islamic empires were the greatest power on earth, and their riches the envy of the world? Poverty and economic and social resentments could not have been the reasons.

In any case, the early Muslim conquests were astonishingly swift, impelled by a furious energy the like of which the world had never seen before (and would never see again). "If someone in the first third of the seventh Christian century," says Hitti, "had had the audacity to prophecy that within a decade or so some unheralded, unforeseen power from the hitherto barbarous and little-known land of the Arabians was to make its appearance, hurl itself against the only two world powers of the age, fall heir to the one (the Sasanid) and strip the other (the Byzantine) of its fairest provinces, he would undoubtedly have been declared a lunatic. Yet that was exactly what happened."[4]

Before the Prophet had been dead ten years, Muslim armies had taken Syria, Egypt, and Persia. Muslim armies conquered Damascus in 635, only three years after Muhammad's death; substantial portions of Iraq in 636; Jerusalem in 638; Caesarea in 641; and Armenia in 643. The conquest of Egypt took place in the same period. The Muslims also won decisive victories over the Byzantines at Sufetula in Tunisia in 647, opening up North Africa; and over the Persians at Nihavand in 642. By 709 they had complete control of North Africa; by 711 they had subdued Spain and were moving into France. Muslim forces first besieged "Caesar's city" of Muhammad's promise, Constantinople, for a full year starting in August 716; but despite repeated subsequent attempts, it would not fall to them for another 700 years. Meanwhile, Sicily fell in 827. By 846 Rome was in danger of being captured by Muslim invaders; repulsed, they "sacked the cathedrals of St. Peter beside the Vatican and of St. Paul outside the walls, and desecrated the graves of the pontiffs."[5]

These were not defensive wars. The Muslims in Arabia were not threatened by either of the two great powers bordering on their lands, Byzantium and Persia, unless one counts the very presence of large neighboring empires to be a threat. These powers were too consumed with each other to pay much attention to the rise of Muhammad's empire.

Nor were they Arab wars; after the conquests, the victors constructed a society based on Muslim, not Arab, hegemony. A convert to Islam from the conquered peoples enjoyed rights far greater than those granted to those of his countrymen who did not convert. The Muslim armies considered themselves to be advancing in the spirit dictated by Muhammad: accept Islam or face war.

The idea that the early jihads were only superficially religious also founders upon the record of the Muslims in India. Muslim forces tried to invade India by sea as early as 634, an astounding achievement in itself for a group made up largely of desert Bedouins—not a people renowned for their maritime exploits. Finally, the Muslims opted to invade by land. They pressed into what is now Afghanistan, Pakistan, and India from the eighth century on, making slow but steady progress. According to the Hindu historian Sita Ram Goel, by 1206, the Muslim invaders had conquered "the Punjab, Sindh, Delhi, and the Doab up to Kanauj."[6] Later waves expanded these holdings to the Ganges and beyond.

Sita Ram Goel concedes that "India before the advent of Islamic imperialism was not exactly a zone of peace.... But in all their wars, the Hindus had observed some time-honored conventions sanctioned by the Sastras. The Brahmins and the Bhikshus were never molested. The cows were never killed. The temples were never touched. The chastity of women was never violated. The noncombatants were never killed or captured. A human habitation was never attacked unless it was a fort. The civil population was never plundered. War booty was an unknown item in the calculations of conquerors." In contrast, says the historian, "Islamic imperialism came with a different code—the Sunnah [tradition] of the Prophet. It required its warriors to fall upon the helpless civil population after a decisive victory had been won on the battlefield. It required them to sack and burn down villages and towns after the defenders had died fighting or had fled. The cows, the Brahmins, and the Bhikshus invited their special attention in mass murders of noncombatants. The temples and monasteries were their special targets in an orgy of pillage and arson. Those whom they did not kill, they captured and sold as slaves. The magnitude of the booty looted even from the bodies of the dead, was a measure of the success of the military mission. And they did all this as *mujahids* (holy warriors) and *ghazis* (*kafir* [unbeliever]-killers) in the service of Allah and his Last Prophet."[7]

Of course, when Hindus fought Hindus they observed these restraints because they shared the same values: both sides revered the same temples, monasteries, and, for that matter, cows. But Sita Ram Goel is right that the actions of the Muslims were in accord with Islamic law and precedent; these actions can't be attributed solely to attempts to end resistance and demoralize the locals. The Muslim invaders' behavior was consistent with the example of the Prophet who once enjoined one of his followers "to attack Ubna in the morning and burn the place."[8] (On another occasion, however, Muhammad forswore the use of fire as a punishment. According to one of his companions, Abu Huraira, "Allah's Messenger sent us in an expedition (i.e., an army unit) and said, 'If you find so-and-so and so-and-so, burn both of them with fire.' When we intended to depart, Allah's Apostle said, 'I have ordered you to burn so-and-so and so-and-so, and it is none but Allah Who punishes with fire, so, if you find them, kill them.'"[9] The great radical Muslim thinker Sayyid Qutb considers this episode an admirable example of the Prophet's adherence to principle.[10])

Muhammad himself often benefited from the booty taken in battles from non-Muslims, even directing his followers to devote some of the booty they won to the cause of Islam. As part of the meaning of "believing in Allah alone," he ordered Muslims to "pay *Al-Khumus*," i.e., "one-fifth of the booty to be given in Allah's Cause"—that is, for the defense of Islamic societies, as well as for mundane matters such as upkeep of mosques, payment of muezzins, and the like.[11] Accordingly, after the conquest of Iraq, the caliph Umar directed that whatever "possessions and horses" the Muslim troops acquired be divided among them, "after taking away one-fifth."[12]

Islamic legislators later set down that "anyone who, despite resistance, kills one of the enemy or effectively incapacitates him, risking his own life thereby, is entitled to whatever he can take from the enemy, meaning as much as he can take away with him in the battle, such as a mount, clothes, weaponry, money, or other."[13]

Hindu temples and monasteries would have been particular targets of the Muslims because they were considered places of idolatry. Historian K. S. Lal explains that Muslim conquerors in India "destroyed temples because it is enjoined by their scriptures. In the history of Islam, iconoclasm and razing other peoples' temples are central to the faith. They derive their justification and validity from the Quranic Revelation and the Prophet's *Sunna* or practice." Consequently, "thousands of Hindu shrines and edifices disappeared in northern India by the time of Sikandar Lodi and Babur"—that is, the early sixteenth century. Lal notes that many mosques and other

Muslim structures were built "from the debris of Hindu temples." He quotes historian Will Durant, "We can never know from looking at India today, what grandeur and beauty she once possessed."[14]

Although the Hindus have often been extended the privileges of the "People of the Book," they aren't officially among the religious groups that are singled out for protection—including some protection for their houses of worship—under Islamic law. At times, having the status of the "People of the Book" was no guarantee of safety anyway, especially in cases in which non-Muslim armies offered stiff resistance to the Muslims; the eighth century Muslim invaders of France burned churches in Bordeaux and Poitiers before they were pushed back into Spain.[15]

Those who deny or minimize the role of Islam in these conquests are faced in such cases with behavior that's otherwise inexplicable: why would the Muslim invaders behave this way when they didn't have to do so in order to gain control of the territory, and indeed when doing so forever hardened a segment of the population against them?

The steady expansion of Muslim holdings in Europe was surely driven by more than a desire for material gain and territory. When the sultan Mehmet laid siege to Constantinople in 1453, the Byzantine Empire was an mere shadow of its former self. Certainly there was immense symbolic value in the capture of the city, but by that time it was of little political or economic significance; Mehmet's Islamic empire was already in firm control of the surrounding territories. The sultan, in accordance with the Sharia, still offered them Muhammad's three-part choice: "surrender of the city, death by the sword, or conversion to Islam."[16]

Some Muslim conquests both in Europe and India, of course, were later lost. The great Islamic empire gradually declined in power and began to lose territory rather than gain it, but it must be emphasized that this was a political, not a theological development. In other words, Muslims didn't stop waging jihad because they ceased to believe in it, but because they were no longer able to do so. The theology that fueled these military campaigns in the first place was never repudiated. The early Muslim conquests followed the pattern delineated by the tenth-century Muslim writer Ibn Abi Zayd al-Qayrawani (922–996), a legal theorist of the Maliki school of jurisprudence (*madhhab*). He was only summarizing the evidence of the Qur'an and the teachings of the Prophet when he wrote, "Jihad is a precept of Divine institution.... We Malikis maintain that it is preferable not to begin hostilities with the enemy before having invited the latter to embrace the religion of Allah except where the enemy attacks first. They have the alternative of either converting to Islam or paying the poll tax [*jizya*], short of which war will be declared against them.... It is incumbent upon us to fight the enemy without inquiring as to whether we shall be under the command of a pious or depraved leader."[17]

Likewise, the great Muslim philosopher Averroes (1126–1198) wrote, "the Muslims are agreed that the aim of warfare against the People of the Book...is twofold: either conversion to Islam, or payment of poll-tax (*jizya*)."[18] The great rigorist jurist of the Hanbali school, Ibn Taymiyya (1263–1328), agreed. He defines jihad as "the punishment of recalcitrant groups, such as those that can only be brought under the sway of the Imam by a decisive fight.... For whoever has heard the summons of the Messenger of God, peace be upon him, and has not responded to it, must be fought, 'until there is no persecution and the religion is God's entirely' (Koran 2:193, 8:39)."[19]

By contrast, the Crusades, which are often blamed for igniting the ongoing hostility between the Muslim world and the West, were never buttressed by anything like this kind of theological elaboration. Despite their role as a whipping-boy in modern-day analyses, the Crusades, for all the abuses of the Crusaders, were actually conceived of as defensive actions against the steadily advancing Muslims. Neither Christianity nor any other religion has ever had a doctrine like jihad. The great medieval Muslim historian Ibn Khaldun acknowledges this, and in fact chalks it up as one of the advantages of Islam. "The other religious groups [that is, besides Islam] did not have a universal mission, and the holy war was not a religious duty to them, save only for purposes of defense. It has thus come about that the person in charge of religious affairs in (other religious groups) is not concerned with power politics at all." But Muslim leaders are quite concerned with "power politics," because Islam is "under obligation to gain power over other nations."[20]

Such scholars are not merely the dead voices of the past. Not only did these ideas and assumptions fuel the conquests; they still live among Muslim radicals. In his 1996 declaration of jihad against the United States, Osama bin Laden praises Ibn Taymiyya for arousing "the Ummah of Islam against its enemies" and calls for an end to the modern-day silence "imposed on the scholars (Ulama) and callers (Da'ees) of Islam by the iniquitous crusaders' movement under the leadership of the USA."[21]

Islamization and dhimmitude

Hand-in-hand with jihad goes dhimmitude, the institutionalized subjugation of non-Muslim minorities. As we have seen, Islamic law regards non-Muslim minorities in Muslim countries, as dhimmis, or "protected people." Muslims and non-Muslim apologists attempt to portray this system as a uniquely generous, fair-minded, and tolerant arrangement—in short, a prototype for today's secular Western societies.

But often left unremarked in such analyses is the fact that this protection came at a price, and did not leave the "protected" people on an equal footing with those who protected them. According to historian Habib C. Malik of the Lebanese American University, "Over the centuries, political Islam has not been too kind to the native Christian communities living under its rule. Anecdotes of tolerance aside, the systematic treatment of Christians and Jews (who fall under the Islamic category of *dhimmi*) as second-class citizens is abusive and discriminatory by any standard. . . . Under Islam, the *dhimmi* are not allowed to build new places of worship or renovate existing ones; *dhimmi* women are available for marriage to Muslims while the reverse is strictly prohibited; the political rights of *dhimmis* are absent; and the targeted *dhimmi* community and each individual in it are made to live in a state of perpetual humiliation in the eyes of the ruling community."

For Malik the implications of all this are clear. "These measures can only spell a recipe for gradual liquidation."[22]

On their way to this fate, these "subject peoples" were required, according to Islamic legal manuals, to "pay the non-Muslim poll tax (jizya)" and had to accept multiple signs of their inferior status, discussed earlier.[23] Details varied, but these laws were generally applied in the Islamic empires, and relaxations invariably met with protests from the Muslim majority.

These regulations were not in place only in the Middle East. In India, dhimmitude status was magnanimously extended to the Hindus, even though they aren't "People of the Book," by Muhammad bin Qasim, who conquered Sind in 712. Later conquerors and rulers followed his example. K. S. Lal emphasizes that this did not grant tolerance and equality to the Hindus; "at the most it allows survival on payment of a poll-tax, *Jiziyah*, and acceptance of a second class status, that of *Zimmi*."[24] Hindus, like Christians and Jews, had to live in a state of perpetual humiliation. They had to pay the *jizya* while being spat upon; Christians and Jews had to pay it while receiving a blow on the head.[25]

Yet conventional wisdom has it that Syria, Egypt, Persia, and the other lands that are now cornerstones of the House of Islam adopted their new faith freely in the wake of the conquests, impelled by its natural attractiveness rather than by social advantage—and certainly not by the sword. Cultural imperialism is a concept that scholars tend to apply only to later, Western empires, and thus it seldom, if ever, enters into the popular mind that these conquests, which after all took place so very long ago, were a species of imperialism. The Metropolitan Museum of Art, in a book for children entitled *Fun with Hieroglyphs*, explains blandly that Egyptians used hieroglyphic writing until around 400 A.D., when Egyptians adopted a modified form of the Greek alphabet. "This late form of Egyptian is called Coptic. Eventually Coptic was replaced by Arabic, the language spoken in Egypt today."[26]

Coptic was indeed replaced by Arabic, but the transition was made not by nature, but by war. One twelfth-century Coptic monk, speaking almost five hundred years after the Muslim conquest of Egypt, still found it within him to assert, "We are the masters of this country, both from the point of view of population as well as for the land tax. The Muslims took it from us, they appropriated it by force and violence, and it is from our hands that they seized power." He also referred to "the massacre that they wrought on our kings and our ruling families during their conquest."[27] In the fourteenth century, an Egyptian Muslim writer noted, "the Copts declare that this country still belongs to them, and that the Muslims evicted them from it unlawfully."[28]

Yet Hitti blandly asserts that "the native Semites of Syria and Palestine, as well as their Hamite cousins of Egypt, looked upon the Arabian newcomers as nearer of kin than their hated and oppressive alien overlords."[29] In this he echoes the English convert to Islam and translator of the Qur'an, Muhammad Marmaduke Pickthall, who asserted in a 1927 lecture on "Tolerance in Islam" that "in Egypt the Copts were on terms of closest friendship with the Muslims in the first centuries of the Muslim conquest, and they are on terms of closest friendship with the Muslims at the present day. In Syria the various Christian communities lived on terms of closest friendship with the Muslims in the first centuries of the Muslim conquest, and they are on terms of closest friendship with the Muslims at the present day, openly preferring Muslim domination to a foreign yoke."[30]

The caliph Umar, who ruled and expanded the empire of Islam from 634 to 644, was more realistic. "Do you think," he asked, "that these vast countries, Syria, Mesopotamia, Kufa, Basra, Misr [Egypt] do not have to be covered with troops who must be well paid?"[31] Why the occupying troops, if the inhabitants welcomed the invaders and lived with them on terms of closest friendship? Why did the Copts still complain centuries after the conquest that their close friends had stolen the land from them?

Numerous histories and descriptions of the Muslim conquests suffer from the same amnesia. Many of these have a scholarly patina. A multi-volume college textbook called *The Cambridge History of Islam* states that after the Muslim conquest of Egypt in 641, "the Christian and Jewish populations obtained the usual lenient treatment regularly accorded to the People of the Book." Elsewhere this lenient treatment is spelled out. "Christians were to be given protection, and to have freedom of worship, paying a tax which in comparison was less heavy than that which in the past they had paid to Byzantium."[32]

Lenient treatment? A more favorable tax than under Byzantium? Amr ibn al-As, the conqueror of Egypt, adhered to the guarantees of protection given to the People of the Book who accepted Muslim rule. He "did not touch the property of the churches, preserved them from all pillage, and protected them during the entire length of his government." This was in accord with the nascent

Muslim laws concerning dhimmis, and it is acknowledged in a seventh-century account by John of Nikiou, a Coptic bishop. But John adds that, in accordance with the Qur'an's directives about the *jizya*, the non-Muslim poll tax (Sura 9:29), "he raised the tax to as much as twenty-two batr of gold, with the result that the inhabitants, crushed down by the burden and in no position to pay it, went into hiding." Others "came to the point of offering their children in exchange for the enormous sums that they had to pay each month."[33]

Despite the claim of *The Cambridge History*, it seems unlikely that the tax could have been uniformly higher under Byzantine rule. In any case, even in quieter times non-Muslims in Egypt had to pay twice what Muslims paid, as a hadith dating from shortly after the conquest specifies. It directs tax collectors to assess Egyptian Muslims "one dinar out of every 40 dinars," while the dhimmis are to be assessed "one dinar on every 20 dinars."[34] That the Muslims would establish a system of taxation based on the religion of the subjects of its empires bears witness to the essentially religious component of their conquests.

Analyses that minimize the resistance and oppression of the native populations don't adequately consider the realities of institutionalized jihad and dhimmitude. The early Muslim conquerors more or less scrupulously observed the regulations regarding dhimmis derived by early Muslim jurists from the Qur'an and the words of the Prophet. There were to be no forced conversions (although this rule was not always obeyed); rather, non-Muslims would suffer so many social and economic disadvantages that conversion would become the sole gateway to a livable existence.

Continuing jihad and dhimmitude

Jihad and dhimmitude have never vanished from Muslim lands—not in the nineteenth century, not in the twentieth century, and not now.

In 1892 a Persian decree reemphasized, among many other niggling regulations designed to reinforce a status of subservience, that Jews "must not wear fine clothes... [and] are forbidden to wear matching shoes.... A Jewish creditor of a Muslim must claim his debt in a quavering and respectful manner.... If a Muslim insults a Jew, the latter must drop his head and remain silent.... It is forbidden for him to have a house higher than his Muslim neighbor."[35] A quite similar edict was promulgated in Yemen in 1905; it also prohibited Jews from saying that a "Muslim law can have a defect."[36] This sort of law put non-Muslims in a double bind. A Muslim could say to a Jew, "If the Sharia has no defect, why don't you confess that Muhammad is the Prophet of Allah? And if you do not confess him, you must in fact believe that it does have a defect." In 1982 two Yemeni Jews recalled that "until our departure from Yemen in 1949, it was forbidden for a Jew to write in Arabic, to possess arms, or to ride on a horse or camel.... We had to lower our head, accepting insults and humiliations. The Arabs called us 'stinking dogs.' Jewish children who became orphans before they were fifteen were forcibly converted to Islam.... The Jews worked in all occupations except agriculture. They made shoes for the Arabs, but they themselves were not allowed to wear them."[37]

A traveler to Morocco in 1880 reported that the local government was intent on making its non-Muslim population "feel themselves subdued." "A deputation of Israelites, with a grave and reverend rabbi at their head," asked the local Muslim ruler to appeal to the sultan for permission "for them to wear their shoes in the town. 'We are old, Bashador,' they said, 'and our limbs are weak; and our women, too, are delicately nurtured, and this law presses heavily upon us.'" Yet the traveler "was glad they were dissuaded from pressing their request, the granting of which would exasperate the populace, and might lead to consequences too terrible to contemplate."[38]

Eight years later the Anglo-Jewish Association pushed for the abolition of dhimmi laws in Morocco, under which Jews were required to "live in the ghetto... On leaving the ghetto they are compelled to remove their footwear and remove their headcovering.... Jews are not permitted to build their houses above a certain height.... Jews 'are not allowed to drink from the public fountains in the Moorish quarter nor to take water therefrom' as the Jews are considered unclean."[39] There were other humiliating regulations as well. Although there were local variations, these laws—because they are grounded in the Sharia—are remarkably consistent throughout the Muslim world. In any case, the Anglo-Jewish Association appeal went nowhere.

In 1894 in another part of the Ottoman Empire, Armenia, the dying Ottoman government initiated genocide based on the long-established stipulation that dhimmis enjoyed protection only as long as they accepted their second-class status. "If non-Muslim subjects of the Islamic state refuse to conform to the rules of Islam," states a legal manual, "or to pay the non-Muslim poll tax, then their agreement with the state has been violated." In that event, the Muslim leadership may deal with them along the lines of the four alternatives delineated for prisoners of war: death, slavery, ransom, or release.[40]

The Ottomans chose death for the Armenians. According to the chief dragoman (Turkish interpreter) of the British embassy, when the Turks initiated the first wave of the Armenian genocide in 1894, they were "guided in their general action by the prescriptions of the Sheri [Sharia] Law. That law prescribes that if the 'rayah' [dhimmi] Christian attempts, by having recourse to foreign powers, to overstep the limits of privileges allowed them by their Mussulman [Muslim] masters, and free themselves from their bondage, their lives and property are to be forfeited, and are at the mercy of the Mussulmans. To the Turkish mind, the Armenians had tried to overstep those limits by appealing to foreign powers, especially England. They therefore considered it their religious duty and a righteous thing to destroy and seize the lives and properties of the Armenians."[41] According to historian Bat Ye'or, "the genocide of the Armenians was a *jihad*. No *rayas* [dhimmis] took part in it."[42] The fact that none of the many non-Muslim minorities in the Ottoman Empire at that time helped the Turks "pacify" Armenia points to the religious character of the whole enterprise.

The missionary Johannes Lepsius, who visited Armenia during World War I, recounts how well the Ottomans did their work, and referred to the cover-up of these horrific events. "Are we then simply forbidden to speak of the Armenians as persecuted on account of their religious belief? If so, there have never been any religious persecutions in the world. . . . We have lists before us of 559 villages whose surviving inhabitants were converted to Islam with fire and sword; of 568 churches thoroughly pillaged, destroyed and razed to the ground; of 282 Christian churches transformed into mosques; of 21 Protestant preachers and 170 Gregorian (Armenian) priests who were, after enduring unspeakable tortures, murdered on their refusal to accept Islam. We repeat, however, that those figures express only the extent of our information, and do not by a long way reach to the extent of the reality. Is this a religious persecution or is it not?"[43]

The *New York Times* reported it in 1915. "Both Armenians and Greeks, the two native Christian races of Turkey, are being systematically uprooted from their homes en masse and driven forth summarily to distant provinces, where they are scattered in small groups among Turkish Villages and given the choice between immediate acceptance of Islam or death by the sword or starvation." The *Times of London* noted somewhat later that Assyrian Christians in what is now Iraq suffered at the hands of the Turks as well. "Telegrams from Mesopotamia state that some 47,000 refugees, largely Nestorians, have come into the British lines after having got through the Turkish lines. Many of these are being taken to camps near Baghdad. A further 10,000 have been absorbed in the towns of Kurdistan or are wandering among the hills. These refugees have come from the Urumia region, which was isolated during the Turkish advance in North-West Persia.... The day after this escape the Turks entered Urumia and massacred 200 unresisting people—mostly old men—while 500 Christian women are reported to have been distributed between the Turkish troops and the Moslem inhabitants."[44]

The *New York Times* predicted that unless Turkey lost the war, "there will soon be no more Christians in the Ottoman Empire."[45] Despite losing the war, postwar secular Turkey substantially fulfilled this prophecy, animated by principles rooted in the Sharia's provisions about religious minorities.

In the genocides of 1915–1916 and 1922–1923, around 1.5 million Armenians were killed. Yet despite mountains of documentation, including photographic evidence and eyewitness testimony, to this day the Turkish government persists in denying that the genocide ever happened. These denials, as craven and outrageous as they are, are not entirely surprising. After all, the West in general is suffering from a case of denial that touches on much more than just Armenia: this persistent and pervasive denial encompasses virtually all the crimes perpetrated anywhere and at any time in the name of Islam. The West flees from sitting in judgment upon any religion—save Christianity—even when that reli-

gion believes, and practices, the idea of holy war against nonbelievers, which means, among others, the secular and Judeo-Christian West.

In our own day, both the denial and the crimes continue. Muslims have slaughtered millions of Hindus in Bangladesh, Kashmir,
and India. In Pakistan, they have regularly targeted Christians for
violence. Thousands of Christians were killed in Cyprus during the
1974 Turkish takeover of the northern part of the island. Assyrian
Christians have been massacred by Muslims in Iraq sporadically
during the nineteenth and twentieth centuries. Conflicts rage today
between Muslims and non-Muslims in Indonesia, the Philippines,
Nigeria, and elsewhere. Samuel Huntington observes in *The Clash
of Civilizations,* "Wherever one looks along the perimeter of Islam,
Muslims have problems living peacefully with their neighbors. . . .
Muslims make up one-fifth of the world's population but in the
1990s they have been far more involved in intergroup violence
than people of any other civilization." Huntington goes on to show
that more than half of the "ethnopolitical" conflicts in the world
involved Muslims and there were "three times as many intercivilizational conflicts involving Muslims as there were conflicts
between all non-Muslim civilizations. The conflicts within Islam
also were more numerous than those in any other civilization. . . .
Conflicts involving Muslims also tended to be heavy in casualties. . . . Three different compilations of data . . . yield the same conclusion: In the early 1990s Muslims were engaged in more
intergroup violence than were non-Muslims, and two-thirds to
three-quarters of intercivilizational wars were between Muslims
and non-Muslims. Islam's borders *are* bloody, and so are its
innards."[46]

Yet the West refuses to acknowledge the facts of Islamic history,
with real world consequences today. Bat Ye'or points out that a
whitewash of history is being used to establish an Islamic state in

Bosnia. In Muslim, pre-Communist Bosnia, Christians lived under the constraints of dhimmitude. But because the West prefers to believe the myth of Islamic "tolerance," Bosnian President Izetbegovic and his supporters repeatedly affirm "that the five hundred years of Christian dhimmitude was a period of peace and religious harmony," and thus provides a model for the future.[47]

In June 2002, the Zayed Center of Washington, D.C., an organization sponsored by United Arab Emirates ruler Sheikh Zayed Bin Sultan Al Nahyan, sponsored a symposium on "The Jews in The Arab World." Blithely ignoring the facts of history, the participants concluded that Jews had it great under Islam, "which rendered an exemplary model of tolerance, understanding, peaceful living, religious and sectarian freedom, in addition to preservation of the rights to privacy."[48]

If this beggars the imagination—especially the last phrase, which absurdly echoes the language of abortion and homosexual rights activists in the West—this is only the beginning of the myth-making, as we'll see.

Chapter Seven

THE MODERN MYTH OF ISLAMIC TOLERANCE

The Fact of Modern Islamic Intolerance

Muslim Spain: the myth

USLIM SPAIN IS A BEACON of hope in a fractious and frightened world. Karen Armstrong, the author of *Islam: A Short History*, wants us to "remember that until 1492, Jews and Christians lived peaceably and productively together in Muslim Spain—a coexistence that was impossible elsewhere in Europe."[1]

This is no new idea. In 1897, historian Stanley Lane-Poole wrote, "for nearly eight centuries, under her Mohammedan rulers, Spain set to all Europe a shining example of a civilized and enlightened state... Whatsoever makes a kingdom great and prosperous, whatsoever tends to refinement and civilization, was found in Moslem Spain." By contrast, the Catholic Spain of Ferdinand and Isabella gave rise to "the abomination of desolation, the rule of the Inquisition, and the blackness of darkness in which Spain has been plunged ever since."[2] Almost a hundred years later Anthony Burgess lamented the vanished "beauty, tolerance, learning and good order" of the Emirate of Cordoba.[3] Even the U.S. State Department, heralding the opening of a museum devoted to Islam and Muslims in that jewel of Islamic culture, Jackson, Mississippi, proclaimed that "during the Islamic period in Spain, Jews, Christians, and Muslims lived together in peace and mutual respect, creating a diverse society in which vibrant exchanges of ideas took place."[4]

By now all this has passed into the popular consciousness. Andalusia under Islamic rule was a proto-multiculturalist paradigm, all the more appealing to modern post-Christian Westerners because this paradise of tolerance was not constructed under the auspices of Christianity, thereby seeming to vindicate their long insistence that all cultures are equal and that some—particularly non-Christian ones—are more equal than others. And at the opposite end of the political spectrum, *National Review* marveled at al-Andalus as "a plush region on Spain's Mediterranean coast with a vibrant economy and an adventurous intellectual community, ruled by a benign Islamic monarch whose Jewish right-hand man helps bring about a mutually beneficial relationship with Orthodox Christians."[5]

It's a potent idea in these post-September 11 days: Osama bin Laden and other terrorists have allegedly given Islam's detractors a fresh excuse to vilify Islam as a violent religion—but al-Andalus shows us a very different, and most inviting, Muslim reality in history. Edward Said, whose *Orientalism* and *Covering Islam* are the twin towers of today's academic Islamophilia, complained early in

2003 that "for almost a year American politicians, regional experts, administration officials, and journalists have repeated the charges that have become standard fare so far as Islam and the Arabs are concerned. Most of this predates September 11 [2001]. To today's practically unanimous chorus has been added the authority of the UN human development report on the Arab world, which certified that Arabs dramatically lag behind the rest of the world in democracy, knowledge, and women's rights." Said decries all this as "vague, recycled Orientalist clichés repeated by tireless mediocrities such as Bernard Lewis" and sneers at "the clash of civilizations that George Bush and his minions are trying to fabricate"—as well as at the idea that the Muslim world needs to "join modernity."[6]

Instead, Said and his own minions call upon the Muslim world to recall the greatness of Islamic civilization. For modern Westerners and many Muslim moderates, this greatness finds its apogee in al-Andalus, a place where Muslims, Christians, and Jews lived and worked together in harmony—and which might hold the key to recovering that peace in our own day.

Or at least so claims scholar María Rosa Menocal, who revived the by-now hoary cultural images of tolerant, vibrant Muslim Spain in a warmly received 2002 study entitled *The Ornament of the World*. Yossi Klein Halevi (the author of a book entitled *At the Entrance to the Garden of Eden: A Jew's Search for God with Christians and Muslims in the Holy Land*) calls it "essential reading" for "all those who believe that religion still has a role to play in helping humanity heal and evolve."[7] Menocal herself speaks of Andalusia as a fount of "our cultural memories and possibilities."[8] In his foreword to Menocal's book, Harold Bloom laments that "there are no Muslim Andalusians visible anywhere in the world today."[9]

But were there ever any Muslim Andalusians?

Muslim Spain: the reality

Menocal paints a romantic, impressionist picture of Muslim Spain, deliberately evoking a mythic past: her book even begins "Once upon a time...."[10] When the Muslim conquerors established their culture of tolerance, they "not only allowed Jews and Christians to survive but, following Quranic mandate, by and large protected them.... In principle, all Islamic polities were (and are) required by Quranic injunction not to harm the dhimmi, to tolerate the Christians and Jews living in their midst."[11] It's refreshing to see Menocal acknowledge that the laws of dhimmitude are still on the books for Islamic polities, and even more refreshing that unlike many writers, she details some of the terms of this "protection":

> The *dhimmi*, as these covenanted peoples were called, were granted religious freedom, not forced to convert to Islam. They could continue to be Jews and Christians, and, as it turned out, they could share in much of Muslim social and economic life. In return for this freedom of religious conscience the Peoples of the Book (pagans had no such privilege) were required to pay a special tax—no Muslims paid taxes—and to observe a number of restrictive regulations: Christians and Jews were prohibited from attempting to proselytize Muslims, from building new places of worship, from displaying crosses or ringing bells. In sum, they were forbidden most public displays of their religious rituals.[12]

So much for a paradise of tolerance and multiculturalism. Historian Kenneth Baxter Wolf observes that "much of this new legislation aimed at limiting those aspects of the Christian cult which seemed to compromise the dominant position of Islam." After enumerating a list of laws much like Menocal's, he adds, "Aside from such cultic restrictions most of the laws were simply designed to underscore the position of the dimmîs as second-class citizens."[13] These laws were not uniformly or strictly enforced; Christians were forbidden public funeral processions, but one contemporary account tells of priests merely "pelted with rocks and dung" rather than being arrested while on the way to a cemetery.[14]

Yet if such laws were on the books in al-Andalus, and, as we have seen, they were elsewhere in the Islamic world up to modern times, then a fundamental premise of Menocal's thesis (or what others have made of it) is undercut. If Muslims, Christians, and Jews lived together peaceably and productively—only with Christians and Jews relegated by law to second-class status—then al-Andalus has precisely nothing to teach our age about tolerance. The laws of dhimmitude give all of Menocal's accounts of Jewish viziers and Christian diplomats the same hollow ring as the stories of prominent American blacks from the slavery and Jim Crow eras. Yes, Frederick Douglass and Booker T. Washington were great men, but their accomplishments not only do not erase or contradict the records of the oppression of their people, but render them all the more poignant and haunting. Whatever the Christians and Jews of al-Andalus accomplished, they were still dhimmis. They enjoyed whatever rights and privileges they had not out of any sense of the dignity of all people before God, or the equality of all before the law, but at the sufferance of their Muslim overlords.

That sufferance, moreover, could be revoked at any time by Muslims who determined that Christians or Jews had overstepped the bounds of their "protection" agreement. If these Christians didn't abide by the restrictions Menocal enumerates, as we have seen, they could in accordance with the Sharia be lawfully killed or sold into slavery.[15]

This happened more than once in al-Andalus, but even on a day-to-day basis the situation of Christians and Jews in Muslim

Spain was not as pleasant as it might seem in *The Ornament of the World*. According to historian Richard Fletcher, "the simple and verifiable historical truth is that Moorish Spain was more often a land of turmoil than it was a land of tranquility." In fact, "Moorish Spain was not a tolerant and enlightened society even in its most cultivated epoch. The Mozarabic Christian communities whom John of Gorse met on his embassy to Córdoba were cowed and demoralized.... The Christians of al-Andalus were second-class citizens like Christians under Muslim rule elsewhere in the world, such as the Copts of Egypt."[16]

Wolf holds out for the old romantic ideal, asserting that "this proliferation of legal restrictions on Christian activity did not necessarily mean that the actual situation of Christians living under Islam deteriorated to any appreciable degree;" paradoxically, however, he also quotes Paul Alvarus, a ninth-century Christian in Cordoba, complaining about the "unbearable tax" that Muslims levied on Christians. After quoting another Christian in Muslim Spain referring to the high tax, Wolf concludes that "there is little doubt, given the tone of victimization that both men adopted when speaking of the levies and the regularity with which they were collected, that *tributum, vectigal,* and *census* were simply Latin synonyms for the universal *dhimmî* tax, the *jizya.*"[17]

Nor were the dhimmi communities free from the most extreme penalties. Menocal notes that Spain's Muslim rulers "had zero tolerance for disparagement of their Prophet."[18] Consequently, according to Wolf, "in the spring of 850, a priest named Perfectus was arrested and later executed for publicly expressing his opinions about the errors of Islam to a group of Muslims. Months later, a Christian merchant named Joannes suffered a severe lashing, public humiliation, and a long prison term for invoking the prophet's name as he sold his wares in the marketplace."[19] This was the beginning of a series of public denunciations of Islam and the prophethood of Muhammad by Christians. All were followed by public execution; Menocal reports that after about fifty such horrifying events, "the passions of the moment passed and life went on as it had before in this city of thriving religious coexistence."[20] But in fact, Christian and Muslim sources contain numerous records of similar incidents in the early part of the tenth century. Around 910, in one of many such episodes, a woman was executed for proclaiming that "Jesus was God and that Muhammed had lied to his followers."[21]

Jews in al-Andalus sometimes had it even worse. On December 30, 1066, hundreds (perhaps thousands) of Jews in Granada were murdered by rioting Muslim mobs. Menocal called this a "relatively isolated Muslim uprising against what had been a warmly favored Jewish community."[22] But Fletcher correctly points out that the political power of the Jewish vizier Samuel ibn Naghrila and his son Joseph, although celebrated by Menocal as an example of Islamic tolerance, was also resented by Muslims as a "breach of *Shari'ah*."[23] Then, as now, Islamic law stipulates that a non-Muslim must not have authority over a Muslim, as the Saudi sheikh and legal expert Manaa K. al-Qubtan stated in a 1993 fatwa. "The command of a non-Muslim over a Muslim is not permitted based on the words of Allah: 'and Allah will not open to the unbelievers against the believers a way.' [Sura 4:140]"[24] In 1066, the angry mob was incited to kill the Jews by a poem composed by the Muslim jurist Abu Ishaq: "I myself arrived in Granada and saw that these Jews were meddling in its affairs. . . . So hasten to slaughter them as a good work whereby you will earn God's favor, and offer them up in sacrifice, a well-fattened ram."[25]

Since the mob was killing dhimmis who were considered to be in breach of their contract of "protection," the attackers could claim that by the light of the Sharia the killings were lawful. Thus even if Menocal's description of it as an isolated incident is correct, the legal justification for such incidents was always present. And the beautiful record of the culture of tolerance in al-Andalus is overshadowed by the fact that if any such tolerance was achieved, it was in spite of Islamic law, not because of it.

Similarly, in 1126 several thousand Christians were sent into Morocco to serve as slaves. Once again, the Muslim leadership was acting within the bounds of its right to kill or enslave dhimmis who violated the terms of their protection agreement.[26]

The sanction in Islamic law for the subjugation of the dhimmis is far different from the Judeo-Christian West, which has evolved a secular system of genuine tolerance. Muslims as well as Christians and Jews can compile atrocity stories, but more important is the question of whether and how such atrocities are likely to be repeated. Christian leaders have apologized for the Crusades, the Inquisition, and other enormities real and imagined. The pope in Rome and Jerry Falwell in Virginia are equally committed to Western ideals of freedom, justice, and the equality of all men before God. But the laws of jihad and dhimmitude remain part of the Sharia. They are the law of Islam.

The dhimmitude of the academics

In the face of all these facts, why is the myth of Muslim Spain so persistent? Fletcher sees the myth as a manifestation of "the guilt of the liberal conscience, which sees the evils of colonialism—assumed rather than demonstrated—foreshadowed in the Christian conquest of al-Andalus and the persecution of the Moriscos (but not, oddly, in the Moorish conquest and colonization). Stir the mix well together and issue it free to credulous academics and media persons throughout the western world. Then pour it generously over the truth."[27]

Historian Bat Ye'or has another explanation for the popularity of this unsavory stew. In a 1995 address to the International Strategic Studies Association, she boldly struck out against the tide and asserted that "the long and agonizing process of Christian annihilation by the laws of jihad and dhimmitude is a taboo history, not only in Islamic lands, but above all in the West. It has been buried beneath a myth, fabricated by Western politicians and religious leaders, in order to promote their own national strategic and economic interests."

The myth "started in Bosnia-Herzegovina in the nineteenth century" as a justification for various geopolitical maneuverings of the day, but it was not restricted to analyses of Islam in the Balkans.[28] "We now have a myth which has taken the place of history, a big myth which has covered three continents: Africa, Asia, and Europe. This myth spans not only three continents but also thirteen centuries, the period of Islamic rule over the Christian world."[29]

This myth "alleges that Turkish rule over Christians in its European provinces was just and lawful. That the Ottoman regime, being Islamic, was naturally 'tolerant' and well disposed toward its Christian subjects; that its justice was fair, and that safety for life and goods was guaranteed to Christians by Islamic laws. Ottoman rule was brandished as the most suitable regime to rule Christians of the Balkans."[30]

Generally, however, "although tolerance existed, it was counterbalanced by a system of oppression that led to the open extermination of Christian populations and the disappearance of the Eastern Christian culture. Tolerance was given to Jews and Christians only on the condition that they would accept and submit to a system of persecution and total inferiority. The governing context for such tolerance was the jihad. The two are linked and cannot be separated."[31]

The myth of tolerance was advanced by Europeans who wanted to forestall Russian advances into southeastern Europe; continuing

Ottoman rule was the chief alternative. "To justify the maintenance of the Turkish yoke on the Slavs," says Bat Ye'or, "it was portrayed as a model for a multi-ethnical and multi-religious empire. Of course, the reality was totally different! First the Ottoman Empire was created by centuries of jihad against Christian populations; consequently the rules of jihad, elaborated by Arab-Muslim theologians from the eighth to the tenth centuries, applied to the subjected Christian and Jewish populations of the Turkish Islamic dominions. Those regulations are integrated into the Islamic legislation concerning the non-Muslim vanquished peoples and consequently they present a certain homogeneity throughout the Arab and Turkish empires."[32]

Bat Ye'or notes that "before the twentieth century, the myth of Islamic tolerance had no currency. It is largely a modern creation." But Western politicians had more incentives than just the politics of southern Europe. "The West's obfuscation was a result of the political and cultural difficulties of colonialism. France had North Africa, Algeria, Morocco, Tunisia, Syria, and Lebanon after World War I. England had a huge Islamic population in India and also in Egypt and Sudan, Iraq and Palestine. They didn't want to confront this population. They didn't want to protect the Christian minorities in these lands because they wanted to have an economically beneficial pro-Arab, pro-Islamic policy."

Consequently, Christian minorities in the Muslim world who had looked with hope to Europe for centuries were on their own. The European powers "didn't want to protect the Christians. They told them, You have to integrate into the Islamic environment; we are no longer protecting you. Therefore, for political, strategic, and economic reasons—mostly related to oil in the Middle East—the Western colonial powers didn't want to antagonize the Muslim countries. As a result, they developed a whole literature praising Islamic tolerance toward Jews and Christians."

There were other reasons for the myth as well. Bat Ye'or suggests that European anti-Zionism found a natural alliance among those whose holy book called the Jews "apes and pigs" (Sura 5:59-60). Christians, who had shared a common fate with Jews in Muslim lands as "People of the Book" for centuries, tried to "integrate themselves into Islamic society by being anti-Zionist." Consequently, "the Jews had to be depicted as the source of all evil in the Middle East, especially as the source of the persecution of Christians. (We hear even today that it is because of the creation of Israel that there is a bad relationship between Muslims and Christians, while, in fact, the source of this persecution of Christians is in dhimmi rules that were established in the eighth century.)"[33] Of course, jihad and dhimmitude are not themselves the "source of all evil in the Middle East," but their role as an obstacle to peace efforts and a source of continuing friction between Jews, Christians, and Muslims has been insufficiently noted.

The Present-day Reality of Dhimmitude in the Middle East

Whatever its causes, the myth of Islamic tolerance has potentially lethal consequences insofar as it diverts attention from the ongoing reality of dhimmitude. Just as jihads are still being waged around the globe today, so also are Christians and Jews discriminated against and treated as second class in many areas of the Islamic world—often in ways that are eerily reminiscent of the chronicles of their forebears in Muslim Spain and elsewhere. And in accordance with dhimmi laws that mandated that they must bear insults in silence, they have often been reluctant to speak out—whether from fear or some other motive. One Lebanese Christian who also lived in Syria for many years said that in those countries and throughout the Middle East today, "we [Christians] have become citizens of second rank, almost foreigners in our

homeland. We have the clear feeling that we are reluctantly tolerated. Christians in the Near East live in a permanent atmosphere
of anxiety. The future seems not only uncertain, but bleak. Listen
to the fiery *khutba* [sermons] delivered in the mosques of most
Middle Eastern countries and North Africa on Fridays. Without the
Western powers, not only the Jews but also the Christians would
be driven into the sea."[34] He declined to be identified by name in
this book for fear of reprisals against his family in the Middle East.

As we have seen, the Saudi sheikh Marzouq Salem Al-Ghamdi
recently reaffirmed the laws of dhimmitude. "If the infidels live
among the Muslims, in accordance with the conditions set out by
the Prophet—there is nothing wrong with it provided they pay
Jizya to the Islamic treasury. Other conditions are...that they do
not renovate a church or a monastery, do not rebuild ones that
were destroyed, that they feed for three days any Muslim who
passes by their homes...that they rise when a Muslim wishes to
sit, that they do not imitate Muslims in dress and speech, nor ride
horses, nor own swords, nor arm themselves with any kind of
weapon; that they do not sell wine, do not show the cross, do not
ring church bells, do not raise their voices during prayer, that they
shave their hair in front so as to make them easily identifiable, do
not incite anyone against the Muslims, and do not strike a Muslim...If they violate these conditions, they have no protection."[35]

The Lebanese Christian with whom I spoke about the Middle
East experienced the same thing. "Yes," he said, "we enjoy religious
freedom, but only to a certain degree. In the Gulf Emirates, there
are a couple of churches, but they are not allowed to have bells.
Reason: ringing bells will hurt the feelings of Muslims! But having
deafening loudspeakers to broadcast the call to prayer and the
praise of the Prophet is normal. Muslim men may marry Christian
women, but Christian men are not allowed to marry Muslim

women. It is laudable to proselytize to convert Christians to Islam, but it is a crime for Christian missionaries to preach to Muslims."

He attributed the rapid decline of the Christian population of the Middle East (fifteen percent of the total population in 1953 and two percent now) to the ravages of Islamic radicalism. "The increasing emigration movement of Christians from the Arab world to Europe, America and Australia is a consequence of their fear. What happened in Iran and Libya may happen in any Arab country. Fundamentalist Muslim regimes may take over. The consequence will be either overt or covert persecution as well as discrimination regarding employment of Christians in the public sector."[36]

Many such restrictions are being applied to non-Muslims today even in the birthplace of Christianity. "With the notable exception of the Christians of Lebanon," says historian Habib C. Malik, "Christian communities native to the Middle East today exhibit the scars of centuries of inferiorization and marginalization. They constitute living relics of the ravages of a system that, although technically abolished in many modern Arab states, continues on the level of official as well as popular attitudes and practices. The Christians of the Holy Land, for example—Palestinian Christians— are symptomatic of this *dhimmi* genre and its attendant complexes."[37]

Muslim radicals have manifested the other side of the same dynamic by consistently mistreating the Christian population of the Middle East, particularly Palestinian Christians. They have even used Christian sites and people as shields against the Israelis. In spring 2002 they appropriated Bethlehem's Manger Square as a base of operations, knowing that Israeli forces would not attack them there and would face international opprobrium if they did. This activity precipitated the siege of the Church of the Nativity in April and May of that year. "For weeks Manger Square had been a refuge for Palestinians like Jihad Ja'ara, a top gunman from al Aqsa Martyrs Brigades. By day they lounged on cheap foam mattresses in the spring sunshine, believing this was one place the Israelis would not dare to strike. By night they sneaked out to the edges of town to shoot across the valley at Gilo, a suburb of Jerusalem built on occupied land."

When, on April 2, "Ja'ara and his gang clashed with the Israelis in the Fawaghreh neighborhood of Bethlehem's Old City," Ja'ara was wounded and he and his comrades fled into the church, where they remained for thirty-nine days, secure in the knowledge that "the Israelis knew they could not storm one of the holiest sites in all of Christianity."[38] Among those inside the church were Nidal Ahmad Isa Abu Gali'f, "senior assistant to Yihia Da'amsa, who is responsible for the recent Jerusalem suicide bombings in Kiryat Yovel and Beit Yisrael neighborhoods;" Muhammad Sa'id Atallah Salem, who was "involved in the planning and dispatching of the two aforementioned Jerusalem suicide bombings;" Ibrahim Muhammed Salem Abyat, "a senior Hamas operative who was in charge of organizing Hamas terror attacks;" and Basem Muhammed Ibrahim Hamud, "a Hamas terror operative who was involved in the preparation of explosives and the dispatching of two Hamas terrorists to carry out a suicide bombing at Jerusalem's International Convention center."[39]

Christians made little protest about this occupation of one of their holiest sites by active terrorists. One Bethlehem priest, however, disputed news reports that portrayed the occupiers of the church as respectful of their surroundings. He also explained why most remained silent. "We [Christians] are a small minority with little rights left, so it's obvious you have to be cautious with what you say. But I would have preferred silence rather than saying that everything is okay. We are worse than cowards, we are lying."[40]

In acquiescing to such lies, Palestinian Christians have, according to Habib Malik, tended to fall back upon "the myth that everything was fine between Christians and Muslims until Israel came along." Even no less a luminary than Jordan's Queen Noor, herself a descendant of Christian Arab dhimmis and a convert to Islam, subscribes to this view. "Jews, Muslims, and Christians had lived peacefully in the Middle East and indeed in Palestine for centuries. It was not until the rise of Zionism and the creation of Israel that animosities took root."[41]

Malik observes, however, that in fact "removing Israel from the equation and satisfying the Palestinians beyond their wildest dreams would not eliminate the violence against non–Muslims inherent in political Islam." He points out that "Egyptian and Lebanese Christians, the largest and most significant Christian communities of the Arab world . . . know better than to believe that once the Palestinian problem is laid to rest all will be well."

In fact, notes Malik, "the history of Palestinian Christianity has, for the most part, been no different from that of *dhimmi* Christianity throughout the Levant. Were Israel not in the picture the problem of *dhimmi* subservience would still exist for Palestinian Christians. And even with Israel as the perceived and proclaimed enemy of both Muslim and Christian Palestinians, the specter of *dhimmi* subjugation continues to lurk just below the surface."

Malik's perspective is borne out by reports from the Palestinian Authority. Although Yasir Arafat takes care to include references to Palestinian Christians and their holy places in his speeches, among Muslim radicals there is no feeling of common cause. Arafat's own regime sends out mixed signals. Early in 2003, Republican Congresswoman Jo Ann Davis of Virginia and the Religious Freedom Coalition asked the Israeli government to come to the aid of two Palestinian converts to Christianity, Saeed and Nasser Salame, who have been imprisoned and threatened by the Palestinian Authority. Nasser Salame was also tortured.[42]

This isn't a new pattern of behavior for Arafat's regime. According to the Foundation for the Defense of Democracies, "Since the December 1995 Palestinian takeover of Bethlehem . . . Palestinian converts to Christianity have been harassed, Christian cemeteries have been destroyed, monasteries have seen their phone lines cut and convents have been broken into. By December 1997 *The Times of London* could report: 'Life in (PA ruled) Bethlehem has become insufferable for many members of the dwindling Christian minorities. Increasing Muslim-Christian tensions have left some Christians reluctant to celebrate Christmas in the town at the heart of the story of Christ's birth.' "[43]

In 1997 came a report that, in accord with classic Sharia directives forbidding conversion from Islam to another religion, the Palestinian Authority was "waging a campaign of intimidation and harassment to push Muslims who have converted to Christianity to renounce their new faith."

According to Mustafa, a Christian convert who refused to give his whole name, "The first time the Palestinian police called me in, they told me I had better become a Muslim again. But when that did not work they would accuse me of being a spy for Israel. Finally, I started to get death threats in the post, so I ran away from my village."

A convert who gave his name as Imad reported physical intimidation. Palestinian police, he said, "gave me a few kicks and a few slaps and asked me what I was doing going around with Christians. Many Christians think the Palestinian Authority is against them and it has made us very fearful." According to the *London Telegraph*, not long after the police incident, Imad's "[tire] repair shop was burnt down, he was beaten up and his car was defaced with Islamic slogans."

"I would love to build a church in my village," said another con-vert, "where we could pray when we wanted, but if I did the church would be burnt down, along with everyone inside." The *Telegraph* noted, "Palestinians suggest that converts are being harassed because Islam demands death for ex-Muslims who do not renounce their new faith. Although the Palestinian Authority does not have any laws making it illegal to convert, religious Muslims may consider the Islamic precepts as a legitimate reason to put pressure on converts."[44]

The Palestinian Ministry of Information dismissed this *Telegraph* story as "a baseless article written in bad faith" and affirmed that "Palestinians are equal before the law, they have the same rights and obligations, their liberty and freedom to worship and to prac-tice their religious beliefs are protected." However, in the very next sentence it stated that "the Palestinian people are also governed by Shari'a law, as the Shari'a law is the law of Islam and is adhered to with regard to issues pertaining to religious matters. According to Shari'a law, applicable throughout the Muslim world, any Muslim who declares changing his religion or declares becoming an unbe-liever is committing a major sin punishable by capital punishment."

The ministry then affirms, "In practice, this has never happened in the Palestinian territories, nor is it likely to happen at all." It is silent, however, about the charges that converts were threatened and intimidated, and declared its unbending allegiance to the Sharia. "Having said that, the PNA cannot take a different position on this matter. The norms and tradition will take care of such situ-ations should they occur. The PNA will apply the law of the land, and will protect its citizens accordingly."[45]

In his book *Green Crescent Over Nazareth: The Displacement of Christians by Muslims in the Holy Land*, Raphael Israeli offers a glimpse into the nature of this protection under the law. "Attacks against and condemnation of Christians are also often heard in mosques, in sermons and in publications of the Muslim Movement. On the eve of the Al-Ad'h Festival in 1996, a leaflet was distributed in Umm al-Fahm, which accused local youth of improper behavior 'mimicking that of Jewish and Christian Unbelievers.' The manifesto reached Nazareth and caused outrage there which was reflected in the local press—which is owned and edited by Christians—such as Al-Sinara and Kul-al-'Arab."

But Palestinian Christians, conditioned by centuries of oppression, were wary of responding in kind. "In response the Christians, far from counter-attacking, reacted like a *dhimmi* people who sing the praise of the ruler as they are being beaten by him. They protested that they were as Arab as all the others, and they pointed out their contributions to Arab culture and history, something that only encouraged more onslaughts upon them."[46]

The sentiments of Palestinian Christians, says Habib Malik, stem "from a deeper *dhimmi* psychological state: the urge to find—or to imagine and fabricate if need be—a common cause with the ruling majority in order to dilute the existing religious differences and perhaps ease the weight of political Islam's inevitable discrimination."

Underscoring this was a 2001 sermon broadcast over Palestinian Authority television. It was preached by an employee of the Palestinian Authority, Sheikh Ibrahim Madhi. "We welcome, as we did in the past," said the Sheikh, "any Jew who wants to live in this land as a Dhimmi, just as the Jews have lived in our countries, as Dhimmis, and have earned appreciation, and some of them have even reached the positions of counselor or minister here and there. We welcome the Jews to live as Dhimmis, but the rule in this land and in all the Muslim countries must be the rule of Allah. . . . Those from amongst the Jews and from amongst those who are not Jews who came to this land as plunderers, must return humiliated and disrespected to their countries."[47]

If Jews are to be subjected to the laws of dhimmitude, there is no reason why Christians wouldn't be. The Sharia makes no distinction between Jews and Christians. Both are "People of the Book"—indeed, they're the "People of the Book" *par excellence.* Sheikh Yussef Salameh, the Palestinian Authority's undersecretary for religious endowment, spelled this out in May 1999. He "praised the idea that Christians should become dhimmis under Muslim rule, and such suggestions have become more common since the second intifada began in October 2000."[48]

In response, the Catholic archbishop of the Galilee, Butrus Al-Mu'alem, was incredulous. "It is strange to me that there remains such backwardness in our society... there are still those who amuse themselves with fossilized notions." Palestinian Christians, he insisted, were not "residues, foreigners, or beggars of mercy."[49]

But instead of speaking out against all this, many Palestinian Christians are voting with their feet. According to the Foundation for the Defense of Democracies, "Christians in the Palestinian territories have dropped from fifteen percent of the Arab population in 1950 to just two percent today. Both Bethlehem and Nazareth, which had been overwhelmingly Christian towns, now have strong Muslim majorities. Today three-fourths of all Bethlehem Christians live abroad, and more Jerusalem Christians live in Sydney, Australia, than in the place of their birth. Indeed, Christians now comprise just 2.5 percent of Jerusalem, although those remaining still include a few born in the Old City when Christians there still constituted a majority."

Those who think this exodus can be attributed solely to the strife in the region have trouble explaining why Christians are leaving Muslim countries all over the world. "And it is not only the Holy Land from which many native Christians have fled. Throughout the entire Middle East, once significant Christian communities have shrunk to a minuscule portion of their former robust selves. In fifty years they may well be extinct."

Why? "The single greatest cause of this emigration is pressure from radical Islam."

The report notes that Christians in Egypt still suffer from the enforcement of dhimmi laws regarding the building and repair of churches. "It is nearly impossible to restore or build new churches at a time while many thousands of new Islamic buildings have been sanctioned by the state." This is part of a larger pattern: "Egyptian Copts... have felt the brunt of both the state and Islamic fundamentalists. Many laws and customs favor Muslims, and the constitution proclaims Islam as the state religion. Muslim, but not Christian, schools receive state funding and Arabic may be taught in schools only by Muslims. Identity cards note the bearer's religion, Christians are frequently ostracized or insulted in public, and laws prohibit Moslem conversions to Christianity. Most frightening of all, Islamic radicals have frequently launched physical attacks on Copts."

Similarly, "in Iran, Christians form a minuscule .4 percent of the population. The tiny Christian population has been treated as second class dhimmis—'people of the Book' who are theoretically protected while officially marginalized. The printing of Christian literature is illegal, converts from Islam are liable to be killed and most evangelical churches must function underground."

Even worse, "in Taliban Afghanistan the application of harsh shari'a law bred such hatred of Christians that there were no longer any open churches or significant numbers of avowed Christians in the country."

The Sharia and dhimmitude in Pakistan

There are many Christians in neighboring Pakistan, but they generally fare little better in what is for many Muslims the "land of the pure," as its name means in Persian. Many of the classic laws of dhimmitude are enforced there today. There are around three million Christians in Pakistan, constituting about two percent of the population. This long-established community, which traces its origin back to the expeditions of the Apostle Thomas to India, is seriously threatened in modern Pakistan.

Tensions increased after September 11, 2001. As Muslims in Pakistan often linked the nation's Christians with the West, Christians became a target of particular wrath once the war on terror began. On October 28, 2001, Muslim gunmen killed seventeen Christians and wounded thirty at St. Dominic's Roman Catholic Church in Bahawalpur, where the Church of Pakistan was holding Sunday services. The following summer, four more were killed in attacks on a Christian missionary school and a Christian hospital and chapel. On September 25, 2002, seven more Christians were killed in Karachi. The Rev. Youngsook C. Kang of the United Methodist Church, a member of a 2002 World Council of Churches delegation to Pakistan, found fear and despair among the nation's Christians. "There was one eight-month pregnant widow, hardly twenty-three or twenty-four years old, whose husband had been killed. Even after a month of the incident she was in a daze, tears gathering in her eyes, hardly able to speak, the tragedy was very ominous. Yet another widow told the delegation, 'If you want to be helpful, take our children and us out of here.'"[50]

As war began in Iraq in early 2003, Pakistani Christians were nervous that Muslim radicals would use the war as a pretext to attack them. "We are very afraid of retaliation by Islamic militants if there is a war in Iraq. We are appealing to the government for more security for Christians," announced Shahbaz Bhatti of the All Pakistan Minorities Alliance. Muslim leaders, he said, were putting Pakistani Christians in a dangerous position by "protesting this war on religious grounds. They're not protesting for peace. They are calling this war a crusade and they are urging the Muslim youth to participate in jihad."[51] In March 2003, the human rights group International Christian Concern called attention to "an intensive hate campaign" that was being conducted "against the Christian minority of Pakistan by various militant Islamic groups. . . . Large demonstrations have been held over the past two weekends in Karachi, Islamabad, and Rawalpindi protesting the expected war in Iraq, and urging citizens to boycott Christians and to wage a jihad against them."[52]

Pakistani Christians have long been objects of controversy as well as outright persecution. The Pakistani intellectual Fazlur Rahman (1911–1988) held that in the modern age the laws of dhimmitude should be relaxed; others, however, insisted that they were needed more than ever.[53] In 1977, the Pakistan National Alliance began a campaign to impose the Sharia on the nation; almost immediately it won concessions from the government. Sharia courts were established and over the years were granted an ever-widening sphere of authority. Finally, in 1998, the National Assembly passed a bill that made "the Qur'an and Sunnah 'constitutionally and legally supreme;" the bill was left unconsidered by the Pakistani Senate, but remained a symbol of the growing power and restiveness of Islamic hardliners in Pakistan.

Those hardliners enforced the Sharia wherever they could within the country, including the laws of dhimmitude. The jizya is not collected in present-day Pakistan, but Christians remain nervous that it will eventually be instituted. Other elements of dhimmitude law remain. Because of the traditional restrictions against non-Muslims holding authority over Muslims (the same laws which sparked anti-Jewish riots in tolerant Muslim Spain a thousand years ago), Christians have had difficulty gaining and holding onto political office in Pakistan. Muslim spokesmen pressed for full enforcement of the Sharia, emphasizing that Christians should "have no voice in the making of laws, no right to administer the law and no right to hold public offices."[54]

Patrick Sookhdeo, the author of *A People Betrayed: The Impact of Islamization on the Christian Community in Pakistan*, reports that "it is difficult to find recent figures, but according to government figures for January 1983, there were no non-Muslims in the two highest grades of federal government civil servants." Similarly redolent of the bad old days of dhimmitude were laws of evidence passed in 1979 to bring Pakistani courts more into line with Islamic norms; these "prohibited non-Muslim witnesses in cases involving a Muslim defendant." And like modern Christians in Egypt and elsewhere who suffer under Sharia laws restricting dhimmis from building new houses of worship, Pakistani Christians have had trouble getting permission from authorities to build new churches. "In some parts of the country," says Sookhdeo, "such as the North West Frontier Province, overt church buildings are not allowed at all. Churches can only be erected if they are described as 'community centers.'"

The same prohibition of non-Muslims holding authority over Muslims underlies Pakistan's long-standing system of separate electorates for religious minorities. According to the U.S. State Department's report on human rights in Pakistan in 2000, "Minorities are underrepresented in government and politics. Under the electoral system, minorities vote for reserved at-large seats, not for nonminority candidates who represent actual constituencies. . . . With separate electorates, representatives have little incentive to promote their minority constituents' interests. Many Christian activists state that separate electorates are the greatest obstacle to the attainment of Christian religious and civil liberties."[55] The Musharraf government abolished the system of separate electorates in 2002, but Christians still had a long way to go to attain equal rights in Pakistan.

In line with the requirement that dhimmis must "feel them-selves subdued" (Sura 9:29), the State Department report stated that "Christians in particular have difficulty finding jobs other than menial labor, although Christian activists say the employment sit-uation has improved somewhat in the private sector. Christians are over-represented in Pakistan's most oppressed social group—that of bonded laborers. . . . [M]any Christians complain about the dif-ficulty that their children face in gaining admission to government schools and colleges, a problem they attribute to discrimination."

Patrick Sookhdeo explains that many Muslims believe that the impurity that Christians are considered to have by the standards of Islamic ritual laws "will be passed on by physical contact with them. A young Christian journalist found that a female Muslim typist would not eat with her for this reason. An elderly Christian man who staffed the press lounge at the National Assembly was banned by the National Assembly staff from touching any canteen utensils or even carrying a tray. A Christian student of science at the Islamia College in Karachi was forbidden by his fellow students to drink from a tap. Five Christian schoolgirls from St. Mary's School in Gujrat, who were taking a Home Economics practical examination on February 25, 1997, found that the Muslim exam-iner would not test or mark the food they had cooked. She ordered the Christians' food to be put into the dustbin, but tested the food of their eight Muslim classmates in the normal way."

A Muslim lawyer remarked in 1992, "Christians must realize that they have become the 'niggers' of this country, even though the cottonfield chores may have been replaced by that of sweep-ing the city streets."[56]

Nor are Christian men permitted to marry Muslim women, again in accord with restrictions enshrined in the Sharia. Accord-ing to the State Department report, "Upon conversion to Islam, the marriages of Jewish or Christian men remain legal; however, upon conversion to Islam, the marriages of Jewish or Christian women, or of other non-Muslims, that were performed under the rites of the previous religion are considered dissolved."[57]

Non-Muslims in Pakistan have the most to fear today from the country's notorious blasphemy laws. According to the State Department, these laws originally reflected secular notions of tolerance but have been progressively Islamized:

> Section 295(a), the blasphemy provision of the Penal Code, originally stipulated a maximum 2-year sentence for insulting the religion of any class of citizens.... In 1982 Section 295(b) was added, which stipulated a sentence of life imprisonment for 'whoever willfully defiles, damages, or desecrates a copy of the holy Koran.' In 1986 another amendment, Section 295(c), established the death penalty or life imprisonment for directly or indirectly defiling 'the sacred name of the holy Prophet Mohammed.' In 1991 a court struck down the option of life imprisonment. These laws, especially Section 295(c), have been used by rivals and local authorities to threaten, punish, or intimidate Ahmadis [a Muslim sect generally considered heretical], Christians, and even orthodox Muslims. No one has been executed by the State under any of these provisions, although religious extremists have killed some persons accused under them.

The report recounted the plight of two Christian brothers whose lives were ruined by an attempt to buy some ice cream. The ice cream vendor seems to have believed, like the Muslims at Islamia College, St. Mary's School, and the National Assembly, that his utensils would be defiled by the Christians; he "allegedly fought with the brothers after he asked them to use their own dishes, stating that his were reserved for Muslim customers." Then he accused them of "desecrating the Koran and blaspheming the Prophet

Mohammed." Both received thirty-five year prison sentences and fines of $1,500.[58] The blasphemy charge is itself a sign of Pakistan's increasing Islamization: Patrick Sookhdeo reports that while there were only six cases of blasphemy in Pakistani courts between 1947 and 1986, from 1986 to 1995 "sixteen blasphemy cases were brought against Christians, at least nine against Muslims and at least one hundred against Ahmadiyyas. By June 1997, three Christians, one Sunni Muslim, and two Shi'a Muslims had been sentenced to death under Section 295-C (defiling the name of Muhammad), though all were acquitted on appeal."[59]

In this, Pakistani law follows the ruling of the Shafi'i school of Islamic legal jurisprudence, which is the school of many Pakistani and Indian Muslims. The Shafi'i teaches that if dhimmis dare to say "something impermissible about Allah, the Prophet, or Islam," the dhimmitude contract is dissolved, and that they are hence able to be put to death.[60] Pakistan could have opted for a less stringent course, since most Pakistanis adhere to the Hanafi school, which considers blasphemy by a non-Muslim par for the course and not the end of his "protection" contract.[61]

Converts from Islam have also faced persecution, in accord with Islam's traditional strictures against apostasy. Although the death penalty for apostates is not enforced in Pakistan, converts are frequently "beaten by their relatives and driven from the home. Other problems included threats from family and community (some vague, some specifically to shoot them), anger and insults from parents and community, having their water supply cut off by other villagers, being pensioned off from a job, and expulsion from school."[62]

Because it is based on the Sharia, what is happening in Pakistan, the Palestinian Authority, and elsewhere in the Islamic world could happen in any Muslim country at any time. Farajollah Parvizian, an Iranian who grew up in the 1940s and 1950s, noted that Iranians behaved according to the laws of dhimmitude even though the laws weren't officially on the books. The Jewish population of Tehran was routinely derided and abused as "dirty Jews" by the Muslim majority. During World War II, as Hitler's armies advanced deep into Russia and seemed destined to cross the Caucasus, one prominent Jewish merchant was approached by his Muslim neighbors. "When Hitler comes," they asked him, "may we have your dining room furniture?" But it wasn't just a case of backing the side they thought was going to win: Christian Armenians in Iran fared little better.[63]

Even today, according to the U.S. Commission on International Religious Freedom, "the government of Iran engages in or tolerates systematic, ongoing, and egregious violations of religious freedom, including prolonged detention and executions based primarily or entirely upon the religion of the victims." Much of this persecution follows predictable patterns of dhimmitude. Jews, Christians, and Zoroastrians are protected as "People of the Book" and granted some freedoms, but "members of these groups are subject to legal and other forms of official discrimination. For example, discrimination against non-Muslims is prevalent in education, government, the armed services, and other aspects of life. Over the past thirteen years, at least eight evangelical Christians have been killed at the hands of government authorities and between fifteen and twenty-three are reported 'missing' or 'disappeared.' According to the UN Special Representative's report, some are said to have been convicted of apostasy."

And that's the tolerance Islamic law mandates for the People of the Book. No such protection is offered to groups that are not considered People of the Book, such as the Baha'is, who are considered to be Muslim heretics. "While all religious minorities suffer, particularly severe violations are principally directed towards the 300,000 to 350,000 followers of the Baha'i faith in Iran. Baha'is are often viewed as 'heretics,' and may face repression on the grounds of 'apostasy.' Government authorities have killed more than 200 Baha'i leaders in Iran since 1979, and more than 10,000 have been dismissed from government and university jobs. Baha'is may not establish houses of worship, schools, or any independent religious associations. In addition, Baha'is are denied government jobs and pensions as well as the right to inherit property, and their marriages and divorces are not recognized. Their cemeteries, holy places, and community properties are often seized and some are destroyed. Members of the Baha'i faith are not allowed to attend university.... As of April 2003, credible sources report that five Baha'is are in prison on account of their religious activities, including a Baha'i who had been imprisoned from June 1999 to May 2000 and held in solitary confinement and beaten, and who was imprisoned again in March 2003 for 'taking part in Baha'i activities.' "[64]

This tendency to regard non-Muslims as second class or worse stems from the status of the Sharia as Islamic law. Although it isn't the primary law of all countries that have Muslim majority populations today, it is still *Islamic* law. That law has not been reformed and by its nature cannot be, as it is considered to be the law of Allah himself. Any group that wishes to restore the Islamic purity of its country, and that has the power to do so, could institute the institutionalized humiliation and oppression of non-Muslims that are mandated by the Sharia. The coming of Islamic law to a nation doesn't herald the reappearance of the mythical tolerance of al-Andalus, but rather the reality of discrimination and persecution that is modern Pakistan. This is not a religious issue. It is a human rights issue.

Chapter Eight

JIHAD IN ECLIPSE
AND RESURGENT

Reevaluating jihad

USLIM ARMIES PLAGUED portions of Europe, India, and elsewhere more or less continuously from the seventh century through the seventeenth. But after the last siege of Vienna was broken on September 11, 1683, a relative calm descended.

Many assume that jihad ended because Islamic theology evolved away from it. However, this period of calm corresponds not to any theological or philosophical fermentation, but rather to the decline and eventual dissolution of the last great Muslim power, the Ottoman Empire. The great European colonial powers arose at the same time. As such, it would be unwise to ascribe to unwillingness what may have arisen from inability.

On the other hand, there were attempts in those days to reform the concept of jihad. One key period of fermentation and innovation came during the British colonial occupation of India.

The early history of the British in India is marked by several revolts by the Muslim population against the colonizers, often in the name of jihad. British supremacy was established in India by 1820, and in 1821 Sayyid Ahmed Barelwi established the Tariqa-i Muhammadi (the Way of Muhammad), a revivalist group. "One should know," he wrote, "that jihad is an advantageous and beneficial institution." These advantages were for everyone, even dhimmis. "The benefits of this great institution are of two kinds: a general benefit in which obedient believers, stubborn unbelievers, sinners, hypocrites and even *djinnis* [spirit beings], human beings, animals, and plants collectively partake, and specific benefits for some groups."

Sayyid Ahmed taught that these advantages would come principally in the form of heavenly blessings. Such blessings would manifest themselves "when the majesty of the Religion of Truth [is upheld], when pious rulers govern in the different regions of the earth, when the righteous community [gains] military strength and when the principles of the *shari'ah* are being propagated in villages and towns."[1] Sayyid Ahmed was killed in 1831 while waging jihad against the Sikhs, in whose territory he had hoped to establish a base for jihad against the British. His struggle, however, went on; the Tariqa-i Muhammadi was not wiped out until 1883. There were other flare-ups against British rule in the same period, including the Sepoy Mutiny of 1857, in which Hindus and Muslims fought together against the colonial enemy.

The Hindus, however, were quickly pacified, while the theology of jihad forced the Muslims into a position of potentially endless holy war against the British, a war many Muslim leaders recognized could not be won, and which, to the more practically minded, was unnecessary. The British were far from anti-Muslim; indeed, they had a predilection in favor of "the warrior races." All jihad would achieve would be to deprive Muslims of the material advantages of British rule.

Faced with economic and social disaster, some Muslim theologians emphasized aspects of jihad that had previously been background themes: defending the faith from critics, supporting its growth and defense financially, even migrating to non-Muslim lands for the purpose of spreading Islam.

The foundation of these alternative approaches to jihad is a remark that modern Muslims, particularly in America and Western Europe, never tire of quoting. Upon his return from a battle, the Prophet Muhammad said, "We are returning from the lesser jihad to the greater one."[2] When his followers asked him what constituted the greater jihad, he replied that it was the struggle to bring the soul into conformity with Allah's will. While the idea of spiritual jihad is comforting or convenient to many observers and to Muslims themselves, its traditional pedigree is far weaker than the tradition of military jihad. Some Muslim scholars and leading radical Muslim theorists, including Hasan al-Banna, the founder of the Muslim Brotherhood, and Abdullah Azzam, Osama bin Laden's friend and intellectual mentor, even deny the authenticity of the saying.[3] The concept of the "greater jihad" as a spiritual struggle was elaborated by the great masters of the mystical Sufi sect al-Hakim al-Tirmidhi (d. 932) and Abu Hamid al-Ghazali (1058–1128), and then spread beyond Sufi circles. Others went further, casting off the settled rulings of classical Muslim scholars and "reopening the gates of *ijtihad*"—that is, subjecting key Islamic ideas to new interpretation.

Islamic tradition holds that the "gates of ijtihad" have been closed since at least the tenth century, so this was no mean undertaking. Among those who attempted it was an Indian Muslim, Sayyid Ahmad Khan (1817–1898). He entered a raging debate over whether British-occupied India was part of the Dar al-Islam, the House of Islam, or Dar al-Harb, the House of War—as Islamic theology divides the world. He argued that as British India offered Muslims peace and freedom and put no restrictions on their faith, it couldn't be part of the House of War.[4]

According to historian Rudolph Peters, Khan taught that "jihad is only allowed in the case of positive oppression or obstruction of the Moslems in the exercise of their faith, impairing the foundation of some of the pillars of Islam."[5] This position became widely enough accepted for Muslims to become generally loyal to British rule, but radical groups such as the Deobandis, founded in 1866, continued to preach more traditional understandings of jihad, albeit unsuccessfully. (The Deobandi school found its place on the world stage much later, when it gave rise to the Taliban rulers of Afghanistan.) Ideas like those of Sayyid Ahmed Khan, along with attendant Western notions of secularism and nationalism, became widespread among Muslims during the colonial period. Against such liberalism, Muslim radicals invoked the Qur'an, the example of the Prophet, Islamic traditions, and a history of Islamic conquest that bridled at being colonized. But it was not until the twentieth century that the jihad revival really caught fire. Among Shi'ite Muslims, the spark came from Iran's Ayatollah Ruhollah Khomeini (1902–1989). For Sunni Muslims, it came from four titanic Muslim thinkers: the Egyptians Hasan al-Banna (1906–1949) and Sayyid Qutb (1906–1966), the Indian Sayyid Abul A'la Maududi (1903–1979), and the Palestinian Abdullah Azzam (1941–1989).

Hasan al-Banna and the Muslim Brotherhood

Hasan al-Banna founded the prototypical Muslim radical group of the modern age, the Muslim Brotherhood, in Egypt in 1928. The Brotherhood emerged as a response to the same colonialism that had produced the relatively gentle Islam of Sayyid Ahmed Khan. But rather than seek accommodation with the West, the Brotherhood was determined to fight Western influence. Al-Banna wrote that "a wave of dissolution which undermined all firm beliefs, was engulfing Egypt in the name of intellectual emancipation. This trend attacked the morals, deeds, and virtues under the pretext of personal freedom. Nothing could stand against this powerful and tyrannical stream of disbelief and permissiveness that was sweeping our country."

He decried Ataturk's abolition of the caliphate in secular Turkey, separating "the state from religion in a country which was until recently the site of the Commander of the Faithful." Al-Banna characterized it as just part of a larger "Western invasion, which was armed and equipped with all [the] destructive influences of money, wealth, prestige, ostentation, power, and means of propaganda."[6]

Al-Banna's Brotherhood had a deeply spiritual character from its beginning, but it didn't combat the "Western invasion" with just words and prayers. In a 1928 article, al-Banna decried the complacency of the Egyptian elite. "What catastrophe has befallen the souls of the reformers and the spirit of the leaders?...What calamity has made them prefer this life to the thereafter [sic]? What has made them...consider the way of struggle *[sabil al-jihad]* too rough and difficult?"[7] When the Brotherhood was criticized for being a political group in the guise of a religious one, al-Banna met the challenge head on:

We summon you to Islam, the teachings of Islam, the laws of Islam and the guidance of Islam, and if this smacks of "politics" in your eyes, then it is our policy. And if the one summoning you to these principles is a "politician," then we are the most respectable of men, God be praised, in politics... Islam does have a policy embracing the happiness of this world.... We believe that Islam is an all-embracing concept which regulates every aspect of life, adjudicating on every one of its concerns and prescribing for it a solid and rigorous order.[8]

Al-Banna's vision was in perfect accord with that of classical Muslim scholars such as Ibn Khaldun, who taught in the fourteenth century that "in the Muslim community, the holy war is a religious duty, because of the universalism of the Muslim mission and (the obligation to) convert everybody to Islam either by persuasion or by force."[9] Al-Banna wrote in 1934 that "it is a duty incumbent on every Muslim to struggle towards the aim of making every people Muslim and the whole world Islamic, so that the banner of Islam can flutter over the earth and the call of the Muezzin can resound in all the corners of the world: God is greatest [*Allahu akbar*]! This is not parochialism, nor is it racial arrogance or usurpation of land."[10] Al-Banna would doubtless therefore have looked kindly upon the Palestinian sheikh Ibrahim Madhi's 2002 call to believers: "Oh beloved, look to the East of the earth, find Japan and the ocean; look to the West of the earth, find [some] country and the ocean. Be assured that these will be owned by the Muslim nation, as the Hadith says... 'from the ocean to the ocean.'"[11]

In the same article, al-Banna insisted that "every piece of land where the banner of Islam has been hoisted is the fatherland of the Muslims"—hence the impossibility of accommodation with Israel, against which the Brotherhood and its offshoots still struggle. But the problem was not just Israel, which after all did not yet exist when the Brotherhood was founded. According to Brynjar Lia, the historian of the Muslim Brotherhood movement, "Quoting the Qur'anic verse 'And fight them till sedition is no more, and the faith is God's' [Sura 2:193], the Muslim Brothers urged their fellow Muslims to restore the bygone greatness of Islam and to re-establish an Islamic empire. Sometimes they even called for the restoration of 'former Islamic colonies' in Andalus (Spain), southern Italy, Sicily, the Balkans and the Mediterranean islands."[12]

Such a call might seem laughable except that the Brotherhood also had weapons and a military wing. Scholar Martin Kramer notes that the Brotherhood had "a double identity. On one level, they operated openly, as a membership organization of social and political awakening. Banna preached moral revival, and the Muslim Brethren engaged in good works. On another level, however, the Muslim Brethren created a 'secret apparatus' that acquired weapons and trained adepts in their use. Some of its guns were deployed against the Zionists in Palestine in 1948, but the Muslim Brethren also resorted to violence in Egypt. They began to enforce their own moral teachings by intimidation, and they initiated attacks against Egypt's Jews. They assassinated judges and struck down a prime minister in 1949. Banna himself was assassinated two months later, probably in revenge."[13]

The Brotherhood was no gathering of marginalized kooks. It grew in Egypt from 150 branches in 1936 to as many as 1,500 by 1944. In 1939 al-Banna referred to "100,000 pious youths from the Muslim Brothers from all parts of Egypt," and although Lia believes he was exaggerating at that point, by 1944 membership was estimated between 100,000 and 500,000.[14] By 1937 it had expanded beyond Egypt, setting up "several branches in Sudan, Saudi Arabia, Palestine, Syria, Lebanon, and Morocco, and one in each of Bahrain, Hadramawt, Hyderabad, Djibouti and," Lia adds matter-of-factly,

"Paris."[15] These many thousands, dispersed around the world, heard al-Banna's call to "prepare for jihad and be lovers of death."[16]

The Brotherhood's ability to attract Muslims in all these disparate societies indicates the power of its religious appeal. It wasn't offering Muslims a new version of Islam, but a deeply traditional one. The call to restore the purity and vitality of Islam has always struck a chord among Muslims; and the Islam the Brotherhood preached was the traditional one of a total Islamic society, one that could not abide accommodation—let alone colonial subjugation—to the West. Al-Banna told his followers, "Islam is faith and worship, a country and a citizenship, a religion and a state. It is spirituality and hard work. It is a Qur'an and a sword."[17]

The Brotherhood's combination of militancy and Sufism is interesting. So strong was the link between the Brotherhood and Sufism that other Salafi movements (that is, movements dedicated to the purification and restoration of Islam and Islamic society) disparaged the Brothers as "dervishes."[18] Sufism has generally stood for a peaceful version of Islam throughout history, but al-Banna and the Brotherhood evidently saw no contradiction between mysticism and jihad.

Al-Banna is a revered figure in the Muslim world today, and by no means only among radicals. His grandson Tariq Ramadan, the well-known European Muslim moderate, praises his grandfather for his "light-giving faith, a deep spirituality, [and] personal discipline...."[19] And many of al-Banna's writings are still in print and circulate widely.

Sayyid Qutb, America, and the Sharia

The Muslim Brotherhood's second great theorist was Sayyid Qutb, "the father of modern [Islamic] fundamentalism." He sharpened his distaste for the West while living in the United States from November 1948 to August 1950.[20] While hospitalized for a respiratory ailment in Washington, D.C., in February 1949, he heard of the assassination of al-Banna, an event that, he later claimed implausibly, set the hospital staff to open rejoicing.[21]

Qutb's disgust with the gaudy materialism of postwar America was intense. He wrote to an Egyptian friend of his loneliness, "How much do I need someone to talk to about topics other than money, movie stars, and car models." Moving to Greeley, Colorado, he was impressed by the number of churches in the city, but not with the piety they engendered. "Nobody goes to church as often as Americans do.... Yet no one is as distant as they are from the spiritual aspect of religion." He was thoroughly scandalized by a dance after an evening service at a local church. "The dancing intensified.... The hall swarmed with legs...Arms circled arms, lips met lips, chests met chests, and the atmosphere was full of love." The pastor further scandalized Qutb by dimming the lights, creating "a romantic, dreamy effect," and playing a popular record of the day: "Baby, It's Cold Outside." Qutb regarded American popular music in general with a gimlet eye. "Jazz is the favorite music [of America]. It is a type of music invented by [American] Blacks to please their primitive tendencies and desire for noise."

Ultimately, Qutb concluded, "I fear that when the wheel of life has turned and the file on history has closed, America will not have contributed anything." He didn't find American prosperity to be matched by a corresponding wealth of spirit. "I am afraid that there is no correlation between the greatness of the American material civilization and the men who created it.... In both feeling and conduct the American is primitive (*bida'a*)."[22]

When he returned to Egypt, Qutb characterized the influence of the West in the Muslim world as an unmitigated evil. He derided "American Islam," a counterfeit of the religion that was designed only to combat communism in Egypt. (In this he may have been referring to the Egyptian dictator Nasser's 1964 overtures to the

Muslim Brotherhood, which he hoped would join an anticommunist alliance.) Even before his stay in the United States, Qutb cautioned that "Islam is a comprehensive philosophy and an homogeneous unity, and to introduce into it any foreign element would mean ruining it. It is like a delicate and perfect piece of machinery that may be completely ruined by the presence of an alien component."[23]

The chief "alien component" was secularism. Qutb regarded Western secularism not as the solution to the problems of the Islamic world (as many have proposed) but as the chief source of the problem: it destroyed the fundamental unity of Islam by separating the religious sphere from that of daily life.

Qutb saw the West's two dominant political and social philosophies, capitalism and communism, as bankrupt and valueless. With notable and often moving passion and vigor, Qutb's influential book *Milestones* explicitly positions Islam as the true source of societal and personal order, as opposed to both capitalism and communism. "Mankind today is on the brink of a precipice," he asserted in the Cold War-era manifesto, "not because of the danger of complete annihilation which is hanging over its head—this being just a symptom and not the real disease—but because humanity is devoid of those vital values which are necessary not only for its healthy development but also for its real progress." Perhaps with his time in America in mind, he went on. "Even the Western world realizes that Western civilization is unable to present any healthy values for the guidance of mankind. It knows that it does not possess anything which will satisfy its own conscience and justify its existence."

To Qutb, both capitalism and communism were spent forces. "Democracy in the West has become infertile to such an extent that it is borrowing from the systems of the Eastern bloc, especially in the economic system, under the name of socialism. It is the same with the Eastern bloc. Its social theories, foremost among which is Marxism, in the beginning attracted not only a large number of people from the East but also from the West, as it was a way of life based on a creed."

With admirable prescience for a man writing in 1964, when Marxism looked to many observers to be still positioned at the vanguard of history, Qutb proclaimed that "now Marxism is defeated on the plane of thought, and if it is stated that not a single nation in the world is truly Marxist, it will not be an exaggeration." He asserted that Marxism was doomed to fail because "on the whole this theory conflicts with man's nature and [his] needs. This ideology prospers only in a degenerate society or in a society which has become cowed as a result of some form of prolonged dictatorship." A quarter-century before the fall of the Soviet Union, Qutb described "the failure of the system of collective farming" as just part of "the failure of a system which is against human nature." He concludes, "It is essential for mankind to have new leadership!"[24]

That new leadership would come from Islam. To Qutb, what the Muslim *umma* needed was a restoration of Islam in its fullness and purity, including all the rules of the Sharia for regulating society. "If we look at the sources and foundations of modern ways of living, it becomes clear that the whole world is steeped in *Jahiliyyah* [Ignorance of the Divine guidance], and all the marvelous material comforts and high-level inventions do not diminish this ignorance. This *Jahiliyyah* is based on rebellion against God's sovereignty on earth. It transfers to man one of the greatest attributes of God, namely sovereignty, and makes some men lords over others."[25]

True freedom could come to man only by restoring the divine sovereignty—that is, the Sharia. To further this end, Qutb formally joined the Muslim Brotherhood shortly after his return to Egypt from the United States.

In articulating his vision for a resurgent Islam that would lead the way to a restoration of civilization and true values in the world, Qutb made one great departure from the thought of other Muslim intellectuals of his day: he classified not only non-Muslim lands but also large portions of the Muslim world as lands of *jahiliyyah*, the Muslim term for the pre-Islamic period of unbelief, ignorance, and darkness. He based this assessment on the fact that most Muslim lands did not follow the Sharia either in whole or part, writing in *Milestones* that "it is necessary to revive that Muslim community which is buried under the debris of the man-made traditions of several generations, and which is crushed under the weight of those false laws and customs which are not even remotely related to the Islamic teachings, and which, in spite of all this, calls itself the 'world of Islam.' "[26]

Qutb advances Islam as "a challenge to all kinds and forms of systems which are based on the concept of the sovereignty of man; in other words, where man has usurped the Divine attribute. Any system in which the final decisions are referred to human beings, and in which the sources of all authority are human, deifies human beings by designating others than God as lords over men."

Islam, says Qutb, in response to this wrongful deification of human beings, must "proclaim the authority and sovereignty of God" and thereby "eliminate all human kingship and to announce the rule of the Sustainer of the universe over the entire earth. In the words of the Qur'an: 'He alone is God in the heavens and in the earth.' (43:84) 'The command belongs to God alone. He commands you not to worship anyone except Him. This is the right way of life.' (12: 40)"[27]

In practice, this meant implementation of the Sharia. Qutb therefore despised democracy for subjecting society to manmade laws that were the product of deliberation by the electorate or the legislature. The laws of Allah were not a matter for majority vote.

He advocated active and all-encompassing resistance to governments in Muslim lands that did not implement the Sharia. He insisted, "We must also free ourselves from the clutches of *jahili* society"—that is, society ordered according to human laws (literally, those of ignorance) rather than divine ones—"*jahili* concepts, *jahili* traditions, and *jahili* leadership. Our mission is not to compromise with the practices of *jahili* society, nor can we be loyal to it. *Jahili* society, because of its *jahili* characteristics, is not worthy to be compromised with. Our aim is first to change ourselves so that we may later change the society."[28]

This resistance must be international, in accord with the traditional Islamic view that religion transcends nationality. "A Muslim has no country except that part of the earth where the Shari'ah of God is established and human relationships are based on the foundation of relationship with God; a Muslim has no nationality except his belief, which makes him a member of the Muslim community in Dar-ul-Islam; a Muslim has no relatives except those who share the belief in God, and thus a bond is established between him and other Believers through their relationship with God."[29]

The idea that Muslim governments lose their legitimacy if they don't enforce the Sharia has recurred throughout Islamic history. The famous medieval scholar Ibn Taymiyya (1263–1328) declared that "a ruler who fails to enforce the shari'a rigorously in all aspects, including the conduct of jihad (and is therefore insufficiently Muslim), forfeits his right to rule."[30] Nevertheless, such a view was relatively unheard of among the secularized, Western-influenced Muslims of Qutb's day; thus it has led numerous analysts of Islamic radicalism to label him an innovator and contrast his views with those of "traditional Islam."

But Qutb's views of the Sharia were not innovative at all. And, he argued, they were not extremist, but simply the rule of Islamic law. "The way to establish God's rule on earth is not that some con-secrated people—the priests—be given the authority to rule, as was the case with the rule of the Church, nor that some spokesmen of God become rulers, as is the case in a 'theocracy.' To establish God's rule means that His laws be enforced and that the final deci-sion in all affairs be according to these laws."[31]

Of course, the distinction between the rule of the Sharia and that of a theocratic ruling elite is exceedingly fine; witness Iran today. Egypt's Arab Socialist ruler, Gamel Abdel Nasser, was well aware of the political implications of Qutb's writings and had him subjected to ten years of imprisonment and torture, and finally ordered him executed in 1966. A year before that, Qutb wrote from his prison cell, "The whole of Egypt is imprisoned.... I was arrested despite my immunity as a judge, without an order of arrest... my sole crime being my critique of the non-application of the Sharia."[32]

Nasser might have been most concerned with Qutb's exhorta-tions to jihad. These were predicated on the idea that the estab-lishment of Allah's rule would not be without obstacles. "Since this movement [Islam] comes into conflict with the *Jahiliyyah*," Qutb wrote, "which prevails over ideas and beliefs, and which has a prac-tical system of life and a political and material authority behind it, the Islamic movement had to produce parallel resources to con-front this *Jahiliyyah*."

Chief among those resources was jihad. In Qutb's view, "This movement uses the methods of preaching and persuasion for reforming ideas and beliefs and it uses physical power and Jihaad for abolishing the organizations and authorities of the *Jahili* system which prevents people from reforming their ideas and beliefs but forces them to obey their erroneous ways and make them serve human lords instead of the Almighty Lord."[33]

Armed struggle—jihad—was a necessity. "The establishing of the dominion of God on earth, the abolishing of the dominion of man, the taking away of sovereignty from the usurper to revert it to God, and the bringing about of the enforcement of the Divine Law (Shari'ah) and the abolition of man-made laws cannot be achieved only through preaching. Those who have usurped the authority of God and are oppressing God's creatures are not going to give up their power merely through preaching; if it had been so, the task of establishing God's religion in the world would have been very easy for the Prophets of God! This is contrary to the evidence from the history of the Prophets and the story of the struggle of the true religion, spread over generations."[34]

Muslims, Qutb says, must not only preach, but also "strike hard at all those political powers which force people to bow before them and which rule over them, unmindful of the commandments of God, and which prevent people from listening to the preaching and accepting the belief if they wish to do so. After annihilating the tyrannical force, whether it be in a political or a racial form, or in the form of class distinctions within the same race, Islam establishes a new social, economic, and political system, in which the concept of the freedom of man is applied in practice."[35]

Qutb's reference to the history of the prophets is one indication of how firmly his view of jihad is based on a close and careful reading of the Qur'an and study of the example of the Prophet Muhammad. In *Milestones* he quotes at length from the great medieval scholar Ibn Qayyim (1292–1350), who, says Qutb, "has summed up the nature of Islamic Jihaad." Ibn Qayyim outlines the stages of the Muhammad's prophetic career. "For thirteen years after the beginning of his Messengership, he called people to God through preaching, without fighting or *Jizyah*, and was commanded to restrain himself and to practice patience and forbearance. Then he was commanded to migrate, and later permission was given to fight. Then he was commanded to fight those who fought him, and to restrain himself from those who did not make war with him. Later he was commanded to fight the polytheists until God's religion was fully established."[36]

Qutb summarizes the stages. "Thus, according to the explanation by Imam Ibn Qayyim, the Muslims were first restrained from fighting; then they were permitted to fight; then they were commanded to fight against the aggressors; and finally they were commanded to fight against all the polytheists."[37]

That these stages of jihad can be found in Qutb, as well as in the writings of the Deobandis, the Wahhabis, and medieval Muslim scholars, underscores the traditional character of contemporary Islamic radicalism. Modern mujahedin are not "hijacking" Islam; they are—at least in their own view—restoring it. Ibn Qayyim, as quoted by Qutb, outlines the conditions of post-jihad society, i.e., dhimmitude. "After the command for Jihaad came, the non-believers were divided into three categories: one, those with whom there was peace; two, the people with whom the Muslims were at war; and three, the Dhimmies. . . . It was also explained that war should be declared against those from among the 'People of the Book' who declare open enmity, until they agree to pay Jizyah or accept Islam. Concerning the polytheists and the hypocrites, it was commanded in this chapter that Jihaad be declared against them and that they be treated harshly."[38]

Ultimately, he explains, those with whom the Muslims were at peace or had treaties became Muslims themselves, "so there were only two kinds [of unbelievers] left: people at war and Dhimmies. The people at war were always afraid of [Muhammad]. Now the people of the whole world were of three kinds: One, the Muslims who believed in him; two, those with whom he had peace and three, the opponents who kept fighting him."[39] In line with this, Qutb says that if someone rejects Islam, "then it is the duty of

Islam to fight him until either he is killed or until he declares his submission."[40]

Qutb's jihad: *not* defensive

Qutb speaks harshly of modernist and moderate Muslims who would recast jihad as a struggle for self-defense. Even while they "talk about Jihaad in Islam and quote Qur'anic verses," he says, they "do not... understand the nature of the various stages through which this movement develops, or the relationship of the verses revealed at various occasions with each stage." In other words, they don't understand that Allah gradually revealed the Muslim's responsibility to wage jihad, as outlined above by Ibn Qayyim.

This leads to further errors. "Thus, when they speak about Jihaad, they speak clumsily and mix up the various stages, distorting the whole concept of Jihaad and deriving from the Qur'anic verses final principles and generalities for which there is no justification. This is because they regard every verse of the Qur'an as if it were the final principle of this religion." This is probably something like what Qutb would say to contemporary Muslim spokesmen who quote the Qur'an's "tolerance verses" without making any mention of the stages of development in the holy book's teachings about jihad.

Qutb ascribes the growth of the idea that jihad is only a struggle for self-defense to a defeatist attitude. "This group of thinkers, who are a product of the sorry state of the present Muslim generation, have nothing but the label of Islam and have laid down their spiritual and rational arms in defeat. They say, 'Islam has prescribed only defensive war!' and think that they have done some good for their religion by depriving it of its method, which is to abolish all injustice from the earth, to bring people to the worship of God alone, and to bring them out of servitude to others into the servants of the Lord." [41]

He inveighs against attempts by "these defeatist-type people [who] try to mix the two aspects," that is, forced conversion and the struggle to establish the sovereignty of Allah alone, and who try to "confine Jihaad to what today is called 'defensive war.' The Islamic Jihaad has no relationship to modern warfare, either in its causes or in the way in which it is conducted."[42] Anyone who understands that jihad is actually a struggle to establish Allah's sovereignty "will also understand the place of *Jihaad bis saif* (striving through fighting), which is to clear the way for striving through preaching in the application of the Islamic movement. He will understand that Islam is not a 'defensive movement' in the narrow sense which today is technically called a 'defensive war.' "[43]

Who is ultimately responsible for this misrepresentation of jihad? Qutb blames "orientalists," Western interpreters of Islam. (Ironically, this is the very same camp blamed by Edward Said—the famous Princeton professor, Palestinian activist, and author of *Orientalism*—for caricaturing jihad as a struggle on the battlefield.) "This narrow meaning," says Qutb, "is ascribed to it by those who are under the pressure of circumstances and are defeated by the wily attacks of the orientalists, who distort the concept of Islamic Jihaad. It was a movement to wipe out tyranny and to introduce true freedom to mankind, using resources according to the actual human situation, and it had definite stages, for each of which it utilized new methods. If we insist on calling Islamic Jihaad a defensive movement, then we must change the meaning of the word 'defense' and mean by it 'the defense of man' against all those elements which limit his freedom. These elements take the form of beliefs and concepts, as well as of political systems, based on economic, racial or class distinctions."[44]

In other words, Qutb will allow for a "defensive jihad" if that means defending mankind from democracy, capitalism, communism, racism, and so on. His views on offensive and defensive jihad

are not innovative: he follows the Shafi'i school of Sunni jurisprudence, which mandates that "jihad had for its intent the waging of
war on unbelievers for their disbelief and not merely when they
entered into conflict with Islam."[45] This Shafi'i school still holds
sway at Cairo's prestigious al-Azhar University.

Orientalists, says Qutb, have distorted the idea of jihad by con-
fusing it with forced conversion, but Muslim scholars have not
responded properly. "The orientalists have painted a picture of
Islam as a violent movement which imposed its belief upon people by the sword. These vicious orientalists know very well that
this is not true, but by this method they try to distort the true
motives of Islamic Jihaad. But our Muslim scholars, these defeated
people, search for reasons of defensive [war] with which to negate
this accusation. They are ignorant of the nature of Islam and of its
function, and that it has a right to take the initiative for human
freedom."[46]

To support his contention that jihad is not solely for the defense
of Muslim lands, Qutb again invokes the early Islamic period. "As
to persons who attempt to defend the concept of Islamic Jihaad by
interpreting it in the narrow sense of the current concept of defensive war, and who do research to prove that the battles fought in
Islamic Jihaad were all for the defense of the homeland of Islam—
some of them considering the homeland of Islam to be just the
Arabian peninsula—against the aggression of neighboring powers,
they lack understanding of the nature of Islam and its primary aim.
Such an attempt is nothing but a product of a mind defeated by
the present difficult conditions and by the attacks of the treacher-
ous orientalists on the Islamic Jihaad. Can anyone say that if [the
first three caliphs] Abu Bakr, 'Umar, or 'Othman had been satisfied
that the Roman and Persian powers were not going to attack the
Arabian peninsula, they would not have striven to spread the message of Islam throughout the world? How could the message of

Islam have spread when it faced such material obstacles as the political system of the state, the socio-economic system based on races and classes, and behind all these, the military power of the government?"[47]

After quoting a number of Qur'anic verses on jihad, Qutb adds, "With these verses from the Qur'an and with many Traditions of the Prophet—peace be on him—in praise of Jihaad, and with the entire history of Islam, which is full of Jihaad, the heart of every Muslim rejects that explanation of Jihaad invented by those people whose minds have accepted defeat under unfavorable conditions and under the attacks on Islamic Jihaad by the shrewd orientalists."

Those who fall for such ideas are (at best) too soft and (at worst) traitors to Islam. "What kind of a man is it who, after listening to the commandment of God and the Traditions of the Prophet—peace be on him—and after reading about the events which occurred during the Islamic Jihaad, still thinks that it is a temporary injunction related to transient conditions and that it is concerned only with the defense of the borders?"[48]

Qutb's disgust for this point of view shows through in many passages of *Milestones*. He contrasts it with the internationalist outlook that Muslims should have, and which we see today in the support Saddam Hussein received from all over the Muslim world in the name of jihad. "Those who would say that Islamic Jihaad was merely for the defense of the 'homeland of Islam,'" Qutb asserts, "diminish the greatness of the Islamic way of life and consider it less important than their 'homeland.' This is not the Islamic point of view, and their view is a creation of the modern age and is completely alien to Islamic consciousness. What is acceptable to Islamic consciousness is its belief, the way of life which this belief prescribes, and the society which lives according to this way of life. The soil of the homeland has in itself no value or weight. From the

Islamic point of view, the only value which the soil can achieve is because on that soil God's authority is established and God's guidance is followed; and thus it becomes a fortress for the belief, a place for its way of life to be entitled the 'homeland of Islam,' a center for the movement for the total freedom of man."[49]

Perhaps with the pan-Arab movements of Nasser and others in mind, Qutb emphasized Islam's universal character and call. "This religion is not merely a declaration of the freedom of the Arabs, nor is its message confined to the Arabs. It addresses itself to the whole of mankind, and its sphere of work is the whole earth.... This religion wants to bring back the whole world to its Sustainer and free it from servitude to anyone other than God."[50]

But what about the Qur'an's command to Muslims not to "begin hostilities?" In his monumental, multi-volume commentary on the Qur'an, *In the Shade of the Qur'an*, completed in Nasser's prison, Qutb explains that Sura 2:190 ("begin not hostilities. Lo! Allah loveth not aggressors") is not a command to Muslims to avoid attacking their opponents, as it was interpreted by many who taught that jihad was only defensive. "'Aggression,'" says Qutb, "implies attacks on noncombatants and peaceful, unarmed civilians who pose no threat to Muslims or to their community as a whole. This includes women, children, the elderly, and those devoted to religious activity, such as priests and monks, of all religious and ideological persuasions. Aggression would also entail exceeding the moral and ethical limits set by Islam for fighting a just war."[51] He pointedly avoids saying that this verse limits jihad to self-defense.

In fact, according to Qutb, the very nature of the call to Islam rules out the idea that jihad could only be for self-defense. "Since the objective of the message of Islam is a decisive declaration of man's freedom, not merely on the philosophical plane but also in the actual conditions of life, it must employ Jihaad. It is immaterial whether the homeland of Islam—in the true Islamic sense, Dar ul-Islam—is in a condition of peace or whether it is threatened by its neighbors."⁵²

What then of non-Muslim countries that do not attack the Muslims? Can they be left alone? Only if they pay the non-Muslim poll-tax (jizya), the crowning symbol of dhimmitude and submission. "It may happen that the enemies of Islam may consider it expedient not to take any action against Islam, if Islam leaves them alone in their geographical boundaries to continue the lordship of some men over others and does not extend its message and its declaration of universal freedom within their domain. But Islam cannot agree to this unless they submit to its authority by paying Jizyah, which will be a guarantee that they have opened their doors for the preaching of Islam and will not put any obstacle in its way through the power of the state."53

Indeed, it is "a basic human right to be addressed with the message of Islam. No authority should deny mankind that right and under no circumstances should any obstacles be allowed to prevent that Divine Message from being delivered." Commenting on Sura 2:191 ("persecution is worse than slaughter"), Qutb says, "Islam considers religious persecution and any threat to religion more dangerous for the future stability and existence of Islam than actual war. According to this great Islamic principle, the survival and prosperity of the faith take precedence over the preservation of human life itself."⁵⁴ Christianity and other faiths, of course, would say the same thing, but none except Islam enjoin in response not the sacrifice of one's own life, but the killing of others.

For Qutb, violent jihad is a necessary part of establishing true peace, which equals the supremacy of the Sharia. "When Islam strives for peace, its objective is not that superficial peace which requires that only that part of the earth where the followers of Islam are residing remain secure. The peace which Islam desires is that the religion (i.e., the Law of the society) be purified for God, that the obedience of all people be for God alone, and that some people should not be lords over others. After the period of the Prophet—peace be on him—only the final stages of the movement of Jihaad are to be followed; the initial or middle stages are not applicable."[55]

That is, as Ibn Qayyim put it, there are now only two kinds of non-Muslims: those at war with Islam and those who have submitted to it. In a report on "the roots of jihad," BBC Middle East analyst Fiona Symon implied that Qutb was breaking with tradition by classifying "all non-Muslims [as] infidels—even the so-called 'people of the book,' the Christians and Jews."[56] But Ibn Qayyim (and other authorities) make it clear that in this Qutb was in full agreement with Islamic tradition.

Not only is the call to Islam universal; it is eternal. "This struggle," says Qutb, "is not a temporary phase but an eternal state—an eternal state, as truth and falsehood cannot co-exist on this earth."[57]

While he insists that jihad is not solely for self-defense, Qutb doesn't deny that defense of Islam is a part of the Muslim's duty—especially given the contemporary state of world affairs. "Today, Muslims continue to be the target of religious persecution under a host of Christian, Zionist, and secular regimes in many parts of the world. This situation makes jihad an incumbent duty on Muslims."[58] But the goal of this jihad, as he makes clear in *Milestones* and elsewhere, is not simply the ending of persecution, but the establishment of the Sharia everywhere.

This absolutist perspective is the view of Islamic radicals today. Qutb is a widely revered figure and his books are easily available in Islamic bookstores even in the United States. In spring 2003 *Milestones* was offered for sale by most online Muslim bookstores. The Muslim Brotherhood still lives, and counts Hasan al-Banna and Sayyid Qutb as its two leading lights. The Brotherhood, as well as Muslims around the world today, hail al-Banna, assassinated under mysterious circumstances, and Qutb, executed by Nasser, as *shahids*, martyrs. Some Muslims even consider Qutb the leading Sunni thinker of the twentieth century. Zafar Bangash, director of the Institute of Contemporary Islamic Thought in London, calls Qutb "a man of impeccable Islamic credentials [who] made an immense contribution to Muslim political thought at a time when the Muslim world was still mesmerized by such western notions as nationalism, the nation-State, and fathers of nations."[59] Qutb's biographer claims that his subject is "the most famous personality of the Muslim world in the second half of the twentieth century."[60]

The Brotherhood, meanwhile, was banned by the Egyptian government in 1948 for its participation in terrorist activities, but al-Banna reacted to the ban by declaring, "When words are banned, hands make their move."[61] In the ensuing years, the Brothers were reinstated and banned again, tried to assassinate Nasser several times, and were promised by Anwar Sadat in 1970 that Sharia would be implemented in Egypt. On October 6, 1981, with the Sharia still not Egypt's sole source of public order, Sadat was assassinated by four members of Islamic Jihad, an offshoot of the Muslim Brothers. The Brotherhood is still a presence in Egypt, continuing a wary give-and-take with the Mubarak government and spreading far and wide the message of Qutb.

Today the Brotherhood proudly takes credit for "liberating Muslim lands from colonialist powers in almost every Muslim country. The ikhwan [Brothers] were active amongst Muslims in Central Asian Muslim republics since the '70s, and their involvement can be seen recently in such republics as Tajikistan. More recently they had a major role in the struggle for Afghanistan and Kashmir." They proclaim: "Allah is our objective. The messenger [Muhammad] is our leader. Quran is our law. Jihad is our way. Dying in the way of Allah is our highest hope."[62]

And in America, we should remember that when spokesmen for American Muslim groups talk about peace and jihad as purely defensive war, they are likely to have read Qutb or at least be conversant with his ideas. Thus: peace means a society under Sharia law. Jihad is war in defense of Allah's law. The imposition of Sharia is the liberation of mankind. Those who currently live under what Qutb would have regarded as the tyranny of the Bill of Rights should take careful note of this.

Sayyid Abul A'la Maududi and the Islamic revolution

Sayyid Abul A'la Maududi was another modern-day leading Islamic thinker and activist. A descendant of both the Prophet Muhammad and of a medieval leader of the Chishti Sufi sect, and the author of several influential books, including *Jihad in Islam* and the massive *Towards Understanding the Qur'an*, Maududi was, like Qutb, not simply a theorist. Influenced by the rigorous Islam of the Deobandi sect, in 1940 he founded the Jamaat-e-Islami (Muslim Party).[63] This organization still exists today in Pakistan, India, and Bangladesh (as well as Kashmir), dedicated to making those countries Islamic states; and Maududi's influence goes well beyond the subcontinent.

One admirer called Maududi "the greatest revivalist of Islam in the twentieth century" and pointed out that his "writings and thoughts inspired similar movements in a large part of the world. Muslim Brotherhood, or Al-Ikhwanul Muslimoon as it is better known, has borrowed a lot from the man who brought a sea change in the Muslim perspective in this part of the world." Maududi effected this change by calling on Muslims "to do some real introspection" and exhorting them "to change themselves and follow true Islamic teachings" rather than the nationalism that preoccupied so much of Indian Muslim political thought in his day. At this time, Muslims were pressing for their own nation, which would successfully be carved out of the old British Raj: Pakistan.[64]

Maududi's concept of jihad is based on an Islam that goes beyond normal boundaries of "religion" and "nation." "In common terminology," he observes, "'religion' means nothing more than a hotch potch of some beliefs, prayers and rituals. If this is what 'religion' means, then, it should, indeed, be a private affair. You should be free to entertain any belief and worship any deity whom your conscience is ready to accept. If you are over-zealous and ardent devotees of this type of religion, go and preach it to the whole world and engage yourselves in declamations with the protagonists of other religions. There is no reason why you should take up a sword. Do you wish to convert people to your faith by killing them? We are forced to admit the point that if you regard Islam as a religion in the conventional meaning of the term and if, indeed, Islam be a conventional type of religion, the necessity for 'Jihad' cannot be justified."

As for the term "nation," he says that it "connotes no more than a homogeneous group of men who have joined themselves in a distinct entity on the basis of fundamental and shared traits." Such a nation has the right to defend itself, he says (although in reference to his contemporary Mahatma Gandhi, he notes that, "some saintly personages have declared even armed self-defense a sin"). However, a nation can't engage in offensive action. "But launching an armed attack on other people with the purpose of snatching away their lawful rights can be justified by no one except a few dictators."

The key point, Maududi declares, is that Islam rejects these common views. "But the truth is that Islam is not the name of a 'Religion,' nor is 'Muslim' the title of a 'Nation.' In reality Islam is a revolutionary ideology and programme which seeks to alter the social order of the whole world and rebuild it in conformity with its own tenets and ideals. 'Muslim' is the title of that International Revolutionary Party organized by Islam to carry into effect its revolutionary programme. And 'Jihad' refers to that revolutionary struggle and utmost exertion which the Islamic Party brings into play to achieve this objective."

This kind of talk is clearly borrowed from Marx and Engels, but Maududi's program is conscientiously Islamic.

As Qutb did later, Maududi firmly rejected nationalism. "Islam has no vested interest in promoting the cause of this or that Nation. The hegemony of this or that State on the face of this earth is irrelevant to Islam." In fact, "Islam wishes to destroy all States and Governments anywhere on the face of the earth which are opposed to the ideology and programme of Islam regardless of the country or the Nation which rules it."

The Sharia will be put in the place of all other governments. "The purpose of Islam is to set up a State on the basis of its own ideology and programme, regardless of which Nation assumes the role of the standard-bearer of Islam or the rule of which nation is undermined in the process of the establishment of an ideological Islamic State."

This is a universal responsibility. "Islam requires the earth—not just a portion, but the whole planet—not because the sovereignty over the earth should be wrested from one Nation or several Nations and vested in one particular Nation, but because the entire mankind should benefit from the ideology and welfare programme or what would be truer to say from 'Islam' which is the programme of well-being for all humanity." Alluding again to Marxism, he says, "The call of Islam is not addressed to the workers, and holders, peasants or industrialists; it is directed to the whole of the human race." This call is meant to allow for "evil and contumacy" to be "wiped out" so that "God's Law [can] be enforced in the world." The call to Islam as a social system must be universal if it is made at all, for "no State can put her ideology into full operation until the same ideology comes into force in the neighboring States. Hence it is imperative for the Muslim Party for reasons of both general welfare of humanity and self-defense that it should not rest content with establishing the Islamic System of Government in one territory alone, but to extend the sway of [the] Islamic System all around as far as its resources can carry it.... Towards this end, Islam wishes to press into service all forces which can bring about a revolution and a composite term for the use of all these forces is 'Jihad.'"

Maududi acknowledges that jihad has a multitude of meanings and can take a variety of forms, including writing controversial literature and offering financial support. But he insisted that "to alter the old tyrannical social system and establish a new just order of life by the power of the sword is also 'Jihad' and to expend goods and exert physically for this cause is 'Jihad' too."

"The old tyrannical social system" doesn't refer only to life under dictators. It refers to any rule according to a law other than that of God. Maududi's thought on the nature of human governments aligns exactly with Qutb's. "No one," Maududi declares, "has the right to become a self-appointed ruler of men and issue orders and prohibitions on his own volition and authority. To acknowledge the personal authority of a human being as the source of commands and prohibitions is tantamount to admitting him as the sharer in the Powers and Authority of God. And this is the root of all evils in the universe."

The Muslims, the party of Allah, is accordingly "left with no other choice except to capture State Authority, for an evil system takes root and flourishes under the patronage of an evil government and a pious cultural order can never be established until the authority of Government is wrested from the wicked and transferred into the hands of the reformers."

Maududi also invokes the Qur'an, Muhammad, and Islamic history to support his exposition of jihad and the ultimate objectives of Muslims. "The Muslim Party will inevitably extend invitation to the citizens of other countries to embrace the faith which holds promise of true salvation and genuine welfare for them. Even otherwise also if the Muslim Party commands adequate resources it will eliminate un-Islamic Governments and establish the power of Islamic Government in their stead." This is, he says, exactly what Muhammad and the first caliphs did. "It is the same policy which was executed by the Holy Prophet (peace of Allah be upon him) and his successor illustrious Caliphs (may Allah be pleased with them). Arabia, where the Muslim Party was founded, was the first country which was subjugated and brought under the rule of Islam."

Maududi refers to the letters Muhammad sent to Heraclius, Chosroes, and other rulers as patterns of action for modern Muslims. "Later the Holy Prophet (peace of Allah be upon him) sent invitations to other surrounding States to accept the faith and ideology of Islam. Where the ruling classes of those countries declined to accept this invitation to adopt the true faith, the Prophet (peace of Allah be upon him) resolved to take military action against them."

After Muhammad's death, according to Maududi, Abu Bakr "launched an invasion of Rome [Byzantium] and Iran, which were under the dominance of un-Islamic Governments." Egypt, Syria, Byzantium, and Persia resisted until, says Maududi, they realized that the Muslims "had come with the sole object of instituting a just system." Thereafter, he asserts, they willingly joined in the struggle.

Maududi rejects the offensive/defensive distinction. "If you carefully consider the explanation given above, you will readily understand that the two terms 'offensive' and 'defensive,' by which the nature of welfare is differentiated, are not at all applicable to Islamic 'Jihad.'" Why not? "Islamic Jihad is both offensive and defensive at one and the same time. It is offensive because the Muslim Party assaults the rule of an opposing ideology and it is defensive because the Muslim Party is constrained to capture State power in order to arrest the principles of Islam in space-time forces."

Again like Qutb, Maududi objects to the Western conflation of jihad with forced conversion. "Islamic 'Jihad' does not seek to interfere with the faith, ideology, rituals of worship or social customs of the people. It allows them perfect freedom of religious belief and permits them to act according to their creed. However, Islamic 'Jihad' does not recognize their right to administer State affairs according to a system which, in the view of Islam, is evil."

That doesn't mean, however, that non-Muslims will be able to operate freely in an Islamic state. "Islamic 'Jihad' also refuses to admit their right to continue with such practices under an Islamic government which fatally affect the public interest from the viewpoint of Islam." Maududi explains that "as soon as the Ummah of Islam captures State power" it will therefore ban various un-Islamic practices: the lending of money at interest, "all forms of business and financial dealings which are forbidden by Islamic Law," gambling, prostitution, "and other vices," and "it will make it obligatory for non-Muslim women to observe the minimum standards of modesty in dress as required by Islamic Law and will forbid them to go about displaying their beauty like the days of ignorance." An Islamic state will also "clamp censorship on the Cinema."

Intolerant? "No creed in the world has shown more tolerance to the votaries of other faiths as has been practiced by Islam. In other places, protagonists of another faith are so repressed that finding existence unbearable they are constrained to emigrate from their homes. But Islam provides full opportunity for self-advancement to the people of other faiths under conditions of peace and tranquility and displays such magnanimity towards them that the world has yet to show a parallel example."[65] Still, in his commentary on the Qur'an he notes that the non-Muslim poll-tax mandated by Sura 9:29 "symbolizes the submission of the unbelievers to the suzerainty of Islam." He sneers at "some nineteenth-century Muslim writers and their followers in our own times" who "never seem to tire of their apologies for *jizyah*." He states that non-Muslims, although they are free to practice their "false, man-made way" have "absolutely no right to seize the reins of power in any part of God's earth nor to direct the collective affairs of human beings according to their own misconceived doctrines." If they do, "the believers would be under an obligation to do their utmost to dislodge them from political power and to make them live in subservience to the Islamic way of life."[66]

Again, Maududi is no dead-letter theorist. The political movement he created, Jamaat-e-Islami, is one of the largest political parties in Pakistan today, and numerous government officials have risen through its ranks. Its current leader in Pakistan, Qazi Hussain Ahmed, states that Jamaat-e-Islami believes "NOT in the Western definition of 'democracy,' which assign[s] (in principle though) all authority to the people. We believe in the Authority of Allah and human being as His vicegerents [sic]. Thus 'democracy' in Islam is guided as well as guarded." The democracy that Qazi envisions will need no voting, for its principles are "quite clearly expounded in the Qur'an and Sunnah."[67] Jamaat-e-Islami calls for "rectification of and change in society, stabilizing it according to Shari'ah."[68] Thus it is working through the current political system in Pakistan in order to destroy the status quo. Fanning the flames of anti-American fervor after September 11, 2001, the party won large gains in the October 2002 elections.

But Jamaat-e-Islami's legitimate political activities don't necessarily indicate that the organization has, even for the moment, entirely forsworn armed jihad. The alleged architect of the September 11 attacks, al Qaeda chieftan Khalid Shaikh Mohammed, was caught (after an international manhunt) in Pakistan, in the home of Ahmed Abdul Qadus, a Jamaat-e-Islami member. On hearing news of the arrest, Jamaat-e-Islami spokesman Amirul Azeem went ballistic—not because Qadus was hiding a prime terror suspect, but because the Pakistani government had cooperated with the United States in efforts to find and arrest him. Khalid Shaikh Mohammed, he said, was a hero, and his arrest constituted a "shameful sell-out" by Pakistani authorities. Referring to al Qaeda, Azeem said, "Those who fought jihad in Afghanistan... who refused to be dictated to by the Americans are heroes of Islam. These man [sic] are the targets of America, but Pakistanis consider them their guests—they are ready to give them refuge."

Moreover, he asserted that this "sell-out" was "not acceptable to the people."[69] He seemed untroubled by the possibility that the people of Pakistan would condemn the September 11 attacks and applaud the arrest of the mastermind behind them.

In January 2003, two other al Qaeda members were nabbed in the home of another Jamaat-e-Islami leader, Sabiha Shahid.[70] According to journalist Gretchen Peters, "The party has also been implicated in other recent terror arrests. A Jamaat member was in the Karachi apartment where police found al Qaeda leader Ramzi Binalshibh, and a doctor arrested in Lahore several months back for al Qaeda ties was also linked to the party."[71]

According to Pakistani author Ahmed Rashid, "The Jamaat has never condemned September 11, and denies that al Qaeda is a terrorist organization. This is a group that believes [the attacks were] carried out by Jews in America. The really scary thing is that this is also the most moderate Islamic party in Pakistan."[72]

Abdullah Azzam, Afghanistan, and Osama bin Laden

Least moderate of all is Sheikh Abdullah Azzam, a Muslim scholar who unites in his person several of the chief radical Islamic organizations. According to *Jane's Intelligence Review*, Azzam was "an influential figure in the Muslim Brotherhood" and "the historical leader of Hamas," as well as the man who shaped Osama bin Laden's view of the world.[73] Born in a Palestinian village in 1941, Azzam was raised in a pious Muslim household and earned a degree in Sharia from the Sharia College of Damascus University in 1966. In 1973 he received a Ph.D. in Islamic jurisprudence from al-Azhar University in Cairo, the oldest, most respected, and most influential institute of higher learning in the Muslim world. While in Egypt, he met members of Sayyid Qutb's family, who revered the author of *Milestones* as a martyr.

Azzam then joined the jihad against Israel, but soon grew frustrated. His fellow mujahedin spent their off-hours gambling and playing music, both forbidden activities according to Islamic law—particularly in the interpretation of the Shafi'i school which holds sway at al-Azhar.[74] Ultimately, Azzam decided that "this revolution has no religion behind it" and traveled to Saudi Arabia to teach.[75] There he taught that the Muslim philosophy in conflicts with non-Muslims ought to be "jihad and the rifle alone. NO negotiations, NO conferences and NO dialogue."[76]

In 1980, attracted by the jihad against the Soviets in Afghanistan, he went to Pakistan to get to know the movement's leaders. He taught for a while at the International Islamic University in Islamabad, but soon resigned in order to devote himself full-time to jihad. Azzam and his "dear friend" Osama bin Laden founded the Mujahedin Service Bureau in order to give aid to those fighting in Afghanistan. However, "this was not enough to satisfy Sheikh Azzam's burning desire for Jihad. That desire inspired him finally to go to the frontline."[77]

Joining the fight in Afghanistan, Azzam declared, "Never shall I leave the Land of Jihad, except in three cases. Either I shall be killed in Afghanistan. Either I shall be killed in Peshawar. Or either I shall be handcuffed and expelled from Pakistan." And indeed, in 1989 he was killed under mysterious circumstances in Peshawar. His followers hail him as a martyr and as "the main pillar of the Jihad movement in the modern times."[78] Ten years later, in an interview broadcast on al-Jazeera television, Osama bin Laden said, "Sheikh Abdullah Azzam was not an individual, but an entire nation by himself. Muslim women have proven themselves incapable of giving birth to a man like him after he was killed."[79] The publisher of *Join the Caravan* in English, evidently believing that Osama's opinion would carry weight, featured this quote as an endorsement for the book.

Azzam truly was an extraordinary man. It is extraordinary indeed that this academic who earned degrees from two major Islamic universities and who taught in four countries would have ended up fighting alongside Osama bin Laden. Why wasn't he upbraided and dismissed by the faculties of any of these universities for his radicalism? Why wasn't he convinced that the way he was thinking of jihad was antiquated and out of step with the Qur'an and the example of the Prophet?

No doubt Azzam met Muslim academics who disagreed with his views of jihad. But the fact that he received his degrees and was able to get employment in Muslim institutions in four different countries illustrates that his perspective wasn't regarded the same way that American academics would regard David Duke or Jean Marie LePen.

This may be at least in part because Azzam, like al-Banna, Qutb, and Maududi, based his teachings firmly on the Qur'an and hadith. His exhortation to Muslims to join the jihad in Afghanistan, *Join the Caravan*, is studded with Qur'anic quotations and references to the life of Muhammad.[80] Azzam denies that Muhammad ever understood jihad solely as a spiritual struggle. "The saying, 'We have returned from the lesser Jihad (battle) to the greater Jihad,' which people quote on the basis that it is a hadith, is in fact a false, fabricated hadith which has no basis. It is only a saying of Ibrahim bin Abi Ablah, one of the Successors, and it contradicts textual evidence and reality." He quotes several authorities charging that hadith narrated by Ibrahim bin Abi Ablah are false, including one who reports, "He was accused of forging hadith." Azzam also invokes Ibn Taymiyya, who wrote: "This hadith has no source and nobody whomsoever [sic] in the field of Islamic knowledge has narrated it. Jihad against the disbelievers is the most noble of actions and moreover it is the most important action for the sake of mankind."[81] The idea that armed warfare against non-Muslims is "the most important action for the sake of mankind" corresponds exactly, of course, to the views of Qutb.

For this important action, jihadis receive special rewards. Azzam held out as enticements to would-be jihadis statements like this from the Prophet Muhammad. "Paradise has one hundred grades [or levels] which Allah has reserved for the *Mujahidun* [warriors of jihad] who fight in His Cause, and the distance between each of two grades is like the distance between the heaven and the earth."[82]

"Jihad and hijrah [emigration] to Jihad," writes Azzam, "have a deep-rooted role which cannot be separated from the constitution of this religion." In this he is exhorting Muslims to emigrate, as he did, to lands where jihad is currently being fought. Young Muslims heeded such calls in large numbers. Abu Abdel Aziz, the Muslim commander who went from Afghanistan to Bosnia in search of jihad, went to Afghanistan in the first place because of Abdullah

Azzam. "One of those who came to our land [presumably Saudi Arabia]," Aziz recounted in a 1994 interview, "was sheikh Dr. Abdallah Azzam—may his soul rest in peace—I heard him rallying the youth to come forth and [join him] to go to Afghanistan. This was in 1984—I think. I decided to go and check the matter for myself. This was, and all praise be to Allah, the beginning [of my journey with] Jihad. I am still following this same path." He then quoted Sura 9:111, which promises Paradise to those who are killed while fighting for Allah.[83]

Azzam brought Sayyid Qutb's teachings to his modern-day radical Muslim audience. After quoting and commenting upon several Qur'anic verses, he quotes Qutb. "If Jihad had been a transitory phenomenon in the life of the Muslim Ummah, all of these sections of the Quranic text would not be flooded with this type of verse! Likewise, so much of the Sunnah of the Messenger of Allah (SAWS) would not be occupied with such matters."[84] Azzam's use of Qutb provides a direct link between the mid-twentieth-century literature of Islamic radicalism to Osama bin Laden and present-day terrorism.

Much of *Join the Caravan* is devoted to convincing Muslims that when non-Muslims dominate any portion of Muslim land, jihad becomes an obligation for every individual (*fard ayn*). Azzam points out that Muhammad himself went on twenty-seven "military excursions," and that "he himself fought in nine of these." After summarizing the Prophet's military career he notes that "this means that the Messenger of Allah (SAWS) used to go out on military expeditions or send out an army at least every two months."[85] He quotes a hadith in which Muhammad says that Islam's "highest peak" is jihad.[86] In another book, *Defence of the Muslim Lands*, he notes that offensive jihad is a general obligation for Muslims, classified according to Islamic theology as *fard kifaya*: that is, if enough Muslims answer the call, the rest are freed from the obligation. He adds, "And the Ulama [Muslim scholars] have mentioned that this type of jihad is for maintaining the payment of Jizya!"[87] This presupposes, of course, the entire legal superstructure of dhimmitude that mandates that non-Muslims pay the tax.

Besides the Qur'an and Hadith, Azzam quotes numerous revered Muslim scholars, including Ibn Taymiyya and the medieval Qur'an commentator Abu Abdullah Muhammad Al-Qurtubi, who declares that "going out for Jihad is compulsory in times of need, of advent of the disbelievers, and of severe furore [sic] of fighting."[88]

This is the theological foundation on which Osama bin Laden based the destruction of the World Trade Center on September 11, 2001.

Part Three

THE GREAT JIHAD
COVER-UP

⊠

Chapter Nine

TERRORISM

Jihad abused?

Is terrorism jihad?

ESPITE THE FACT THAT Osama bin Laden has praised Abdullah Azzam, who clearly has an intellectual debt to the other great twentieth-century figures of Islamic radicalism, many analysts conclude that the actions of the world's most famous terrorist are not in fact consistent with their teachings. Scholar Hamid Algar, a Muslim convert, summed up this view in a letter to the *New York Times Magazine*, commenting on an article about Qutb. The article, according to Algar, "failed to show any line of filiation from Qutb, executed in 1966, to al Qaeda, established in the 1980s. Nowhere in Qutb's writings—several of which I have translated—can one find a parallel to al Qaeda's advocacy of mass slaughter." The article, Algar argues, "exemplifies the tendency to conflate into a malevolent blur all Muslims regarded as troublesome."[1]

We have just seen that Azzam, a friend and colleague of bin Laden, used Qutb's arguments to buttress his own. If nothing else, Qutb, al-Banna, Maududi, and other radical Islamic intellectuals articulated a vision of jihad that led scholars like Azzam to forsake the classroom for the battlefield, and which led, at least indirectly, to the September 11 attacks. But would they have applauded what they had wrought?

Algar, of course, puts his finger on the problem: jihad and the Sharia are one thing, but "advocacy of mass slaughter" is another. Many Muslims have pointed out since the September 11 attacks that Islam forbids killing women, children, and the innocent in jihad.

Of this there is no doubt, but there is a key distinction: the Shafi'i school of Sunni Muslim jurisprudence stipulates that "it is not permissible... to kill women and children unless they are fighting against the Muslims." The Hanbali jurist Ibn Taymiyya, a favorite of modern Muslim radicals, directed that "as for those who cannot offer resistance or cannot fight, such as women, children, monks, old people, the blind, handicapped and their likes, they shall not be killed unless they actually fight with words (e.g., by propaganda) and acts (e.g., by spying or otherwise assisting in the warfare)."[2]

So were the workers in the World Trade Center "fighting against the Muslims?" Radical Muslims, including Osama, have answered yes. The November 2002 communiqué purporting to be from Osama states that "the American people are the ones who pay the taxes which fund the planes that bomb us in Afghanistan, the tanks that strike and destroy our homes in Palestine, the armies which occupy our lands in the Arabian Gulf, and the fleets which ensure the blockade of Iraq. These tax dollars are given to Israel for it to continue to attack us and penetrate our lands. So the American people are the ones who fund the attacks against us, and they are the ones who oversee the expenditure of these monies in the way they wish, through their elected candidates."[3] Under this logic, there is no such thing as an innocent American. According to a sermon in the Al-Manshawi mosque in the holy city of Mecca by a Saudi cleric, Sheikh Wajdi Hamza Al-Ghazawi, one man's terrorism is another man's jihad:

> The [kind of] terror [in Arabic, "striking of fear"] that Islamic religious law permits is terrifying the cowards, the hypocrites, the secularists, and the rebels by imposing punishments according to the religious law of Allah.... The meaning of the term "terror" used by the media... is Jihad for the sake of Allah. Jihad is the peak of Islam. Moreover, some of the clerics... see it as the sixth pillar of Islam. Jihad—whether Jihad of defense of Muslims and of Islamic lands such as in Chechnya, the Philippines, and Afghanistan, or Jihad aimed at spreading the religion—is the pinnacle of terror, as far as the enemies of Allah are concerned. The Mujaheed who goes out to attain a martyr's death or victory and returns with booty is a terrorist as far as the enemies of Allah are concerned.... Accordingly, the believer must not use this word.... Jihad, oh believers, is an integral part of our religion. The word "terror" is used to damage this mighty and blessed foundation....[4]

This sermon was posted on a Saudi website on October 6, 2001, less than a month after the September 11 attacks.

Suicide bombing

The September 11 attacks were the ultimate suicide bombing, and, of course, innumerable Muslim spokesmen and scholars have pointed out that suicide is sinful in Islam. They quote the Qur'an: "O ye who believe! Eat not up your property among yourselves in vanities. . . . Nor kill (or destroy) yourselves: for verily Allah hath been to you Most Merciful! If any do that in rancor and injustice, soon shall We cast them into the Fire: And easy it is for Allah" (Sura 4:29-30). Also, the Prophet said, "He who commits suicide by throttling shall keep on throttling himself in the Hell-fire (forever), and he who commits suicide by stabbing himself shall keep on stabbing himself in the Hell-fire."[5]

The problem, however, is that there are Muslim defenders of suicide bombing. They deny that those who blow themselves up in public places are actually committing suicide at all, since their intention is not to kill themselves but to use their bodies as an instrument to kill unbelievers. As such, the bombers are martyrs. Those who make this argument point to other Qur'anic verses, including the one invoked by Commander Abu Abdel Aziz in explaining why he decided to become a mujahid. "Allah hath purchased of the believers their persons and their goods; for theirs (in return) is the garden (of Paradise): they fight in His cause, and slay and are slain: a promise binding on Him in truth . . ." (Sura 9:111).

What does Allah promise to those who "slay and are slain" for Allah? "When ye meet the Unbelievers (in fight), smite at their necks. . . . But those who are slain in the Way of Allah, He will never let their deeds be lost. Soon will He guide them and improve their condition, and admit them to the Garden which He has announced for them" (Sura 47:4-6). We have seen that defenders of suicide bombing also invoke Muhammad, saying that those killed while fighting for Allah go straight to Paradise.

This idea is widespread in the Islamic world. In June 2002, a London-based Arabic-language newspaper carried an interview with Umm Nidal, the mother of Muhammad Farhat of Hamas, who carried out a suicide attack on March 3, 2002. Umm Nidal said, "Jihad is a [religious] commandment imposed upon us. We must instill this idea in our sons' souls, all the time. . . . What we see every day—massacres, destruction, bombing [of] homes—strengthened, in the souls of my sons, especially Muhammad, the love of Jihad and martyrdom. . . . Allah be praised, I am a Muslim and I believe in Jihad. Jihad is one of the elements of the faith and this is what encouraged me to sacrifice Muhammad in Jihad for the sake of Allah. My son was not destroyed, he is not dead; he is living a happier life than I."

Umm Nidal was referring to the Qur'an: "And say not of those who are slain in the way of Allah: 'They are dead.' Nay, they are living, though ye perceive (it) not" (Sura 2:154).

Umm Nidal continued, "Because I love my son, I encouraged him to die a martyr's death for the sake of Allah. . . . Jihad is a religious obligation incumbent upon us, and we must carry it out. I sacrificed Muhammad as part of my obligation. This is an easy thing. There is no disagreement [among scholars] on such matters."

Didn't Umm Nidal know that suicide was forbidden in the Qur'an? How did she arrive at this serene certainty that all Muslim scholars agreed with her point of view? There is no doubt that she viewed her son's action from a perspective of deep Islamic piety. "I prayed from the depths of my heart that Allah would cause the success of his operation. I asked Allah to give me ten [Israelis] for Muhammad, and Allah granted my request and Muhammad made his dream come true, killing ten Israeli settlers and soldiers. Our God honored him even more, in that there were many Israelis wounded."[6]

Likewise Seyf al-Islam ("Sword of Islam") Qaddafi, the son of Libyan dictator Muammar Qaddafi, refused to condemn suicide bombing when given the opportunity by journalist Amir Taheri. The author of *Holy Terror: The Inside Story of Islamic Terrorism*, Taheri has noted that "Islamic religious law...does not permit suicide under any circumstances. In Islam, suicide is an 'unpardonable sin' (*zunb layughfar lah*), in the same category as denying the Oneness of God. People who commit suicide cannot be buried in a Muslim graveyard and are put to rest away from human habitation and in unmarked tombs."[7]

However obvious and straightforward this perspective may seem to be, Taheri didn't find Seyf al-Islam Qaddafi inclined to buy it. When Taheri asked him if he approved of suicide bombings by Palestinians, Qaddafi replied, "It is not a question of approval or disapproval. They have a philosophy behind what they do. They are acting in accordance with the holy Koran and the law of retribution." When Taheri challenged this, invoking the Qur'an's prohibitions of suicide and the killing of noncombatants, Qaddafi replied, "We obviously have different readings of the Koran." He also echoed bin Laden's justification for attacks on American civilians. "There are no civilians in Israel. All Israelis are either in the army or have been or shall one day be soldiers."[8]

The Saudi Sheikh Mohsin Al-'Awaji related suicide bombing directly to the teachings of Muhammad. "The Saudis believe," he asserted in an interview with al-Jazeera televison, "that the glory of the [Islamic] nation appeared when our Prophet taught us the industry of death—when he taught us how to create death. Then life became cheap in our eyes....When one of the sons of our nation is killed, he says, 'I won,' and the master of the Ka'aba [Muhammad] swears that he had won. This we see as the industry of death."

Speaking from wealthy Saudi Arabia, he characterized suicide bombing not as a matter of poverty but rather of preference. "We in Saudi society and in other Islamic societies have finally realized that this is the right path to tread in order to deal with today's deadly strategic weapons. If America has intercontinental missiles and bombs, then our bombs are the Jihad fighters, whom America has called 'suicide attackers' and we call 'martyrs.'"[9]

Not only the sheikh, who is opposed to the Saudi regime, but even the Saudi newspaper *Al-Jazirah*, which is controlled by the Saudi government, registered its approval for suicide bombing as a form of jihad. Dr. Khalil Ibrahim Al-Sa'adat wrote in glowing terms about 'Abd Al-Baset 'Oudeh, "the quiet hero" who blew himself up at a Passover Seder in an Israeli hotel. "You defended your religion, your homeland, and your people. You attached no importance to [any] Arab summit; you did not wait for international agreements; you did not follow television interviews; you did not pause because of dead Arab and international reactions that neither help nor hinder. Courageously, full of willingness to [wage] Jihad, and with faith filling your heart, you executed your assignment and sacrificed your pure soul for your religion and your homeland.... You knew that the Zionists do not honor treaties, promises, and agreements, and understand only the language of resistance and Jihad."[10]

It is easy to find Muslims in the United States and elsewhere who, like Taheri, condemn suicide bombing by invoking the Qur'an's prohibition of suicide. Notable among them is the Albanian-born Imam Muhammad Naasir ud-Din Al-Albani (1914–1999), who taught for a time at the University of Medina in Saudi Arabia and lectured to Muslims internationally.

However, there is no central authority in Islam to make a definitive ruling about the permissibility or impermissibility of suicide attacks. The views of Muslims like Taheri and al-Albani have no greater *a priori* claim to represent true Islam than do those of Umm

Nidal and Dr. Khalil Ibrahim Al-Sa'adat. Those who support suicide bombing aren't listening to cooler heads. They don't tend to find moderate Muslim protestations about the prohibition against suicide convincing, since these generally fail to explain why the suicide prohibition would apply to those who are not committing an act of despair or hopelessness, but rather one that they think will bring them the highest reward available to human beings.

As such, the debate within the Muslim world is at an impasse—and the bombings continue, not only in Israel but also in Kashmir, Chechnya, and other battlegrounds of jihad. Recently, U.S. military personnel have been targeted in Iraq and even in the land of our putative friend and ally Saudi Arabia. On May 12, 2003, "attackers shot their way into three housing compounds in synchronized strikes in the Saudi capital and then set off multiple suicide car bombs, killing twenty people, including seven Americans. Saudi officials said nine attackers also died."[11] The attackers are believed to have been affiliated with al Qaeda.

Suicide bombing has a disturbingly wide appeal. According to Mahmoud Al-Zahhar of Hamas, a 2002 call for suicide bombers at the University of Alexandria in Egypt resulted in two thousand students signing up "to die a martyr's death."[12] The sheer magnitude of the phenomenon of suicide bombing, the variance in the circumstances in which it is carried out, and, above all, its theological underpinnings should make clear that this is not simply a last desperate resort of the poverty-stricken oppressed; rather, it springs from an understanding of Islam that is, however much we would wish it away, founded on traditional concepts and rooted in the deepest longings of many Muslims.

"The Americans love Pepsi-Cola, we love death," said Maulana Inyadullah of al Qaeda in the aftermath of the September 11 attacks. Said Ismail Haniya of Hamas, "[Jews] love life more than any other people, and they prefer not to die."[13] Inyadullah and

Haniya love death, and are ready to bring it upon others, in line with their understanding of the ways of Allah. "Those who love the life of this world more than the Hereafter, who hinder (men) from the Path of Allah and seek therein something crooked: they are astray by a long distance" (Sura 14:3).

Despite the strong evidence that suicide bombing has a foundation in jihad theology, and the signs that the Islamic world is sharply divided about the propriety of the practice, most Western analysts dismiss it as a byproduct of poverty and desperation. Alleviate the economic and social misery of the bombers, they say, and the problem will disappear.

This myth has shown a stubborn resistance to fact. When research scientist Scott Atran published findings in the *New York Times* showing that suicide bombers were actually most often from educated and relatively affluent backgrounds, he provoked a hail of indignant letters to the editor. "Scott Atran may be right that many suicide bombers are educated, not impoverished, and asocial," huffed one, "but this does not rule out ignorance, poverty, and alienation as underlying causes of terrorism. Nor does it mean that religious martyrdom is the main motivation of these attacks." Another sniffed, "It should be obvious by now that the most effective way to deal with terrorism is to deal with the injustices that motivate so much of it."[14]

But the writings of Islamic radicals that we examined in Chapter Nine, particularly Qutb's *Milestones* and the immense and scholarly *In the Shade of the Qur'an*, are not disguised calls to alleviate poverty or injustice, or to return stolen land, or even to eliminate real or perceived colonialism (except insofar as any authority other than that of the Sharia would be inadmissible). Nor are they exercises in the canny manipulation of those who are easily led; on the contrary, they presuppose a thorough and familiar knowledge of the Qur'an, the life and career of the Prophet Muhammad, and Islamic history.

Khomeini, al-Banna, Qutb, Maududi, Azzam, and other Islamic leaders call on Muslims to subdue all people, by violence if necessary, to obey Allah; and they couch this call in terms that are entirely religious. It is condescending, ethnocentric, and ultimately baseless to insist that this religious motivation is really a cover for something else.

Jihad: *not* holy war?

It's the same with jihad in general. Many modern analysts seem to assume that the religious struggle of Muslim radicals is really a disguised call for something else, perhaps because they themselves articulate a vision of jihad that Osama and other radicals would hardly recognize, much less accept.

"Islamic tradition does not have a notion of holy war. *Jihad* simply means to strive hard or struggle in pursuit of a just cause.... Holy war (*al-harb al-muqaddasah*) is not an expression used by the Qur'anic text or Muslim theologians. In Islamic theology war is never holy; it is either justified or not."[15]

These are the words of Khaled Abou El Fadl, a widely respected authority on Islam who teaches at the University of California at Los Angeles. El Fadl's emotional reaction to the September 11 terrorist attacks was quoted around the country by people across the political spectrum. He recounted what he called "a prayer, a wish, a plea: 'Please, God, not Muslims. [Do not let it be] Muslims who have done this, or anyone who is calling themselves a Muslim.'" But El Fadl admitted he was prepared for the worst. "Something in my heart just told me that I know it's going to turn out to be someone who believes himself a Muslim to have done this. I wept for a good hour. It was so much suffering. As a professor who teaches in this field, and as a Muslim who is committed to this religion, for it to all to come to this."

Come to what? El Fadl wasn't crying over the attacks as such. "It wasn't just that I was crying about the planes or the fear or the anxiety. . . . I was crying over what has happened to Muslim civilization. Where are we now? I was crying over the fate of something that I love dearly, and that is Islam."

In El Fadl's view, Muslim civilization didn't begin to go wrong on September 11, 2001; he enumerates earlier events that caused him pain. "Well before this, there was the destroying of the Buddha statues; there [was] the oppression of women in Afghanistan; there [was] the decision to have Christians and Jews wear distinctive marks in Afghanistan. It's ugliness after ugliness after ugliness."[16]

These expressions of regret are laudable as far as they go, but they leave the impression that violent Islamic intolerance is a relatively recent phenomenon. After all, the Taliban didn't originate the idea that Muslim women should be heavily restricted, or that Christians and Jews in Muslim lands should wear distinctive marks. Even before Iran became Khomeini's laboratory of the new Islamic state, in some areas of Iran Jews were made to wear distinctive yellow patches on their clothing as late as 1950.[17] Nor was Iran or Afghanistan innovative in this; such laws are rooted in the classic directives of the Sharia for religious minorities. Distinctive dress for Muslims and Jews was first mandated over a millennium ago by the caliph Ja'far al-Mutawakkil (847–861).[18] We have seen how the oppression of the dhimmis has played out in history.

In addition, El Fadl's assertion that Islam doesn't have a tradition of holy war suggests an unwillingness to face uncomfortable facts of Islamic history and theology. It's unclear what term he would prefer to use for conquests of pagan Arabia by the Prophet Muhammad; the early Muslims' extension of those conquests into

Syria, Egypt, and eventually all of the Middle East and North Africa; the continuing pressure upon Christian Europe by the House of Islam—pressure that resulted in the conquest of Spain (later lost), Eastern Europe, and Constantinople, the jewel of Christendom. Whether or not El Fadl will admit it, all of this and more was done in the name of jihad.

Of course, El Fadl's claim that jihad doesn't mean holy war isn't his own invention, but is common in modern Muslim writings. Even the great theorist of radical Islam Sayyid Abul A'la Maududi spoke contemptuously of the equation of jihad with holy war. "The word 'Jihad' is commonly translated into English as 'the Holy War' and for a long while now the word has been interpreted so that it has become synonymous with a 'mania of religion.' The word 'Jihad' conjures up the vision of a marching band of religious fanatics with savage beards and fiery eyes brandishing drawn swords and attacking the infidels wherever they meet them and pressing them under the edge of the sword for the recital of Kalima [the Muslim confession of faith]. The Artists have drawn this picture with masterly strokes and have inscribed these words under it in bold letters: 'The History of this Nation is a tale of Bloodshed.'"

Maududi blamed Western colonialism for forcing apologies from Muslims. "When we saw this picture of ours painted by the foreigners, we...started offering apologies in this manner—Sir, what do we know of war and slaughter? We are pacifist preachers like the mendicants and religious divines. To refute certain religious beliefs and convert the people to some other faith instead, that is the be-all and ends all [sic] of our enthusiasm. What concern have we with sabers!"

Maududi also ascribed "defensive jihad" and the predominance of nonviolent forms of jihad to this Muslim cringing before colonial masters. "Yes, indeed, we plead guilty to one crime, though, that whenever someone else attacked us, we attacked him in self-defense. Now, of course, we have renounced that also. The crusade which is waged by swords has been abrogated for the satisfaction of your honor. Now 'Jihad' only refers to waging war with the tongue and pen. To fire cannons and shoot with guns is the privilege of your honor's government and wagging tongues and scratching with pens is our pleasure."[19]

The Muslim scholar M. Amir Ali, founder of the Chicago-based Institute of Islamic Information and Education, is one of those who insist jihad does not equal holy war. He is not cringing under Western imperialism, but trying to win over Western liberals. "In the West," he writes in an essay titled "Jihad Explained," " 'jihad' is generally translated as 'holy war,' a usage the media has popularized. According to Islamic teachings, it is UNHOLY to instigate or start war; however, some wars are inevitable and justifiable. If we translate the words 'holy war' back into Arabic, we find 'harbun muqaddasatu,' or for 'the holy war,' 'al-harbu al-muqaddasatu.' WE CHALLENGE any researcher or scholar to find the meaning of 'jihad' as holy war in the Qur'an or authentic Hadith collections or in early Islamic literature." (Capitalizations are in the original). Only a fool would take him up on his challenge, of course, for the word *jihad* indeed cannot properly be translated as "holy war."

Ali strenuously denies that jihad involves forced conversion. "Islam does not teach, nor do Muslims desire, conversion of any people for fear, greed, marriage, or any other form of coercion."

Ali goes on to say that some Muslims use the term "holy war" because they have adopted the language of the oppressor. "Unfortunately, some Muslim writers and translators of the Qur'an, the Hadith and other Islamic literature translate the term 'jihad' as 'holy war,' due to the influence of centuries-old Western propaganda. This could be a reflection of the Christian use of the term 'Holy War' to refer to the Crusades of a thousand years ago. However, the Arabic words for 'war' are 'harb' or 'qital,' which are found in the Qur'an and Hadith. For Muslims the term JIHAD is applied to all forms of STRIVING...."[20] The media establishment has followed along with the idea that to consider jihad as holy war is a misapprehension. In a backgrounder to *Muhammad: Legacy of a Prophet*, a hero-worshipping documentary, the Public Broadcasting System asserted that "had the assassination plot against [Muhammad] in 621 succeeded, his religious career would have been similar in broad outline to that of Jesus." However, later, when Muhammad and the new Muslim community "came under formal military attack for the first time in Medina," the Prophet had to adapt to changed circumstances. "Consequently, the Qur'an and Muhammad's teaching also focused on delineating the concept of the just war."

PBS maintains that even while elaborating this limited defensive concept, the Qur'an "does not abandon the notions of spiritual striving and God consciousness that were hallmarks of the Meccan Period. Even the concept of defensive warfare is placed within the larger concept of jihad as striving for what is right. Though jihad might involve bloodshed, it has the broader meaning of exerting an effort for improvement, not only in the political or military realm, but also in the moral, spiritual, and intellectual realms. Muhammad is often cited in Islamic tradition for calling the militant aspect of jihad the 'minor' or 'little' jihad, while referring to the improvement of one's self as the 'greater' jihad." PBS dismisses radical Islam as already discredited by "most religious scholars around the world."[21] Would that it were so.

In a piece published a week after the September 11 attacks, a Reuters article explained: "The Arabic word 'jihad' is often translated as 'holy war,' but a more accurate translation is 'holy struggle.'" The news service joins M. Amir Ali in blaming Christians for this misunderstanding. "Islamic scholars say the term 'holy war' was actually coined in Europe during the Crusades to mean a war against the Muslims. In a purely linguistic sense, the word 'jihad' means struggling or striving. There are two different, unrelated words which mean war."[22]

Thus Muslims easily fit into the liberal categorization of yet another victim group.

This approach is, needless to say, popular in Western media and is widely used by Muslim spokesmen in the West.

The CAIR jihad cover-up

In presentations purporting to correct American misperceptions of Islam, two American Muslim advocacy groups, the Council on American Islamic Relations (CAIR) and the International Institute of Islamic Thought (IIIT), also insist that "jihad does not mean 'holy war.' Literally, jihad in Arabic means to strive, struggle, and exert effort. It is a central and broad Islamic concept that includes struggle against evil inclinations within oneself, struggle to improve the quality of life in society, struggle in the battlefield for self-defense, or fighting against tyranny or oppression."[23]

This is in line with CAIR's full-page ad in the *New York Times*, which claims that American Muslims have "a shared commitment to our nation's safety and prosperity."[24]

Yet CAIR has never addressed the existence of elements of radical Islam in the United States—indeed, CAIR officials have treated questions about the loyalty of American Muslims as evidence of "anti-Muslim bigotry." For example, on February 25, 2003, I appeared on MSNBC's *Nachman* show with CAIR's Ibrahim Hooper. In the course of the discussion, I referred to Sheikh Muhammad Hisham Kabbani's 1999 statement at a State Department Open Forum that eighty percent of American mosques were under control of extremists.

Kabbani, a Naqshbandi Sufi, has been a vocal and energetic foe of radical Islam. At the State Department, he said, "The most dangerous thing that is going on now in these mosques, that has been sent upon these mosques around the United States...is the extremist ideology. Because [radical Muslims] are very active they took over the mosques; and we can say that they took over more than eighty percent of the mosques that have been established in the U.S. And there are more than three thousand mosques in the U.S. So it means that the methodology or ideology of extremists has been spread to eighty percent of the Muslim population, but not all of them agree with it."[25]

When I referred to Kabbani's assertion, Hooper bristled, and countered, "It's just a falsehood. It's one of those standard lines put out by hate-mongers like Mr. Spencer." When asked again about the eighty percent figure, Hooper replied, "It's a bunch of baloney...When people don't have information about the real Islam, the real experience of the American-Muslim community, when somebody comes to them and makes the false claim that eighty percent of mosques are extremist, they go, 'Well, really? I don't know about Islam, so maybe that's true.' But if they have some contact with Muslims, if they know about Islam, if they understand what's really happening and they understand the agenda of those who are putting forward this hate and this misinformation, they can make a reasoned decision. But if they don't have that information, again, they're vulnerable to this."[26]

Yet Kabbani, the actual source of the "eighty percent" assertion, is intimately familiar with Islam and American Muslims. After visiting 114 mosques around the country, he said that "ninety of them were mostly exposed, and I say exposed, to extreme or radical ideology."[27] Nor is Kabbani the only one who has noticed. Saudi Wahhabis are aggressively spreading their version of Islam in the United States through groups such as the Islamic Society of North America (ISNA). According to the *St. Petersburg Times*, "ISNA is subsidized by the Saudi government. An ISNA subsidiary called the

North American Islamic Trust owns about twenty-seven percent of the estimated 1200 mosques in the United States, says a report by the Council on American-Islamic Relations."[28]

It's intriguing that CAIR itself acknowledges that there are more than three hundred mosques in the United States funded by Wahhabis, yet they've taken a consistent and vocal stance against any monitoring of what is being preached and taught in those mosques. The reasons why stem from the nature of CAIR itself. The organization's board chairman, Omar Ahmed, uttered these sentiments in a speech before a Muslim audience in 1998: "Islam isn't in America to be equal to any other faith, but to become dominant. The Koran should be the highest authority in America, and Islam the only accepted religion on earth."[29] Ahmed has claimed that his remarks were misrepresented, but the reporter says she remembers his statement, if not his exact words, and declines to retract her story.[30]

Nor is Ahmed's an isolated statement. Radical Islam has been a troubling element of the Council on American Islamic Relations from the beginning: CAIR's founder and Executive Director, Nihad Awad, has repeatedly declared his support for the terrorist group Hamas. Former CAIR communications specialist Ismail Royer was recently arrested for his role in a terrorist "Virginia jihad network." Royer's indictment charges that he stockpiled arms and planned "to prepare for and engage in violent *jihad* on behalf of Muslims in Kashmir, Chechnya, the Philippines and other countries and territories, against countries, governments, military forces and peoples that the defendants and their conspirators believed to be enemies of Islam."[31] In March 2003, Bassem K. Khafagi, who has been identified in news reports as the community affairs director for CAIR's national office in Washington, was arrested on charges of bank fraud. An organization he helped found, the Islamic Assembly of North America, is suspected of providing websites for two radical

Sheikhs with ties to Osama bin Laden. Siraj Wahaj, who has served as a member of CAIR's Board of Advisors, in the early 1990s sponsored talks by the blind Sheikh Omar Abdel Rahman in mosques in New York City and New Jersey. Rahman was later convicted for conspiring to blow up the World Trade Center in 1993, the first time Muslim terrorists attempted it. This was before CAIR was established, but it may be revealing of the perspectives of at least some of those active in the group. Yet CAIR is still accepted by the mainstream media as a neutral civil rights advocacy group. One of CAIR's allies, the American Arab Anti-Discrimination Committee (ADC), goes even farther than CAIR in minimizing or denying altogether the Qur'anic and traditional sources of Islamic radicalism. The ADC originated as a group to represent the entire Arab population in the United States, which is overwhelmingly Christian. Increasingly, however, the ADC has become a group for Muslims only. At its website this organization reproduces a *Detroit Free Press* publication, *100 Questions and Answers About Arab Americans*, which asserts flatly: "The Quran teaches nonviolence. Throughout history, political groups and leaders have used Islam and other religions to justify many things, including violence."[32] It is hard when reading this sort of thing not to think of the Shi'ite Muslim doctrine of *taqiyyeh*, shared by many Salafi radicals, which permits Muslims to prevaricate about their religious beliefs when under pressure.[33] It is founded on the Qur'an: "Anyone who, after accepting faith in Allah, utters unbelief,—except under compulsion, his heart remaining firm in Faith—but such as open their breast to unbelief, on them is wrath from Allah, and theirs will be a dreadful penalty" (Sura 16:106).

Nonetheless, Christian churches, eager to be peacemakers, pursue this line as well. According to the Presbyterian News Service, "jihad refers primarily to the inner struggle of being a person of virtue and submission to Allah in all aspects of life. This is some-

times described as 'jihad of the heart.'" The Reverend Stephen Van
Kuiken of Mt. Auburn Presbyterian Church in Cincinnati agreed.
"The term jihad is often distorted to mean 'holy war,' but it has a
deeper meaning . . . the struggle with our own selves. Literally, it
means 'exertion' or 'to struggle.' It means spiritual warfare, to battle with one's own demons in order to give ourselves over to God,
in order to place ourselves," he added with a New Age twist, "in
'the arms of the wind.'"

The United Church of Christ in Vancouver, Washington, likewise objected that to equate jihad with holy war would be to "distort its spiritual significance and connotation." Rather, the church
asserted, jihad referred to the effort to restore "equilibrium within
the inner being of man as well as in the human society in which
that person functions." The UCC even implied that non-Muslims
could and should wage jihads of their own, in accord with their
characterization of jihad as "a reflection of Divine Justice and a
necessary condition for peace in the human domain."

The National Council of Churches added, "Jihad means struggle or exertion in the way of God. The 'greater jihad' is the struggle against temptation and evil within oneself. The 'lesser jihad' is
working against injustice or oppression in society."[34]

The scholars speak

University students around the country have attended (sometimes
as a required part of their course of study) lectures such as one
given in January 2003 at Northern Illinois University by an under-
graduate named Hadam Soliman. According to news reports, Soliman "described jihad's meaning as 'to strive to one's utmost' or 'to
struggle.' This is different from the commonly accepted definition
of 'holy war.' Jihad can be used against one's self, against the devil,
against unbelievers, or against one's oppressors, he said. 'Jihad is not
a means to force others into Islam,' Soliman said."[35]

He's right, of course. Islamic law has consistently forbidden forcible conversion, even though this law has often been broken, and we have seen how even an interpreter as fire-breathing as Sayyid Qutb insisted that jihad was not to be fought to force people into Islam. El Fadl and the others are also right: the word "jihad" is not properly rendered into English as "holy war." El Fadl's assertion that "holy war (*al-harb al-muqaddasah*) is not an expression used by the Qur'anic text or Muslim theologians" is correct.

However, these facts are being used today to try to prove more than they legitimately can. The fact that jihad doesn't mean holy war doesn't do anything to negate the fact that Muslims throughout history have fought wars in the name of their religion. History and contemporary events clearly show that "jihad" is, in practice, the word Muslims themselves use to justify and describe "holy war." That forced conversions are prohibited by the Sharia does not abolish the historical record that jihad was used to establish the supremacy of Islamic law and the subjugation of non-Muslims.

Still, for many American scholars of Islam, spiritual jihad is the only meaning of jihad that has any legitimacy. Karen Armstrong, a noted American apologist for Islam, warns us, "The primary meaning of the word jihad is not 'holy war' but 'struggle.'"[36] According to Joe Elder, a professor at the University of Wisconsin, defining jihad as holy war constitutes a "gross misinterpretation." Elder insists it should be interpreted as a "religious struggle, which more closely reflects the inner, personal struggles of the religion."

Dell DeChant of the University of South Florida asserts that jihad is "usually understood" to be "a struggle to be true to the will of God and not holy war." Wellesley College's Roxanne Euben concurs. "For many Muslims, jihad means to resist temptation and become a better person." Georgia Southern University's John Parcels says that jihad means the struggle to control "the appetites and your own will." According to Harvard dean Michael Shinagel, jihad refers to the effort "to promote justice and understanding in ourselves and in our society."

Two academics went even farther into politically correct fantasy land. Auburn Seminary's Farid Eseck defined jihad as "resisting apartheid or working for women's rights." Duke University's Bruce Lawrence defined jihad as "being a better student, a better colleague, a better business partner. Above all, to control one's anger."[37] He even tried to transform jihad into a weapon of the academic Left, calling for a "jihad that would be a genuine struggle against our own myopia and neglect as much as it is against outside others who condemn or hate us for what we do, not who we are."[38]

The godfather of all these academics is Georgetown University's John Esposito, the Clinton administration's Islamic expert and a continuing media favorite. Martin Kramer makes a blistering analysis of Esposito's thought in his courageous examination of the academic establishment in Islamic studies, *Ivory Towers on Sand.* According to Kramer, Esposito's peculiar genius was in convincing people that "Islamist movements were nothing other than movements of democratic reform."[39] In the 1990s, Esposito discouraged academic investigations of Muslim radicalism. Quoting from the 1992 edition of Esposito's since-revised book *The Islamic Threat: Myth or Reality?* Kramer says, "As for Islamist violence, this was deemed beyond the bounds of approved research. Dwelling upon it would only reinforce stereotypes. After all, announced Esposito, 'most' Islamic movements had reached the conclusion that violence was 'counterproductive.' 'They speak of the need to prepare people for an Islamic order rather than to impose it.' Therefore, promised Esposito, the violence that had marred the 1980s would recede, and 'the nineties will prove to be a decade of new alliances and alignments in which the Islamic movements will challenge rather than threaten their societies and the West."[40] It's clear why Esposito saw a need for revisions.

In a similar vein, Noah Feldman, author of *After Jihad: America and the Struggle for Islamic Democracy*, acknowledges that "for more than a decade after the Iranian Revolution of 1979, many Islamists sought to emulate the Iranian model by Islamizing their own countries through the revolutionary transformation of violent jihad." However, he now claims to see "the Islamists' call for democratic change in the Muslim world"—as exemplified by their participation in Algerian elections and Pakistani politics—as "a fundamental shift in their strategy."[41] Yet he offers no evidence that such democratic participation is not simply a means to an end, not a thoroughgoing rejection of the absolutism of the Sharia. Nor does he give any indication that these groups have renounced violent jihad.

There is an Orwellian flavor to the assessments of the academics—"We have *never* been at war with Eurasia!"—which denies the obvious fact that while jihad has meant spiritual struggle, it has also meant war, conquest, violence, and the subjugation of nonbelievers. It's unlikely that when Sheikh Muhammad Saleh Al-Munajjid declared that Muslims must "educate the children to Jihad and to hatred of the Jews, the Christians, and the infidels," that he meant teaching children to control their anger, be better business partners, or work for women's rights. It's doubtful even that he meant teaching them to resist temptation and become better people. On the contrary, this sheikh and others (such as Laskar Jihad's Jaffar Umar Thalib and the British rabble rouser Abu Hamza al-Masri) mean by jihad precisely what the academics' definitions reject: holy war.

As the great ex-Muslim scholar Ibn Warraq puts it, "The theory and practice of jihad was not concocted in the Pentagon.... It was taken from the Koran, the Hadith and Islamic tradition. Western liberals, especially humanists, find it hard to believe this. . . . It is extraordinary the amount of people who have written about the 11th of September without once mentioning Islam. We must take seriously what the Islamists say to understand their motivation, [that] it is the divinely ordained duty of all Muslims to fight—in the literal sense—until man-made law has been replaced by God's law, the Sharia, and Islamic law has conquered the entire world."

What of the academics' innocuous jihad? "For every text the liberal Muslims produce, the mullahs will use dozens of counter-examples [that are] exegetically, philosophically, historically far more legitimate."[42]

A risky whitewash

Whatever the motives of the whitewash of jihad in the West, it could be lethal if it causes America to underestimate or misunderstand altogether the size of the international jihadist threat or the ultimate goals of Islamic terrorists.

An example of this risk was recently provided by the prison chaplain Warith Deen Umar. Early in 2003, Umar told a *Wall Street Journal* reporter that the terrorists of September 11 were martyrs. "Without justice," he explained, "there will be warfare, and it can come to this country, too." Umar, of course, is the man who claimed that "even Muslims who say they are against terrorism secretly admire and applaud" the September 11 terrorists.[43] When he was criticized by Muslims and non-Muslims alike for all this, Umar said his words were taken (surprise!) "out of context."[44]

However, even as he announced (after the *Journal* story broke) that Umar would no longer be allowed into the prisons, James Flateau, chief spokesman for the New York State Department of Correctional Services, declined to investigate the many Muslim prison chaplains that Umar brought into the system. According to an Associated Press report, "Flateau said it would be a 'dangerous philosophy' to assume they shared Umar's 'extremist views.' "[45]

Dangerous for whom? Was Flateau considering the danger that could arise from an army of mujahedin rising up out of the nation's prisons? Umar, after all, was no lone wolf: not only did he recruit other chaplains for the New York prisons, but he himself studied in Saudi Arabia. The Saudi government even paid for Umar and other chaplains to come to Saudi Arabia for pilgrimage and instruction in Wahhabi Islam.

Nor is the problem limited to the Wahhabis. Yes, the Saudis are exporting violent Wahhabi Islam around the world, but the violence doesn't originate in Wahhabism; nor is it limited to it. It is not money alone that makes the Wahhabi version of Islam so compelling to Muslims around the world; it is its apparent accord with the Qur'an, the example of Muhammad, and Islamic history. Even journalist Stephen Schwartz, a convert to Islam and the author of a book-length critique of Wahhabism entitled *The Two Faces of Islam*, acknowledges that "military jihad cannot be written out of Islam. The prophet Mohammed himself led armies."[46] And the Prophet's example invites legions of his imitators to take up arms themselves today. They're motivated, in the words of Sohail H. Hashmi in the *Encyclopedia of Politics and Religion*, by "the final years of the Prophet's life," in which "jihad clearly meant the struggle to propagate the Islamic order worldwide."[47]

Ultimately, self-appointed analysts who recast contemporary jihads as sublimated struggles for better plumbing, bigger schools, or cable access do so at their own risk. For the radicals don't offer a vision of peaceful coexistence. The only peace that mujahedin will ultimately accept from non-Muslims is that of those who submit to Islamic rule. Short of submission only war is offered. Those who do not accept the radical Muslim vision of God or of the world simply aren't given the chance to opt out of the game.

Chapter Ten

EVERYBODY MUST GET STONED

The Strange Alliance Between Radical Islam and the Post-1960s Left

T HE PROBLEM OF RADICAL Islam is not a liberal or conservative issue. It's a human rights issue. But it's one about which
the Left is strangely silent, with no protest marches, no
angry full-page ads in the *New York Times*. The oppression of Christians by Muslims in East Timor, Sudan, Nigeria, and elsewhere
doesn't seem to rate a solidarity campaign or even a bumper
sticker. Whenever the Left does notice an adulterous woman being
stoned to death under Sharia law, or some other apparent outrage
in the Islamic world, it is usually dismissed as the work of a radical
faction or somehow blamed on their all-purpose bogeyman: the
United States government. Why?

Because, to the Left, any conflict in the world must be the result of Western aggression, either historic (the Crusades, colonialism) or current.

Anti-antiterrorism

"The demise of the Cold War involving the USA and the Soviet Union at the beginning of the 1990s left military strategists in the West searching for a new enemy."

This is the assessment of Abdus Sattar Ghazali, a Pakistani journalist who has served as assistant editor for the Pakistani daily *Dawn* and editor-in-chief of Kuwait TV's *English News*. But, of course, it didn't originate from Ghazali; it has become a commonplace notion not only among Muslim analysts but among Westerners as well. Ghazali sees it as part of a conscious and long-range strategy:

> To borrow [from] Richard Conder, author of the Munchurian [sic] Candidate: "Now that the communists have been put to sleep, we are going to have to invent another terrible threat." Former U.S. Secretary of Defence [sic] McNamara, in his 1989 testimony before the Senate Budget Committee, stated that defense spending could safely be cut in half over five years. For the Pentagon it was a simple choice: either find new enemies or cut defense spending. Topping the list of potential bogeymen were the Yellow Peril, the alleged threat to U.S. economic security emanating from the East Asia, and the so-called Green Peril (green representing Islam). The Pentagon selected "Islamic fundamentalism" and "rogue states" as the new bogeymen."[1]

But in determining to combat Islamic terrorism, was the Pentagon anointing a new bogeyman or confronting a real threat to the United States? The facts spoke for themselves long before

September 11, 2001. Ghazali was writing in 1999—well after the 1998 bombings of the American embassies in Tanzania and Kenya, the 1993 World Trade Center bombing, and other notorious incidents of Islamic terror, including incidents dating back to the Cold War days themselves: the Iran hostage crisis of 1979, the attack on the Marine barracks in Beirut in 1983, the hijacking of TWA flight 847 and the hijacking of the *Achille Lauro* in 1985, the bombing of Pan Am flight 103 in 1988, and so on. Ghazali was also writing after Samuel P. Huntington had published his book *The Clash of Civilizations and the Remaking of World Order*, which showed, with hard statistics as noted earlier, that far more than any other civilization, modern Islam was violent, that "Islam's borders *are* bloody, and so are its innards."

Ghazali concedes that radical Islam "has not been invented by Western politicians"—in the face of all this and more, how could he not? But he adds that even though politicians didn't invent it, radical Islam "is being used by them." Used for what? Ghazali cites the German scholar Jochen Hippler, editor of a volume titled *The Next Threat: Western Perceptions of Islam*, which argues, in a similar vein, that the Islamic threat is a convenient invention designed to fill the gap left by the end of the Cold War. Invoking Hippler, Ghazali concludes that "instead of reducing the military apparatus in the West to a symbolic vestige or getting rid of it altogether and thinking about 'security' completely afresh, new threats are being invented to serve the old purpose. This is our main problem, not an Islamic fundamentalist threat which, in any case, could only be dealt with by political and economic means."[2]

Still, all that was written two years before the Twin Towers were destroyed. One would think it would be harder after the September 11 attacks to argue that the West's military apparatus should be reduced to a symbolic vestige or scrapped altogether. Certainly anyone familiar with the Hamas charter should understand that the threat of Islamic radicalism cannot be dealt with solely through political and economic means. But none of that stopped the renowned linguist, gadfly, and indomitable icon of the American Left, Noam Chomsky. As the first anniversary of the September 11 attacks approached, Chomsky wrote, "September 11 shocked many Americans into an awareness that they had better pay much closer attention"—not to the motivations and goals of radical Muslims, but "to what the United States Government does in the world and how it is perceived." After listing a number of areas in which he contends that American power supports corrupt and repressive regimes (although Saudi Arabia doesn't even make his list), he recounts a twenty-year-old assessment from Yehoshaphat Harkabi, former chief of Israeli military intelligence. "To offer an honourable solution to the Palestinians, respecting their right to self-determination—that is the solution of the problem of terrorism. . . . When the swamp disappears, there will be no more mosquitoes." Chomsky applies the metaphor not just to Israelis and Palestinians, but globally. "If America insists on creating more swamps, there will be more mosquitoes, with awesome capacity for destruction."[3]

Chomsky repeatedly returns to the fact that the United States supported Islamic radical groups fighting in Afghanistan against the Soviet Union two decades ago. "Radical Islamist extremists, often called 'fundamentalists,' were U.S. favorites in the 1980s, because they were the best killers who could be found." He characterizes the September 11 attacks as "blowback from the radical Islamic forces organized, armed, and trained by the U.S., Egypt, France, Pakistan, and others."[4]

He also dismisses the idea that the September 11 attackers acted out of hatred for the freedom that the United States represents. Such a view, Chomsky says, "happens to be completely at variance with everything we know, but has all the merits of self-adulation and uncritical support for power."[5]

Glaringly absent from this analysis is the possibility that the attackers acted not out of hatred for American policies or American freedoms as such, but out of hatred and contempt for America as the foremost representative of the unbelieving world, the world that Muslims must fight against. If jihadist teachings were any part of their motivation, and quite clearly they were, then it is irrelevant that the United States twenty years ago gave training to Muslim radicals, or even that America is free except insofar as that freedom is an indication that America is not Islamic.

But for Chomsky and many others on the Left, America and America only (which he calls "one of the most extreme fundamentalist cultures in the world") has essentially created the problem of modern-day Islamic terrorism.[6] Apparently also only America can end it. If the cloak-and-dagger types in Washington didn't select Islamic radicalism as the new enemy, they created this enemy indirectly by pursuing policies that only increase resentment of the United States around the world. This is a curiously America-centric perspective from the multiculturalist element that bemoans Western cultural hegemony—yet it is the prevailing view today of the American political Left. Instead of seeing radical Islam as a cardinal threat to the security and peace not just of Americans but of all non-Muslims around the world, they see it merely as a reaction by oppressed people to their oppression. Remove the oppression, and the reaction will disappear.

Blaming America was predictable from post-Vietnam leftists in the United States who seem to identify their own country as the cause of most, if not all, of the world's ills. But some have gone further. Large sections of the "peace movement" have manifested a curious tendency to side with radical Islam against the United States. In this sense, those who claim that Islam has replaced communism as a new totem are right: just as twentieth-century leftists prostrated themselves before the "progressive" Soviet Union and its satellites, so too does the twenty-first century Left prefer Islam— with its presumed, romanticized history of "tolerance," despite all evidence to the contrary—to the West. Just as the Left was anti-anticommunist, so too then are they anti-antiterrorist.

Thus it is the U.S., not, say, radical Islam or the Stalinist remnant of North Korea, that is the world's biggest problem, according to Carrie Benzschawel of the Peace Action Education Fund. "The biggest nuclear threat we now face doesn't come from some 'rogue' nation, but from the radical unilateralists within the Bush administration."[7]

Likewise the Student Peace Action Network (SPAN), a "grass-roots peace and justice organization working from campuses across the United States," states its mission in these terms: "*We organize* for an end to physical, social, and economic violence caused by militarism at home and abroad. *We campaign* for nuclear abolition, disarmament, and an end to weapons trafficking. *We support* a foreign policy based on human rights and international cooperation, and a domestic agenda that supports human and environmental concerns, not Pentagon excess. War is not inevitable. *We push for practical alternatives.*" (Emphasis in the original.)[8]

Does SPAN's concern for human rights lead it to take a stand against jihadist terrorism? Not quite. According to a statement from the group, "SPAN's recent work has focused on ending the so-called 'war on terrorism,' which we believe is making the world less secure, not more."[9]

Allying with America's enemies

Anti-antiterrorism in its extreme form has led leftists to identify themselves explicitly with those who wish to destroy the United States. Nicholas De Genova, an assistant professor of anthropology at Columbia University in New York and author of the essay "Check Your Head: The Cultural Politics of Rap Music," took anti-antiterrorism to its logical endpoint on March 26, 2003. Speaking at a "teach-in" at Columbia, De Genova declared, "The only true heroes are those who find ways that help defeat the U.S. military." Referring to the 1993 ambush of U.S. troops in Somalia in which eighteen servicemen were killed and eighty-four wounded, he added, "I personally would like to see a million Mogadishus."

Not only did the professor go on record as wishing for eighteen million American deaths; he also seemed to be calling for the disappearance of America altogether. He explained "peace" in terms that would have warmed the heart of Sayyid Qutb. "Peace is not patriotic. Peace is subversive, because peace anticipates a very different world than the one in which we live—a world where the U.S. would have no place."[10]

When a chorus of voices around the nation called upon De Genova to follow the advice of his rap music essay and "check his head," he charged that his remarks had been taken (of course) out of context and clarified them in an interview in the *Chronicle of Higher Education*. In it he attacked the reporter who originally publicized his remarks as a "a devious yellow journalist from a tabloid newspaper" and claimed for himself the mantle of the entire contemporary peace movement. "There are people with a very vested interest in exploiting this issue and manipulating it for their own ends, and attacks against me are therefore attacks against the entire antiwar movement."

But did he mean to call for American soldiers to be killed? "No, precisely not. That's one of the reasons I am against the war. I am against the war because people like George Bush and his war cabinet are invested in needlessly wasting the lives of people who have absolutely no interest in perpetrating this war and should not be there. And any responsibility for the loss of their lives will rest in the hands of the war makers on the side of the U.S." Expanding his vision from Mogadishu to Vietnam, he explained, "What I was intent to emphasize was that the importance of Vietnam is that it was a defeat for the U.S. war machine and a victory for the cause of human self-determination."[11]

Does De Genova really believe that Saddam Hussein's Iraq offered its citizens a real opportunity for "human self-determination?" He doesn't say. Nor does he seem particularly concerned about the fact that jihadist groups worldwide are interested in anything but human self-determination. One may generously assume that if there were any serious chance of a Sharia regime coming to power in the United States, De Genova would energetically oppose it. But for now, he seems to be operating on the old principle that the enemy of my enemy is my friend.

This principle seems to be shared by many, if not most, of the Americans who work with the International Solidarity Movement (ISM), a self-described "Palestinian-led movement of Palestinian and International activists working to raise awareness of the struggle for Palestinian freedom and an end to Israeli occupation." The organization says that it uses "nonviolent, direct-action methods of resistance to confront and challenge illegal Israeli occupation forces and policies."

Where ISM's sympathies lie as they pursue these "nonviolent, direct-action methods" was made clear in spring 2003 by the American ISM activist Rachel Corrie, who was killed on March 16, 2003, while trying to stop an Israeli military bulldozer. The precise circumstances of her death are hotly disputed, but not in dispute is the fact that just a few weeks before her death, on February 15, 2003, wire services carried two photos of her standing in a crowd of Palestinian children and burning a paper drawing of an American flag. While some have contended that this picture was fabricated, the ISM admits its authenticity in a statement released after

Corrie's death. It scolds those who find the photos of her flag-burning significant. "Trying to use this picture to somehow indicate that Rachel deserved to be run over by a bulldozer is an appalling act of demonization that infers that forms of protest which include flag burning are capital offences." That is true: no one deserves to be run over by a bulldozer, no matter how many flags she burns. But it is ultimately beside the point. The ISM explanation goes on to quote Corrie's parents saying of the flag-burning that "while we may disagree with it, [it] must be put into context."

The context? "In protest over a drive towards war and her government's foreign policy that was responsible for much of the devastation that she was witness to in Gaza, she felt it OK to burn the picture of her own flag."[12] Maybe this was indeed what Corrie was thinking, but these subtleties were probably lost on the children who surrounded Corrie as she burned the mock flag. Most likely they saw it as an expression of hatred for the United States. By fostering this hatred, Corrie became in her own way an obstacle, like Hamas, to the Palestinian homeland that the United States is trying to help establish through peaceful negotiations.

Meanwhile, numerous cracks have appeared in ISM's nonviolent façade. On March 27, 2003, Israeli soldiers arrested Shadi Sukia, a senior member of the terrorist group Islamic Jihad (for which his duties evidently included recruiting suicide bombers) in the ISM offices in Jenin.[13] ISM members claim that Sukia showed up at their door just moments before the arrest, and was not being sheltered in the organization's offices; however, there are other connections between the supposedly nonviolent ISM and terrorism. Israeli authorities several times attempted to deport an American ISM activist, Susan Barclay, who let Sukia into the ISM offices that day, for working openly with Hamas and Islamic Jihad.[14] After this incident, Barclay was successfully deported. She is now on the lecture circuit, billed as a "long time anti-occupation activist."[15]

The stakes

In November 2002, Nigerian journalist Isioma Daniel wrote a feature for the Lagos daily *This Day* on the Miss World pageant, which was to be held in Nigeria in December. She wrote, "What would Mohamed think? In all honesty, he probably would have chosen a wife from one of them."[16]

Muslims were enraged. A Muslim official in the Nigerian state of Zamfara called for Daniel to be killed for her blasphemy against the Prophet. *This Day's* offices were burned. In the riots that followed, according to Andrew Sullivan, the noted author, gay activist, and former editor of the *New Republic*, "Christians were attacked, dozens of churches were burned, and some Christians fought back. As many as five hundred people were killed in the rampage, and there are reports that Christians are now fleeing the area entirely." The Miss World pageant was hastily transferred to London.

Sullivan crisply states the larger significance of these events. "Radicalized Islam—on every continent—is stepping up its assault on Western freedoms. The Miss World contest and *This Day* are just the latest targets. The act of putting on a beauty pageant or writing a column are now subject to the approval of radical religious fanatics. Those who do not please these fanatics will not be criticized or campaigned against or smeared or railed at. They will be killed." Sullivan was not a voice of leftism protesting intolerant Islam. He considers himself a conservative and a Catholic and wrote a doctoral thesis at Harvard on the conservative philosopher Michael Oakeshott.

But what was the response of the establishment liberal media to all this? They blamed Isioma Daniel, or the Miss World pageant for offending the fragile sensitivities of Nigeria's Muslims, or even the contestants for being provocative. Sullivan is blunt:

This is what cultural relativism, p.c. journalism and decadent feminism amounts to: a failure to grasp that freedom is under attack. The only reason I am writing this column is because I live in a free society. One of the keys to that free society is freedom of the press—even to be disrespectful, annoying, blasphemous. What just happened in Nigeria is that a newspaper's offices were burned to the ground, a journalist has had a death sentence pronounced on her, and hundreds of people have been killed because of radical Islam's hatred of our freedoms. The propriety, politics, and principles of a beauty pageant are utterly irrelevant. If I don't like such a pageant, I have many ways to protest. But killing people isn't one of them. That isn't so hard a line to grasp. So why have so few grasped it?

Sullivan, author of a book on gay marriage, *Virtually Normal*, demonstrated a unique (and virtually unknown on the Left) awareness of the difference between those who oppose gay marriage laws and those who stone homosexuals to death when he made this trenchant observation. "When it comes to a far, far deadlier menace to our freedoms than fundamentalist Christianity, much of the left is silent or, worse, making excuses for this Islamist threat."[17]

Freedom is under attack by the warriors of jihad; and the battle lines do indeed resemble those of the Cold War, a fierce division between the West, standing for freedom, and the East, standing for a totalitarian society. "There are very useful analogies to be drawn between communism and Islam," says Ibn Warraq. "Communism has been defeated, at least for the moment; Islamism has not, and unless a reformed, tolerant, liberal kind of Islam emerges soon, perhaps the final battle will be between Islam and Western democracy."[18]

This is the war we're in now.

Chapter Eleven

HOW TO FIGHT
THE WAR WE'RE IN

"O Lord, deal with your enemies, the enemies of religion, including
infidels, atheists, Americans, British, and others. Shake the land under
their feet, kill them one by one and leave no one alive."[1]

T HIS WAS THE PRAYER of the Yemeni Sheikh Ahmad Abd-al-
Razzaq al-Ruqayhi during a sermon in the Grand Mosque
in Sanaa shortly after the end of the Iraq war. The sermon
was carried on Yemen's official TV station. Sheikh Ahmed seems
to be well aware of what few in the West want to admit: like it or
not, the clash of civilizations is upon us. Which civilization will
ultimately prevail has less to do in the long run with might and
munitions than with will.

A tough approach has everything to recommend it. When the
Bush administration cracked down on terrorism at home and
abroad to a degree unprecedented in modern American history,

terrorist attacks decreased. According to the State Department's annual report on global terrorism, terrorist attacks decreased by forty-four percent in 2002 to the lowest figure since before 1972.[2] As George W. Bush said at the conclusion of major hostilities in Iraq, "The war on terror is not over, yet it is not endless."[3]

Still, there is a great deal more that must be done to relegate terrorism to the history books. The first thing we must do is end our myopic complacency and accept the nature of the threat from radical Islam. American Muslim groups have not only sold the American public a drastically incomplete and misleading picture of Islam; they've also succeeded in recasting the national debate. Every new terrorist threat gives rise to a renewed voicing of fears that Americans will react violently against innocent Muslims in the United States. This is a legitimate—if exaggerated—concern, but we must be mindful of the proper focus: the death toll resulting from Islamic jihad and terrorism, in the United States and around the world, is far, far larger than that of the reprisals, which have been substantially fewer than the media attention to them might suggest. Any murder is a crime against humanity, but our anxiety to prevent one could end up allowing for thousands.

Practically, this involves monitoring what is being preached and taught in mosques, carrying out serious background checks on Muslim immigrants, and encouraging moderate voices at home and in the Islamic world—that is, leaders who explicitly renounce jihad ideology and the elements of the Sharia that are incompatible with the UN Declaration of Human Rights. This will involve, among other things, ending alliances with any states for which the Sharia is the law of the land.

These alliances are doomed anyway; witness the continuing duplicity of Saudi Arabia over the hatred and violence that continues to be preached in its mosques. After the May 2003 al Qaeda attacks that killed thirty-five people and injured two hundred in

Riyadh, spokesman Adel al-Jubeir said, "We have looked more intensely in terms of what is being said in our mosques and trying to curb incitement."[4] He doesn't have to look far: just six days before he said this, a preacher whose sermon was carried on Saudi government television prayed, "O God, strengthen Islam and Muslims, humiliate infidelity and infidels, and destroy Islam's enemies, including the vile Jews." Another called on Muslim countries "to stick to the Islamic law, without which no security can be achieved."[5] It's unlikely that these sentiments are going to disappear from Saudi sermons, and equally unlikely that the U.S. can maintain a lasting alliance with any nation in which they are widespread.

Monitoring mosques

There are several terms commonly used for Islamic radicals, our opponents in this conflict, which I never use. The most inaccurate and yet perhaps most common one is "Arabs." In fact, most Muslims in the world are not Arabs and most Arabs in the United States are not Muslims. We are facing a Muslim threat, not an Arab one. Another inaccurate term is "Muslim fundamentalists." While it is true that Muslim radicals hold firmly to the fundamentals of Islam, those fundamentals are in reality only peripherally involved with the issues really at hand for the radicals. The divide in the Islamic world is not between those who hold to the "fundamentals" of the faith and those who don't. To call Muslim radicals "fundamentalists" is really just a Leftist slap at Christian fundamentalists, trying to equate the two—and exposing instead the parochialism, petty-mindedness, and ignorance of the Left.

The third and final misnomer for Muslim radicals is "Islamists." This actually is a useful term as far as it goes and is the appellation of choice for Islamic radicals among many analysts of the Islamic world who are far more perceptive and capable than I. I bow to their expertise but hesitate to use the word because it is very difficult to find, anywhere in the world, a self-proclaimed "Islamist" mosque or society or club or organization. The term is imposed from without, and there is nothing that distinguishes Islamists from ordinary Muslims. They go to the same mosques and read from the same Qur'an. If Sheikh Muhammad Hisham Kabbani is correct that eighty percent of American mosques are controlled by extremists, that means that Islamists are preaching and defining Islam to an audience made up primarily of people who, presumably, are not Islamists. We have seen several now notorious American Muslims, such as Hasan Akbar and Maher Hawash, who surprised their friends and family by suddenly identifying themselves with the most extreme Muslims in the world. Men like these didn't decide at some point: "I am going to become an Islamist," the way someone else may decide to become a Democrat or a vegetarian. They became radicals because they became serious about their religion and took seriously the obligations of jihad.

That is not to say that all Muslims are potential terrorists. Obviously they aren't. But there is unmistakable evidence that Islamic radicalism may have penetrated deeply into the fabric of American Islam: the assessment of Kabbani about extremist control of mosques; the Wahhabi bankrolling of American mosques; the hate-filled textbooks being used in some American Muslim schools; the rejection of American identity by Muslim Student Association speakers and other American Muslims; the alleged sedition and support for terrorism carried out by Professor Sami Al-Arian in an Islamic center in Florida; the al Qaeda cell in the mosque in Lackawanna, New York; the American Muslims who have been charged with conspiring to wage war against the United States (and whose bookshelves were filled with radical Muslim literature extolling jihad); John Walker Lindh, the "Marin County mujahid" whose teenage conversion to Islam ultimately led him to Afghanistan, the

Taliban, al Qaeda, and war against his own country; Brooklyn's al-Farooq mosque that was funding al Qaeda (apparently unbeknownst to the mosque, although Sheikh Omar Abdel Rahman, mastermind of the 1993 World Trade Center bombing, frequented it in the early 1990s); and other American Muslims who knowingly funded terrorist groups.[6]

Unmoved by all this, Democratic congressmen John Conyers Jr. of Michigan and Jerrold Nadler of New York, and Democratic senator Russell D. Feingold of Wisconsin wrote to Attorney General John Ashcroft: "We ask you to immediately terminate the Justice Department's new policy directing the fifty-six FBI field offices to count the number of mosques and Muslims, as well as other community groups and religious organizations, in their areas."

Why? Because in their view the policy targets innocent people. "We cannot sanction the targeting of Muslim populations and mosques, or any other community group or institution, to gather intelligence without any suspicion or cause that a specific individual or group of individuals, or a particular mosque or religious organization, is engaging in terrorist activities. We urge you to follow the constitutionally prescribed channels of investigation to ensure that the rights of American citizens are not violated."[7]

Certainly this monitoring must be careful and respectful. And above all it is vital to follow constitutionally prescribed channels of investigation. But it is not clear that counting mosques and Muslims violates the Constitution in any way. Conservative and liberal groups have expressed concern with some provisions of the Patriot Act, and it is essential to preserve our freedoms and roll back any parts of the act that truly encroach upon them. But thus far the act has been successful as a weapon against terrorism. "The results speak for themselves," says columnist Michelle Malkin, author of *Invasion: How America Still Welcomes Terrorists, Criminals, and Other Foreign Menaces to Our Shores.* According to Malkin:

— The feds have busted more than twenty suspected al Qaeda cell members from Buffalo, New York, to Detroit, Seattle, and Portland, Oregon

— More than one hundred other individuals have been convicted or pled guilty to terrorist related crimes

— The United States has deported 515 individuals linked to the September 11 investigation

— Hundreds of foreign criminals and suspected terrorists, plus one known member of al Qaeda, were prevented from entering the country thanks to the National Entry-Exit Registration System—which Senator Ted Kennedy attempted to sabotage earlier this year

— Long-overdue fingerprint cross-checks of immigration and FBI databases at the border have resulted in the arrest of more than five thousand fugitives wanted for crimes committed in the United States

— And nearly two years after the September 11 attacks, there has not yet been another mass terrorist attack on our homeland[8]

But monitoring public speech in mosques doesn't interfere with the right of Muslims in America to practice their religion—except if such practice crosses the line into sedition or other lawbreaking. If a mosque is stockpiling AK-47s or preaching jihad against the United States, law enforcement has a duty to pay attention—and act. Granted, many will offer the following objections:

⊠ **Not all Muslims are terrorists.** This is, of course, true. But what, ultimately, does it prove? Islam may be just as much of a religion of peace as President Bush insists it is and that would still not change the fact every one of the September 11 terrorists were Muslims, and that one hundred percent of those who are currently waging war on the United States are also Muslims. This is the only identifying feature the FBI has to go on.

🗷 **Not only Muslims commit terrorist acts.** Timothy McVeigh, we are told, was a Christian. McVeigh's actual religious affiliation is disputed, but this much is certain: Christianity was not a motivation for his terrorist attack; Christianity doesn't have a developed doctrine, tradition, and sustained history of war against unbelievers; there is no commandment in Christianity to wage jihad; there is no branch of Christianity of any consequence that supports anything remotely like jihad; and there is no worldwide network of McVeigh-inclined Christians who have vowed to bring down our nation. There is, however, such a network of violent-minded Muslims.

🗷 **This kind of monitoring will result in the jailing or deportation of innocent people.** While no system is perfect, particularly when it's run by fallible human beings, there is no necessary reason why this need be true. Illegal immigrants will be the primary group accidentally discovered and deported, but, sad to say, they are already breaking the laws of the United States.

🗷 **To single out mosques for scrutiny is discrimination.** The cult of victimhood has preached so much nonsense over the last few decades about what constitutes "bigotry" that it's virtually impossible for Americans to think straight about such questions. But to monitor mosques is not to deprive the Americans in them of due process, freedom of religion, or any of their other rights and privileges as citizens. The safeguards of the Bill of Rights are still in place.

The September 11 terrorists' Muslim identity was not incidental to their terrorism; it was central to what they did on that terrible day. They were part of an explicitly Muslim organization—one that justifies its actions with quotations from the Qur'an and references to the traditional Islamic theology of jihad as armed struggle. It is no double standard for American law enforcement to monitor mosques for the preaching of such doctrine here. Christian churches, after all, are already subject to scrutiny. When they engage in political activity they risk losing their tax-exempt status. Monitoring mosques involves little more than the same. Such monitoring is also important in order to protect Muslim moderates. If the members of al-Farooq mosque, a source of funding for al Qaeda, were shocked when they discovered that their money was going to Osama bin Laden, isn't it important to enforce existing law to ensure that their money doesn't go to al Qaeda again?[9] And if they were not shocked, shouldn't American law enforcement know that, as the *New York Post* put it, "a jihad grows in Brooklyn?" Monitoring mosques will establish that most American Muslims are law-abiding citizens—something that CAIR and Muslim advocacy groups have failed to establish by their own questionable rhetoric. As such, monitoring mosques is in the best interests of American Muslims themselves.

Also, we must resist attempts by American Muslim advocacy groups to mischaracterize these law enforcement efforts in attempts to whip up popular hysteria. In the spring of 2003, CAIR and its allies launched a campaign to block President Bush's nomination of Islamic terrorism expert Daniel Pipes to the U.S. Institute of Peace. Among many other smears of Pipes, CAIR charged that Pipes "refused to condemn the internment of Japanese-Americans in World War II."[10] This is a distortion of what Pipes really said, but it's more important for the liberal buttons it attempts to push: the implication is that Pipes would support internment for

Muslims during the war on terror, although neither he nor any other serious analyst has ever suggested such a possibility. In raising these substanceless specters, CAIR successfully diverts attention from what we really must do in order to fight, and win, the war we're in: meet the challenge of radical Islam with honesty, justice, and strength of will and purpose.

Immigration controls

The September 11 attacks were largely a result of faulty immigration controls. Most of the terrorists involved were in the United States on visas issued in Saudi Arabia. Media analyst William McGowan pointed out that the many "holes and weaknesses in the immigration system were major keys to the terrorists' success. The lapses they cited involved dysfunction and corruption in the visa-issuance process, a failure to monitor student visa holders, and poor controls on visa overstays. Other shortcomings included illegal access to state driver's licenses useful in establishing false identities, and municipal 'sanctuary' policies that protect illegal immigrants by barring local police from communicating with their state and federal counterparts and with the Immigration and Naturalization Service."[11]

The ensuing avalanche of calls for tighter immigration controls came at the same time as seven thousand men from countries on the State Department's al Qaeda "watch list"—including Afghanistan, Iran, Iraq, and Libya—legally entered the United States. A State Department official noted that in the months after the attacks, visas were granted according to the same criteria that were in place before September 11, 2001. "The only difference is that we have implemented new enhanced name-check procedures as a temporary measure."[12] Despite tighter controls thereafter, a February 2002 report by the General Accounting Office concluded that "immigration fraud is rampant, even helping to open the door for terrorism, and that the Immigration and Naturalization Service has no idea how to get it under control."[13]

Debate continues to rage about how exactly to get it under control. "On one side," says McGowan, "are those favoring as open a system as possible, who claim the borders need not be closed, even after September 11, and that law-enforcement and intelligence agencies already have the tools to fight terrorism if they would just do their jobs well. On the other side are restrictionists, insisting that American citizens have a right to protection from the depredations of noncitizens and that limitations on immigration, including a more selective approach to certain Middle-Eastern nationals, are the only way to ensure that protection."[14]

Calls for such restrictions touch a nerve. Racism is the great trauma of American domestic history. Many in America today would rather die than do anything that will get them accused of racism. Immigration controls on Muslim countries are supposedly racist, even though Muslims are not members of any single race or ethnic group. Screening entrants into the United States on the basis of religion is an even less viable option. But at the very least, immigration officials can conduct serious and thorough background checks on visa applicants and immigrants from Muslim countries—*including* allegedly U.S.-friendly Muslim countries like Saudi Arabia that are hotbeds of Islamic extremism.

The greatest amount of damage control, however, must be done with the Muslim immigrants who are already in the United States. Multiculturalism has relegated the idea of assimilation to the dustbin of history. But that is precisely what is needed. American Muslims need to become assimilated to the American ideals enumerated in the Constitution. Those ideals are, presumably, why they have chosen to make their home here; and that Constitution, and our country, is what they have sworn allegiance to when they become citizens. American Muslims don't need to leave behind their culture, their language, or even their style of dress. But it is not asking too much to call upon American Muslim groups, in the name of universal human rights, to also make a formal renunciation of jihad and dhimmitude theology, and to expect them to follow through with these renunciations in their mosques and schools. Muslim groups that simply deny that this theology exists are not making this renunciation. The statements on jihad from CAIR and other groups are more deception than renunciation. Let the mosques of America clearly proclaim a message renouncing jihad and dhimmitude. Is this impossible to achieve? No. Many American Muslims understand that jihad and dhimmitude theology puts Islam on a collision course with Western republican government, and they have already discarded that theology in order to live in peace. Some are in the United States precisely in order to escape those who enforce—or preach—the supremacy of the Sharia. We cannot assume that all American Muslims have done so; but it must be made clear that any Muslim who wants to be an American citizen needs to accept the Western ideals of toleration, freedom of thought and association, republican government, due process, and secular law. Other "peoples of the book" have done this—indeed, they have in many cases recognized these ideals as being implicit or inherent in their faiths. For Muslims the challenges might be greater, but it is up to them to make the choice: jihad, dhimmitude, and Sharia, or the freedom offered by the West.

Encourage moderate Islam at home and abroad

We do not encourage moderate Islam by pretending Islam is something it isn't or by referring to "Judeo-Christian-Islamic values," as CAIR, the American Muslim Alliance, and other Islamic advocacy groups in the United States would have us do (actually, would compel us to do, by politically correct coercion).[15]

It serves no purpose to proffer politically correct untruths of the sort uttered by Abdulwahab Alkebsi of the Center for the Study of Islam and Democracy. According to Alkebsi, the essentials of democracy were "consistent with Islam's clarion call for justice, equality, and human dignity.... According to the Qur'an, one of the explicit purposes of God's messengers is to offer mankind liberty, justice, and equality." Islam, he said, "lays the ground for the values of freedom, justice, and equality that are essential to democracy, more so than any other religion or dogma."[16]

If this is so, why didn't the Islamic world ever give rise to a democracy until the establishment of secular Turkey, which was heavily influenced by the West—where ideals like democracy, freedom, justice, and equality run from the classical Greeks, through the Christian era, through today? Alkebsi also doesn't make clear whether the Qur'an's offer of freedom, justice, and equality to mankind extends to all regardless of creed, or is conditional upon conversion to Islam. Whether they were intentionally deceptive or simply a massive exercise in wishful thinking, Alkebsi's words on behalf of moderate Islam ring hollow not only for informed non-Muslims, but, more importantly, for radical Muslims as well.

Ultimately, if moderate Islam is ever to become the dominant form of Islam around the world, the impetus must come from Muslims themselves. They must do it by explicitly renouncing some aspects of Islamic tradition and history—most especially jihad and dhimmitude—and by combating them when they appear as terrorism. Many are taking this initiative. But what the West means by terrorism is not always synonymous with what Muslims mean by it. The Saudi-based Muslim World League said in May 2003 that "terrorism was the most dangerous challenge facing Muslim countries and called for a broadly-based front to eradicate it."[17] The league's secretary general, Sheikh Abdullah al-Turki, lamented that "the events of September 11 have aroused some fear and mistrust between people in the Muslim World and the West." Of Muslim radicals he said, "It is unfair to take such individuals as representatives of Islam and Muslims."[18]

Yet al-Turki's Muslim World League (MWL) continues to spread Wahhabi Islam, with its insistence on traditional faith and practice (including, presumably, traditional teachings on jihad and dhimmitude) around the globe. On March 20, 2002, federal agents raided the MWL offices in Virginia on the suspicion that the league had ties to terrorist groups.[19] They had good reason to think they might find something there. Mohammad Jafal Khalifa, Osama bin Laden's brother-in-law, "through his foundation, has allegedly been supplying arms and other logistics to Abu Sayyaf bandits" in the Philippines, "some of whom also claim to have been trained in bin Laden's terrorist camps in Afghanistan." Khalifa's "foundation" is the International Islamic Relief Organization (IIRO), the self-described "social arm" of the Muslim World League.[20]

Such endeavors are fraught with other perils as well. If moderates are perceived as tools of the United States, they risk losing all credibility among their own people—particularly the radicals whose minds they have to change. In declaring his support for jihad against American forces in Iraq, Sheikh Muhammad Abu Al-Hunud of the Palestinian Authority referred to American protests against material in Saudi textbooks and issued a warning against moderate or "Americanized" Islam. "The aggression against Iraq is an assault on Islam, the Koran and the message of Muhammad.... If, God forbid, something happens to Iraq, the aggression and the Crusade will turn tomorrow against the Koran. Prior to the attack on Iraq, Allah's enemy and the enemy of His Prophet . . . called to change the religious education systems in the Arab and Islamic countries. Today, God forbid, his second assault is on the Koran, [he wants] to change verses and to mess with Allah's book, to Americanize the region, Americanize the religion, Americanize the Koran, Americanize Muhammad's message."[21]

There is an increasingly heated battle for the soul of Islam. "What matters now," says Hasan al-Banna's grandson Tariq Ramadan, "is that Muslims abandon their fear that self-criticism plays into the hands of the West." Some Muslims and ex-Muslims are ready to engage in that criticism in order ultimately to bring health and true peace to Islamic society. According to Iranian philosopher Dariush Shayegan, "We have sanctified the Sharia. But the Sharia is very cumbersome in the Islamic world! It keeps society from moving. This kind of Islam, it is sclerotic Islam, petrified! The time has come for us to break the taboos." Boualem Sansal, an Algerian writer, calls for a new interpretation of Muslim sources— *ijtihad*. "For lack of ijtihad," he says, "Islam is out of step with the times. It crushes more than it elevates; it controls more than it liberates." He said that Muslim countries were "led by bloody charlatans," aided in their oppression by the Qur'an, which "lends itself to all bad interpretations." He noted that "contempt for women" is buttressed by "hundreds of verses."

Concludes Ibn Warraq, "It is time for moderate Muslims to question honestly the principles of their faith. To admit the role of the Qur'an in the propagation of violence. For them to see this text for what it is: a human text, containing serious moral, historic, and scientific errors."[22]

Moderate Islam needs to be encouraged internationally. The Tunisian writer Al-'Afif Al-Akhdar recently attacked in print Muslims who "generate terror through religious Jihad education—an education which all Arab countries implement, except Tunisia."[23] May other countries follow Tunisia's example.

One way America can help is by reconfiguring its alliances with the Muslim world. Any state that prefers the Sharia to friendship with the United States should be dropped as an ally. Painful as this might be in the short term, to do otherwise is self-defeating, as America has presumably learned in Saudi Arabia; moreover, it is one very tangible way to encourage moderation in the Islamic world.

This fact renders the fate of postwar Iraq all the more urgent. On April 8, 2003, Kadhem al-Husseini al-Haeri, an Iraqi Shiite mullah living in Iran, issued a fatwa declaring that Shiites must "seize the first possible opportunity to fill the power vacuum in the administration of Iraqi cities." He spoke directly about resisting American designs for Iraq. "People have to be taught not to collapse morally before the means used by the Great Satan if it stays in Iraq." He directed Iraqi clerics to "raise people's awareness of the Great Satan's plans and of the means to abort them."[24] And in varying guises, many Muslim leaders in Iraq say the same thing. The reconstruction of Iraq along democratic lines will be an enormous experiment of extreme importance for the future of Islam—will it in fact be possible to create a democratic Iraq that will not elect a government intent on imposing the Sharia, and its attendant theologies of dhimmitude and jihad?

Evidence of the human cost of jihad and dhimmitude is all around us, from the World Trade Center to more recent terrorist attacks around the world. There is no reason to think that these attacks are going to end in the foreseeable future. After the spring 2003 attacks in Morocco and Saudi Arabia, al Qaeda remains a powerful worldwide force, with as many as 18,000 members.[25] Other jihad groups still operate around the globe, and are not clamoring for negotiations or ballots. As the Saudi Sheikh Nasser Muhammad Al-Ahmad put it, "There is no solution to... any problem to which the infidel enemy is party, except by waving the banner of Jihad."[26] After the Morocco attacks in May 2003, Abu Seif al-Islam ("Father of the Sword of Islam") of Morocco's Salafi movement declared, "After September 11, the jihad has become open everywhere.... Henceforth the battle is global."[27]

If the mujahedin around the world wage their jihads successfully, the rights of non-Muslim minorities will never be respected. The dreams of Sharia rule shared by the Ayatollah Khomeini, Sayyid Qutb, Osama bin Laden, Iraq's Mohammed Bakr al-Hakim, and all the rest will bring the rest of the world nothing but more of the blood, terror, and oppression that jihad has already wrought.

The United Nations Universal Declaration of Human Rights, adopted in 1948, declares: "All human beings are born free and equal in dignity and rights." It also says: "Everyone has the right to freedom of thought, conscience, and religion; this right includes freedom to change his religion or belief, and freedom, either alone or in community with others and in public or private, to manifest his religion or belief in teaching, practice, worship, and observance."[28]

The Sharia transgresses this declaration in innumerable ways, from its laws about the treatment of women to its death sentence for converts from Islam to another religion. But the legal superstructure of jihad is the worst offender. It ordains that the wars of mankind must not cease until this equality of dignity and rights is denied to whole classes and races of people, who must forever be consigned to humiliating second-class status unless and until they are willing to deny their conscience and identity.

The theology and history of Islam bear out that this is how all too many Muslims have always understood their law. Until Islam undergoes a definitive and universal reform, this is how the warriors of jihad understand it today and will continue to understand it. This is the version of Islam that radical Muslims are pressing forward with bombs and guns and threats around the world.

That is why the struggle against jihad is the struggle of every true lover of freedom.

ENDNOTES

Introduction

1. Bill Guerin, "Poisoning the Peace in the Spice Islands," *Asia Times Online*, January 24, 2003, www.atimes.com.
2. Amy Chew, "Militant Laskar Jihad group disbands," www.cnn.com, October 16, 2002; Daniel Pipes, "What is Jihad," *New York Post*, December 31, 2002; Rod Dreher, "Do Christians Bleed?," *National Review*, September 16, 2002.
3. "Hamas: Charter (August 1988)," in Walter Laquer and Barry Rubin, editors, *The Israeli-Arab Reader: A Documentary History of the Middle East Conflict*, sixth revised edition, (New York: Penguin, 2001), 342.
4. Qassam Brigades Military Communiques found at Hamas: The Islamic Resistance Movement, Palestinian Information Center, http://www.palestine-info.co.uk/hamas/index.htm.
5. Sakina Security Services, "The Ultimate Jihad Challenge," www.sakina.fsbusiness.co.uk. British authorities have shut down this site.
6. Yvonne Ridley, "CIA hit squad accused of London assassination," www.ummahnews.com, January 6, 2003.
7. Brian Ross, "Preparing for Jihad . . . in Alabama," www.abcnews.com, July 25, 2002.
8. Middle East Media Research Institute (MEMRI), "Friday Sermons in Saudi Mosques."
9. Samuel P. Huntington, *The Clash of Civilizations and the Remaking of World Order*, (New York: Touchstone, 1997), 209.

Chapter 1

1. David Zucchino, "Suspect in attack reportedly made anti-US remarks," *Los Angeles Times*, March 24, 2003.
2. Beth Bow, "Second Officer Dies From Grenade Attack," The Associated Press, March 26, 2003.
3. Anne Hull, "U.S. Soldier Detained In Attack Is Identified," *Washington Post*, March 24, 2003.
4. Tim Reid, "US Muslim soldier kills officer and wounds 16," *TimesOnline*, March 24, 2003.
5. Kimberly Hefling, "Officers Describe Kuwait Grenade Attack," The Associated Press, June 17, 2003.

6. Imam Muslim, Sahih Muslim, Abdul Hamid Siddiqi, trans., Kitab Bhavan, revised edition 2000, book 32, no. 6336.

7. "Attitude Problem? Family: Soldier Accused in Grenade Attack Troubled Over Race & Religion Issues," ABCNews.com, March 25, 2003.

8. Muhammed Ibn Ismaiel Al-Bukhari, Sahih al-Bukhari: The Translation of the Meanings, translated by Muhammad M. Khan, Darussalam, 1997, vol. 1, book 2, no. 36. The explanatory parenthetical phrases are added by the translators to bring out the sense of the original.

9. Ahmed ibn Naqib al-Misri, Reliance of the Traveller ('Umdat al-Salik): A Classic Manual of Islamic Sacred Law, translated by Nuh Ha Mim Keller. Amana Publications, 1999. Section o9.0.

10. 'Umdat al-Salik, o9.8.

11. 'Umdat al-Salik, o9.6.

12. Imam Muslim, Sahih Muslim, Abdul Hamid Siddiqi, trans., Kitab Bhavan, revised edition 2000, book 19, no. 4294.

13. Al-Hidayah, vol. Ii., 140, in Thomas P. Hughes, "Jihad," in *A Dictionary of Islam*, (W.H. Allen, 1895), 243-248.

14. Ibn Khaldun, *The Muqaddimah: An Introduction to History*, translated by Franz Rosenthal; edited and abridged by N. J. Dawood, (Princeton: Princeton University Press) 1967, 183.

15. Ibn Taymiyya, "Jihad," in Rudolph Peters, *Jihad in Classical and Modern Islam*, (Princeton: Markus Wiener Publishers) 1996, 49.

16. Middle East Media Research Institute (MEMRI), "Saudi Opposition Sheikhs on America, Bin Laden, and Jihad," MEMRI Special Dispatch No. 400, July 18, 2002. www.memri.org.

17. Cecil Angel, "Terror terms ruled out of trial," *Detroit Free Press*, November 5, 2002; "Detroit Muslim Claims Knowledge of Terrorism," NewsMax.com, July 26, 2002.

18. The Islamic Development Bank, "IDB in Brief," http://www.isdb.org/english_docs/idb_home/backgrnd.htm#Establishment.

19. Paul Sperry, "U.S.-Saudi oil imports fund American mosques," WorldNetDaily.com, April 22, 2002.

20. "Q & A with W.D. Mohammed," *Los Angeles Times*, May 15, 1999. Reprinted at http://www.sunnah.org/publication/salafi/WDMuhammad_saudi.htm.

21. This sermon is undated. Like the others quoted here, it was posted at the Saudi website Al-Minbar (www.alminbar.net).

22. Middle East Media Research Institute Special Report No. 10, "Friday Sermons in Saudi Mosques: Review and Analysis," www.memri.org, September 26, 2002.

23. "Transcript: Saudi Foreign Policy Adviser Adel al-Jubeir on Fox News Sunday," FoxNews.com, May 18, 2003.

24. According to the IBTS website, http://www.ibtsonline.com/page/page/411740.htm.

25. Larry Cohler-Esses, "Sowing seeds of hatred: Islamic textbooks scapegoat Jews, Christians," *New York Daily News*, March 30, 2003.

26. "Saudis Spread Hate Speech in U.S.," Saudi Institute, September 9, 2002. http://www.saudiinstitute.org/hate.htm.

27. Steven Stalinsky, "Preliminary Overview—Saudi Arabia's Education System," Middle East Media Research Institute (MEMRI), Special Report No. 12, December 20, 2002. www.memri.org.

28. Joel Mowbray, "The House that Raised Akbar: An army sergeant's ties to Saudi Arabia," *National Review Online*, April 3, 2003.

29. Frank J. Gaffney Jr., "The 'Fifth Column' syndrome," *Washington Times*, March 25, 2003.

30. Aaron Klein, "Soda, pizza and the destruction of America," WorldNet Daily.com, March 18, 2003.

31. Tim Timmons, "Terrorists Under the Radar Screen in the USA," ASSIST News Service, December 7, 2001.

32. Daniel Pipes Interview with Ahmed Yusuf, "Ahmad Yusuf: 'Hamas Is a Charitable Organization,'" *Middle East Quarterly*, March 1998.

33. Marc Fisher, "Muslim Students Weigh Questions Of Allegiance," *Washington Post*, October 16, 2001.

34. El-Masri, posts to www.clearguidance.com, March 16,2003, http://clearguidance.blogspot.com/. The writer, "El-Masri," claimed to be Ahmed Eissa, head of the Muslim Student Association at Green Valley State University in Allendale, Michigan. When the messages were posted at the popular news commentary site "Little Green Footballs," Eissa denied that he had written them, claiming to have been the victim of a hacker, although his explanation left nagging questions: see his posts on "MSA President at ClearGuidance," March 23, 2003. http://littlegreen-footballs.com/weblog/?entry=5933_MSA_President_at_ClearGuidance.

35. Jeff Jacoby, "The Islamist connection," *Boston Globe*, February 27, 2003.

36. Stephen Buckley, "The Al-Arian argument," *St. Petersburg Times*, March 3, 2002.

37. "Third 'Buffalo Six' Member Pleads Guilty," The Associated Press, March 25, 2003; "New York Man Admits to Attending Al Qaeda Camp," *New York Times*, March 26, 2003.

38. United States District Court Western District of Washington at Seattle, *United States of America v. Earnest James Ujaama*. http://news.findlaw.com/cnn/docs/terrorism/usujaama82802ind.pdf.

39. "Activist James Ujaama Pleads Guilty to Conspiring to Aid Taliban," The Associated Press, April 14, 2003.

40. United States District Court for the District of Oregon, *United States of America v. Jeffrey Leon Battle, Patrice Lumumba Ford, Ahmed Ibrahim Bilal, Muhammad Ibrahim Bilal, Habis Abdulla al Saoub, October Martinique Lewis*. No. CR02-399HA. October 3, 2002. http://news.findlaw.com/hdocs/docs/terrorism/usbattle100302ind.pdf.

41. John Perazzo, "American Al-Qaeda," FrontPageMagazine.com, May 6, 2003.
42. Scot J. Paltrow, "Immigrant's Path: From Tech Success To Terror Charges," *Wall Street Journal*, April 29, 2003.
43. Paul Barrett, "MSA Figure Seized By FBI," *Wall Street Journal*, May 29, 2003
44. Dan Hansen, Benjamin Shors and Thomas Clouse, "UI student arrested on visa fraud charge," The Spokesman-Review.com, February 27, 2003.
45. "Global Relief Foundation Urges Americans to Never Forget September 11," *Business Wire*, December 11, 2001.
46. "Muslim charity sues U.S. over financial sanctions," *Chicago Tribune*, January 29, 2002.
47. Judy Aita, "Global Relief Foundation Placed on U.N. Terror List," U.S. Department of State International Information Programs, October 24, 2002.
48. Paul M. Barrett, "How a Chaplain Spread Extremism To an Inmate Flock," *Wall Street Journal*, February 5, 2003.
49. Middle East Media Research Institute (MEMRI), "The Arab Press on the War and News from Iraqi Television," MEMRI Special Dispatch No. 484, March 21, 2003.
50. "Saddam: Attack is 'Crime,'" Sky News, March 19, 2003.
51. "Text of Saddam Hussein's Speech," The Associated Press, March 19, 2003.
52. "Iraqis pledge to die for Saddam," ninemsn, March 19, 2003, http://news.ninemsn.com.au/World/story_46803.asp.
53. MEMRI Special Dispatch No. 484.
54. Frank Gardner, "Grand Sheikh condemns suicide bombings," BBCNews, December 4, 2001.
55. Douglas Jehl, "Moderate Muslims Fear Their Message Is Being Ignored," *New York Times*, October 21, 2001.
56. Middle East Media Research Institute (MEMRI), "Jihad Against the U.S.: Al-Azhar's Conflicting Fatwas," MEMRI Special Dispatch No. 480, March 16, 2003. www.memri.org.
57. 'Umdat al-Salik, p. xx and section o9.1.
58. Ibn Taymiyya, "The Religious and Moral Doctrine of Jihad," in Rudolph Peters, *Jihad in Classical and Modern Islam: A Reader*. (Princeton: Markus Wiener Publishers) 1996, 53.
59. Rudolph Peters, *Islam and Colonialism: The Doctrine of Jihad in Modern History*, (The Hague: Mouton Publishers) 1979, 86.
60. Ibid., 90.
61. "Muslim rage takes on stronger religious tone," The Associated Press, March 24, 2003.
62. For information on Kuftaro and the papal visit, see http://www.kuftaro.org/.

63. Liza Porteus, "Officials: Syria Sending Equipment to Iraq," FoxNews.com, March 27, 2003.

64. Independent Media Review Analysis (IMRA), "Arab World Sermons: O Lord, deal with the enemies of Islam including Zionists and Americans," April 21, 2003. www.imra.org.il.

65. "Muslim rage takes on stronger religious tone," The Associated Press, March 23, 2003.

66. Kate Jaimet, "Ottawa imam supports jihad," *Montreal Gazette,* April 7, 2003.

67. Aamir Ashraf, "Pakistani Muslims seek jihad for Iraq, others pray," Reuters, March 25, 2003.

68. Farhan Reza, "Karachi clerics call for jihad against US," *Daily Times* (Pakistan), March 25, 2003.

69. Oliver Teves, "ARMM chief: Jihad justified over Iraq," The Associated Press, March 25, 2003.

70. "Indonesia and the war," The Religion Report, April 2, 2003, http://www.abc.net.au/rn/talks/8.30/relrpt/stories/s822518.htm.

71. See *Just War and Jihad : Historical and Theoretical Perspectives on War and Peace in Western and Islamic Traditions,* edited by John Kelsay and James Turner Johnson, Greenwood Publishing, 1991.

72. Council on American Islamic Relations, "About Islam and American Muslims," http://www.cair-net.org/asp/aboutislam.asp.

73. Osama bin Laden,"Letter to the American People," November 24, 2002. http://www.observer.co.uk/worldview/story/0,11581,845725,00.html.

74. Middle East Media Research Institute (MEMRI), "Islamist Leader in London: No Universal Jihad As Long As There is No Caliphate," MEMRI Special Dispatch No. 435, October 30, 2002.

75. "Suicide bombers will have no effect on US war plans: General Brooks," Agence France-Presse, March 31, 2003; Tanalee Smith, "Arab volunteers return home disillusioned," The Associated Press, April 11, 2003.

76. "Four killed as anti-war protests erupt across Middle East," Agence France Presse, March 21, 2003.

77. "Ignore call for jihad," Islamic Republic News Agency, March 21, 2003. http://www.irna.com/en/head/030321113121.ehe.shtml.

78. "Mahathir: Going to Iraq for 'jihad' is a dumb idea," *Straits Times,* February 12, 2003.

79. MEMRI Special Dispatch No. 484.

80. Almin Karamehmedovic, "Iraq Says Suicide Strikes Are 'Policy,'" The Associated Press, March 29, 2003.

81. Hamza Hendawi, "Saddam Vows to Crush Allied Forces," The Associated Press, March 24, 2003; "Saddam speaks, exhorts troops," MSNBC News, March 24, 2003.

82. Middle East Media Research Institute (MEMRI), "The Muslim Woman Magazine: Hosted by Doaa 'Amer," May 7, 2002. www.memri.org.

83. Aluma Solnick, "Based on Koranic Verses, Interpretations, and Traditions, Muslim Clerics State: The Jews Are the Descendants of Apes, Pigs, And

Other Animals," MEMRI Special Report No. 11, November 1, 2002. www.memri.org.

84. Middle East Media Research Institute (MEMRI), "Ramadan Sermon From Iraq," MEMRI Special Dispatch No. 438, November 8, 2002. www.memri.org.

85. Youssef M. Ibrahim, "Democracy: Be Careful What You Wish For," *Washington Post*, March 23, 2003.

86. Chew, "Militant Laskar Jihad group disbands," Pipes, "What is Jihad," Dreher, "Do Christians Bleed?"

87. Gilles Kepel, *Jihad: The Trail of Political Islam*, translated by Anthony F. Roberts. (Cambridge: The Belknap Press) 2002, 250.

88. Tawfiq Tabib, "Interview with Sheikh al-Mujahideen Abu Abdel Aziz," Al-Sirat Al-Mustaqeem (The Straight Path), August 1994. Reprinted at http://www.seprin.com/laden/barbaros.html.

89. Kerim Fenari, "The Jihad of Imam Shamyl," Q-News, reprinted at http://www.amina.com/article/jihad_imamshamyl.html.

90. Mark Riebling and R.P. Eddy, "Jihad @ Work," *National Review Online*, October 24, 2002.

91. Caroline Hawley, "Islamic militants re-evaluate tactics," BBC News, November 17, 1999.

92. "The Amir of the Mujahideen Party: 'The People of Kashmir Are Determined to Continue The Jihad Regardless of The Price,'" Nida'ul Islam magazine, August-September 1995. Reprinted at http://islam.org.au/articles/older/INT-KSHM.HTM.

93. "Pakistani minister supports Kashmir 'jihad,'" BBCNews, June 21, 2002.

94. "Attack on Kashmir radio station, other violence leaves 14 dead," Agence France-Presse, April 26, 2003.

95. "Mindanao Muslims and the global Ummah," Muslimedia, April 1-15, 1999. Reprinted at http://www.muslimedia.com/archives/sea99/milf-intv2.htm.

96. John Eibner and Charles Jacobs, "'Old Europe' and Sudan's Jihad," *Boston Globe*, March 15, 2003.

97. "Saving Sonti's Orphans: Moving Forward with ICC's Total Redemption Project," International Christian Concern, http://www.persecution.org/concern/2001/05/p4.html.

98. "Islamists burn to death Christian pastor, family," WorldNetDaily.com, June 4, 2003.

99. Steven Emerson, "How a terrorist enterprise was created, maintained, financed, and coordinated from the safety of the United States," *Jewish World Review*, February 25, 2003.

100. Jerry Guidera and Glenn R. Simpson, "U.S. probes terror ties to Boston software firm," *Wall Street Journal*, December 6, 2002.

101. "Jail Imam Barred for 'Terror' Link," *New York Post*, March 22, 2003.

102. Eastern District of Michigan Southern Division, *United States of America v. Karim Koubriti, Ahmed Hannan, Youssef Hmimssa, Abdella Lnu, Farouk Ali-Haimoud.* No. 01-80778. August 28, 2002.
103. Michael G. McGovern and Jonathan S. Kolodner, Assistant United States Attorneys, Before Honorable Michael H. Dolinger, United States Magistrate Judge, Southern District of New York, *The United States of America v. Ali Saleh Kahlah Al-Marri,* December 2002.
104. Niraj Warikoo, "Cleric makes case for freedom," *Detroit Free Press,* October 2, 2002.
105. U.S. Department of Justice Press Release, "Guilty Plea in Conspiracy to Damage Property by Explosives," August 8, 2002. Reprinted at http://www.usdoj.gov/usao/fls/Mandhai.html.
106. "Hezbollah: 'A-Team Of Terrorists'," CBSNews.com, April 18, 2003.
107. MEMRI Special Dispatch No. 435.

Chapter 2

1. Andrew Osborn, "'I shot Fortuyn for Dutch Muslims,' says accused," *The Guardian,* March 28, 2003. http://www.guardian.co.uk/international/story/0,3604,924324,00.html.
2. Kirsty Lang, "Pim Fortuyn: Maverick Dutch rightwinger poised for success," *The Guardian,* May 8, 2002. http://www.guardian.co.uk/farright/story/0,11981,711529,00.html.
3. Charles Paul Freund, "Fortuyn's Folly: How an assassinated Dutch politician frustrated journalists," *Reason* magazine, May 7, 2002.
4. John Hooper, "More to Fortuyn than anti-immigrant populist," *The Guardian,* May 8 2002. Reprinted at http://www.smh.com.au/articles/2002/05/08/1019441505948.html; Osborn, "'I shot Fortuyn for Dutch Muslims,' says accused."
5. Lang, "Pim Fortuyn: Maverick Dutch rightwinger poised for success."
6. Osborn, "'I shot Fortuyn for Dutch Muslims,' says accused,"
7. "Fortuyn killer now has doubts," The Associated Press, March 31, 2003.
8. "Dutch politician's killer gets 18 years," *London Evening Standard,* April 15, 2003. http://www.thisislondon.com/news/articles/4363884?source=Evening%20Standard.
9. Pierre-Antoine Souchard, "Mayor of Paris stabbed," The Associated Press, October 7, 2002.
10. Abigail Levene, "Anti-gay talk sparks Dutch outcry," Reuters, May 10, 2001.
11. Oussama Cherribi, "Imams and Issues: The Politics of Islam in European Public Space," presentation at the American Political Science Association, San Francisco, California, August 30–September 2, 2001. Reprinted at http://pro.harvard.edu/papers/033/033005CherribiOu.pdf.
12. 'Umdat al-Salik, o12.1.

13. Hani Ramadan, "La charia incomprise," *Le Monde*, September 10, 2002.
14. "A constitutional dilemma," Radio Netherlands, November 5, 2002, http://www.rnw.nl/hotspots/html/ned021105.html.
15. John L. Allen, Jr., "Europe's Muslims worry bishops," *National Catholic Reporter*, October 22, 1999.
16. Simon Mann, "Hatred mongers exploit freedom of speech," *Sydney Morning Herald*, September 22, 2001.
17. Jon Ronson, *Them: Adventures with Extremists*, (New York: Simon & Schuster) 2002, 23.
18. Jon Dougherty, "Muslim leaders pledge to 'transform West,'" WorldNet-Daily.com, August 13, 2002.
19. Anton La Guardia, Said Ghazzali, Ohad Gozani, and Sean O'Neill, "British bombers posed as peace activists," *Telegraph*, May 2, 2003. http://news.telegraph.co.uk/.
20. "Body on Tel Aviv Beach ID'd As Bomber," The Associated Press, May 19, 2003.
21. "Radical cleric 'taught' bomb suspects," BBCNews, May 2, 2003.
22. Sarah Lyall, "What Drove 2 Britons to Bomb a Club in Tel Aviv?" *New York Times*, May 12, 2003.
23. David Bamber, Daniel Foggo and Martin Bentham, "MI5 admits: we let suicide bombers slip through net," *Telegraph*, May 4, 2003.
24. Lyall, "What Drove 2 Britons to Bomb a Club in Tel Aviv?"
25. "Firebrand cleric of London mosque," www.cnn.com, January 20, 2003, http://www.cnn.com/2003/WORLD/europe/01/20/uk.hamzaprofile/.
26. "Profile: Abu Hamza," BBCNews, January 17, 2003.
27. "Mosque Raid Arrests," www.skynews.com, January 20, 2003; "Timeline: UK ricin terror probe," www.cnn.com, January 23, 2003.
28. Michael Petrou, "'It's OK to kill non-Muslims': Says Radical Cleric," *Ottawa Citizen*, November 24, 2002. Reprinted at http://www.johnathangaltfilms.com/4canada.html.
29. Abu'l Hasan al-Mawardi, al-Ahkam as-Sultaniyyah (The Laws of Islamic Governance), (London: Ta-Ha Publishers) 1996, 192.
30. Ibid., 28.
31. Steve Zwick, "The Thinker," in "The Many Faces of Islam," *Time Europe*, December 16, 2002.
32. Christopher Caldwell, "Allah Mode: France's Islam problem," *Weekly Standard*, July 15, 2002.
33. Howard Schneider, "For First Time, a Pope Sets Foot in a Mosque," *Washington Post*, May 7, 2001.
34. Middle East Media Research Institute Special Report No. 10, "Friday Sermons in Saudi Mosques: Review and Analysis," www.memri.org, September 26, 2002.
35. 'Umdat al-Salik, w4.1(2).
36. Damon Johnston, "WTC Survivor's Son Leaves NY To Fight With Taliban," *The Courier Mail*, November 7, 2001.

37. Sayyid Qutb, "A Muslim's Nationality and His Belief." Reprinted at http://www.witness-pioneer.org/vil/Articles/politics/nationalism.htm.
38. Caldwell, "Allah Mode: France's Islam problem,"
39. Tariq Ramadan, *To Be a European Muslim: A Study of Islamic Sources in the European Context*, The Islamic Foundation, 1999, 165.
40. Ibid., 172.
41. Xavier Ternisien, "Le 'double langage' de Tariq Ramadan en procès à Lyon," *Le Monde*, September 27, 2002.
42. Paul Donnelly, "Tariq Ramadan: The Muslim Martin Luther?," Salon.com, February 15, 2002.
43. Martin Kramer, *Ivory Towers on Sand: The Failure of Middle Eastern Studies in America*, Washington Institute for Near East Policy, 2001, 56.
44. Xavier Ternisien, "Le 'double langage' de Tariq Ramadan en procès à Lyon." *Le Monde*, September 27, 2002.
45. Ramadan, *To Be a European Muslim*.
46. Ibid., 176.
47. Sami A. Aldeeb Abu-Sahlieh, *Muslims in the West: Redefining the Separation of Church and State*, translated by Sheldon Lee Gosline, (Warren Center: Shangri-La Publications) 2002, 96.
48. Joseph Algazy, "'My fellow Muslims, we must fight anti-Semitism,'" *Haaretz*, May 26, 2002.
49. Tariq Ramadan, "Foreword," in Hassan al-Banna, Al-Ma'thurat, Awakening Publications, 2001. Reprinted at http://www.tariq-ramadan.org/document.asp?fichier=foreword&d=38
50. Hasan al-Banna, "On Jihad," in *Five Tracts of Hasan al-Banna*, translated by Charles Wendell, Berkeley, 1978, 142, 150, 154. Reprinted at http://www.nmhschool.org/tthornton/hasan_al.htm.
51. Hani Ramadan, "La charia incomprise," *Le Monde*, September 10, 2002.
52. "Lapidation: Tariq Ramadan se distancie de son frère Hani," *Le Courrier*, November 13, 2002.
53. Tariq Ramadan, *To Be a European Muslim*.
54. Ayub Khan, "Muslim Philosopher Addresses Islam and the West," Islam-Online, April 6, 2002. http://www.islam-online.net/English/News/2002-04/06/article31.shtml.
55. Martin Kramer, *Ivory Towers on Sand: The Failure of Middle Eastern Studies in America*, Washington Institute for Near East Policy, 2001, 54.
56. Christopher Caldwell, "Allah Mode Part 2," *Weekly Standard*, July 6, 2002.
57. Alexis Amory, "Islamofascism Rising in Holland," FrontPageMagazine.com, March 6, 2003; Marlise Simons, "Belgium's Malcolm X: Immigrant activist sets out to 'rock the boat,'" *New York Times*, March 5, 2003.
58. Jennifer Ehrlich and Tom Vandyck, "'Belgian Malcolm X' seeks office," *Christian Science Monitor*, May 16, 2003.

59. Caldwell, "Allah Mode: France's Islam problem,"

60. Dyab Abou Jahjah, "Our Own Agenda: Is the Arab world Europe's nemesis, or its last hope?," *Al-Ahram Weekly*, September 12, 2002. Reprinted at http://www.bintjbeil.com/articles/en/020912_aboujahjah.html.

61. Amnesty International, "AI Report 1997: France," http://www.amnesty.org/ailib/aireport/ar97/EUR21.htm.

62. Arab European League, "Vision and Philosophy," http://www.arabeuropean.org/aboutus.html.

63. Marlise Simons, "Belgium's Malcolm X: Immigrant activist sets out to 'rock the boat,'" *New York Times*, March 5, 2003.

64. "Belgians reject Arab nationalist," The Associated Press, May 19, 2003.

65. U.S. Department of State, Office of the Coordinator for Counterterrorism "2001 Report on Foreign Terrorist Organizations," October 5, 2001.

66. John Miller, "The Activist," in "The Many Faces of Islam," *Time Europe*, December 16, 2002.

67. Ambrose Evans-Pritchard, "Ex-Hezbollah charged with inciting rioting," *London Daily Telegraph*, November 30, 2002.

68. Elaine Sciolino, "French Rallies Against War Shift Focus To Israel," *New York Times*, March 30, 2003.

69. Caldwell, "Allah Mode Part 2."

70. Omer Taspinar, "Europe's Muslim Street," *Muslim News*, March 11, 2003.

71. Andrew Morse and Richard Gizbert, "Opposite Sides: Anti-Semitic Violence Erupts in France, Amid Mideast Conflict," ABCNews.com, April 3, 2002.

72. Caldwell, "Allah Mode: France's Islam problem."

73. "Rabbi stabbed at Paris synagogue," BBCNews, January 4, 2003.

74. Craig S. Smith, "French Jews Tell of a New and Threatening Wave of Anti-Semitism," *New York Times*, March 22, 2003.

75. Alexis Amory, "Islamofascism Rising in Holland," Simons, "Belgium's Malcolm X: Immigrant activist sets out to 'rock the boat,'"

76. Marlise Simons, "Behind the Veil: A Muslim Woman Speaks Out," *New York Times*, November 9, 2002.

77. Geraldine Coughlan, "Somali woman heads for Dutch parliament: Pim Fortuyn's murder made tolerance a key issue," BBCNews, January, 3, 2003.

78. "Dutch 'ex-Muslim' lawmaker to be investigated over alleged anti-Islamic remarks," The Associated Press, January 27, 2003.

79. Abu Hamid al-Ghazali, Ihya' ulum al-din, Cairo, n.d., 4:747, in Hamdun Dagher, The Position of Women in Islam, http://www.light-of-life.com/eng/reveal/r5405efc.htm.

80. 'Umdat al-Salik, m.10.4.

81. Norma Khouri, *Honor Lost: Love and Death in Modern-Day Jordan*, (New York: Atria Books, 2003), 11.

82. Abu-Dawud Sulaiman bin Al-Aash'ath Al-Azdi as-Sijistani, Sunan abu-Dawud, Ahmad Hasan, translator, Kitab Bhavan, 1990. Book 2, no. 641.

83. Muhammed Ibn Ismaiel Al-Bukhari, Sahih al-Bukhari: The Translation of the Meanings, translated by Muhammad M. Khan, Darussalam, 1997, vol. 5, book 64, no. 4213.

84. Andrew Osborn, "Unlikely martyr who battled the mullahs forced to flee for her life," *The Observer*, November 10, 2002.

85. Andrew Osborn, "Woman in hiding after she lambasts Islam," *The Observer*, October 6, 2002.

86. 'Umdat al-Salik, o8.1.

87. Khaled Shawkat, "Dutch MP Creates Seismic Waves by Insulting Prophet Muhammad," IslamOnline, January 27, 2003. http://www.islam-online.net/english/news/2003-01/27/article09.shtml.S

88. Eva Cahen, "Report Records 'Explosion' of Anti-Semitic Violence in France, CNSNews.com, March 28, 2003.

89. Elizabeth Bryant, "Fallaci goes on trial for anti-Muslim book," United Press International, October 9, 2002.

90. "Brigitte Bardot unleashes colourful diatribe against Muslims and modern France," Agence France Presse, May 12, 2003.

91. "The Many Faces of Islam," *Time Europe*, December 16, 2002.

92. "Egyptian volunteers line up to fight in Iraq," Agence France-Press, April 8, 2003.

93. Caldwell, "Allah Mode: France's Islam problem."

94. Caldwell, "Allah Mode Part 2."

95. Kim Housego, "France May Expel Islamic Extremists," The Associated Press, April 16, 2003.

96. Sciolino, "French Threaten Expulsions After Islam Radical Victory."

97. Caldwell, "Allah Mode: France's Islam problem."

98. Hugh Schofield, "France's Islamic heartland," BBCNews, April 18, 2003.

99. Kim Housego, "France May Expel Islamic Extremists," The Associated Press, April 16, 2003.

100. Sciolino, "French Threaten Expulsions After Islam Radical Victory,"

101. Ian Johnson and David Crawford, "In 'Law' Seminars, A Saudi Group Spreads Extremism," *Wall Street Journal*, April 15, 2003.

102. John L. Allen, Jr., "Europe's Muslims worry bishops," *National Catholic Reporter*, October 22, 1999.

Chapter 3

1. "Two deminers shot and wounded in Afghanistan," Reuters, April 23, 2003; "U.S. military says it has killed murderer of Red Cross worker," The Associated Press, April 23, 2003.

2. Carlotta Gall, "In Afghanistan, Violence Stalls Renewal Effort," *New York Times*, April 26, 2003.
3. Andrew North, "Pro-jihad website draws readers: Azzam.com criticises moderate Muslims," BBCNews, February 15, 2002.
4. Independent Media Review Analysis (IMRA), Interview with Dr. Raphael Israeli, March 26, 1996. Excerpted at http://www.cdn-friends-icej.ca/isreport/hamas.html.
5. Yasir Arafat, Address to the United Nations General Assembly, November 13, 1974, in *The Israel-Arab Reader: A Documentary History of the Middle East Conflict*, edited by Walter Laquer and Barry Rubin, (New York: Penguin, sixth revised edition, 2001), 181.
6. "The charter of Allah: The Platform of the Islamic Resistance movement (Hamas)," translated and annotated by Raphael Israeli, The International Policy Institute for Counter-Terrorism, April 5, 1998. http://www.ict.org.il/documents/documentdet.cfm?docid=14.
7. Sahih Muslim, book 41, no. 6985.
8. Middle East Media Research Institute (MEMRI), "Friday Sermon on Palestinian Authority TV," MEMRI Special Dispatch No. 370, April 17, 2002. www.memri.org.
9. Hamas, "The charter of Allah: The Platform of the Islamic Resistance movement"
10. 'Umdat al-Salik, o11.3, 5.
11. Joseph Farah, "The Truth About Christians in 'Palestine,'" WorldNet-Daily.com, February 28, 2003.
12. Hamas, "Statement of Hamas for the Negotiations with the Palestinian Authorities," June 25, 1998. Reprinted at http://www.ict.org.il/documents/documentdet.cfm?docid=11.
13. "PM says will make every effort to reach accord with new PA cabinet," Haaretz.com, April 24, 2003.
14. Nissan Ratzlav-Katz, "Laundering Abu Mazen: A Holocaust revisionist, a conspiracy theorist, and a promoter of terrorism," *National Review Online*, March 19, 2003; Lamia Lahoud, "Hamas, Jihad: We won't hand over weapons," *Jerusalem Post*, April 30, 2003.
15. Mark Lavie, "Sharon takes hard line on settlements ahead of meeting with Palestinian prime minister," The Associated Press, May 13, 2003.
16. Peters, *Islam and Colonialism: The Doctrine of Jihad in Modern History*.
17. Middle East Media Research Institute (MEMRI), "PA TV Broadcasts call for Killing Jews and Americans," MEMRI Special Dispatch No. 138, October 13, 2000. www.memri.org.
18. MEMRI Special Report No. 10, "Friday Sermons in Saudi Mosques: Review and Analysis."
19. Saudi Information Agency, "Saudi Telethon Host Calls for Enslaving Jewish Women," *National Review Online*, April 26, 2002.
20. 'Umdat al-Salik, o9.13.

21. Itamar Marcus, "The Indoctrination of Palestinian Children to Seek Death for Allah—Shahada," Palestinian Media Watch, http://www.pmw.org.il/new/ASK%20FOR%20DEATH.htm.

22. Bat Ye'or, "Myths and Politics: Origin of the Myth of a Tolerant Pluralistic Islamic Society," address to The International Strategic Studies Association, August 31, 1995. Reprinted at http://www.srpska-mreza.com/library/facts/Ye_Or.html.

23. J. E. Blunt to Sir Henry Bulwer, "Answers to Queries," in Bat Ye'or, *The Decline of Eastern Christianity Under Islam: From Jihad to Dhimmitude*, (Rutherford: Fairleigh Dickinson University Press, 1996), 418-419.

24. Ibid., William R. Holmes to Sir Henry Bulwer, 427.

25. Ibid., James Zohrab to Sir Henry Bulwer, 423.

26. Reuven Paz, "Islamic Groups: the International Connection," The International Policy Institute for Counter-Terrorism, January 3, 1999. http://www.ict.org.il/articles/articledet.cfm?articleid=66.

27. Tawfiq Tabib, "Interview with Sheikh al-Mujahideen Abu Abdel Aziz," *Al-Sirat Al-Mustaqeem* (The Straight Path), August 1994. Reprinted at http://www.seprin.com/laden/barbaros.html.

28. Joseph Farah, "Land for peace, again," WorldNetDaily.com, March 8, 2002.

29. "Albanian politicians are helping Bin Laden," World Tribune.com, November 17, 1999.

30. Marcia Christoff Kurop, "Al Qaeda's Balkan Links," *Wall Street Journal Europe*, November 1, 2001.

31. Peter Finn, "Suspects in Macedonia Turned Over to U.S.: 4 Arrested Near Ambassador's Residence," *Washington Post*, March 7, 2002.

32. Craig Pyesjosh Meyer and William C. Rempe, "Bosnia: Bin Laden's Terrorist Base," *Los Angeles Times*, October 7, 2001.

33. Yossef Bodansky, Some Call It Peace: Waiting For War In the Balkans, International Strategic Studies Association, 1996. Reprinted at http://members.tripod.com/Balkania/resources/geostrategy/bodansky_peace/index.html.

34. Alija Izetbegovic, The Islamic Declaration: A program for the Islamization of the Muslims and the Muslim Peoples, Bosna, Sarajevo, 1990. Reprinted at http://www.balkan-archive.org.yu/kosta/licnosti/izetbegovic.2.html.

35. Bodansky, Some Call It Peace.

36. Christian Jennings, "Fear over Islamic terror groups using Macedonia as base," *The Scotsman*, March 4, 2002.

37. Osama bin Laden, "Declaration of War Against the Americans Occupying the Land of the Two Holy Places," August 23, 1996. Reprinted at http://www.terrorismfiles.org/individuals/declaration_of_jihad1.html.

38. Osama bin Laden, "Text of Fatwah Urging Jihad Against Americans," Al-Quds al-'Arabi , February 23, 1998. Reprinted at http://www.ict.org.il/articles/fatwah.htm.

39. 'Umdat al-Salik, o11.6.

40. See Michael Dobbs, "Inside the Mind of Osama Bin Laden: Strategy Mixes Long Preparation, Powerful Message Aimed at Dispossessed," *Washington Post*, September 20, 2001. Evidence of the wide diffusion of this notion can be found in the Indian writer M. J. Akbar's *The Shade of Swords: Jihad and the Conflict Between Islam and Christianity* (London: Routledge, 2002), in which it is cited as axiomatic (197), Dilip Hiro's article "Bush and Bin Laden" (The Nation, September 20, 2001) and elsewhere.

41. Sahih Muslim, book 19, no. 4366.

42. Jonathan Adelman and Agota Kuperman, "Christian Exodus from the Middle East," Foundation for the Defense of Democracies, December 19, 2001. Reprinted at: http://www.defenddemocracy.org/publications/publications_show.htm?doc_id=155713.

43. Stephen Schwartz, "Let America Be America the Liberator Again!" FrontPageMagazine.com, April 11, 2003.

44. Sir Richard F. Burton, *Personal Narrative of a Pilgrimage to Al-Madinah & Meccah*, volume 2, Dover, 1964, 267.

45. Michael Dobbs, "Inside the Mind of Osama Bin Laden: Strategy Mixes Long Preparation, Powerful Message Aimed at Dispossessed," *Washington Post*, September 20, 2001.

46. Middle East Media Research Institute (MEMRI), "Saudi Opposition Sheikhs on America, Bin Laden, and Jihad," MEMRI Special Dispatch No. 400, July 18, 2002. www.memri.org.

47. Adnan Malik, "At Least 20 Die in Saudi Arabia Bombings," The Associated Press, May 13, 2003.

48. Sarah El Deeb, "Al-Qaida Operative Warned of Attacks," The Associated Press, May 13, 2003.

49. John J. Lumpkin, "FBI Scales Back Saudi Investigative Team," The Associated Press, May 14, 2003.

50. John Eibner, "The Old Turkey: Turco-American alliance in disarray," *National Review Online*, April 14, 2003.

51. Suzy Hansen, "Bush is an idiot, but he was right about Saddam," Salon.com, March 22, 2003.

52. Bernard Lewis, *The Multiple Identities of the Middle East*, (Schocken Books, 1998), 26.

Chapter 4

1. Quoted in Donna Abu-Nasr, "Bin Laden's Empire Widespread," The Associated Press, September 19, 2001.

2. Rohan Gunaratna, "Tackling Terror—To win the war on terrorism, Asia's governments must join forces," TimeAsia.com, December 2, 2002.

3. Susan Dominus, "Everybody Has a Mother," *New York Times Magazine*, February 9, 2003.

4. "Jihad in the Qur'an and Ahadeeth," www.waaqiah.com, 2002.

5. Ibn Warraq, "Introduction," *What the Koran Really Says: Language, Text, and Commentary*, Ibn Warraq, editor, (Amherst: Prometheus Books, 2002), 26.

6. *Detroit Free Press*, 100 Questions and Answers About Arab Americans, http://www.freep.com/jobspage/arabs.htm, 2001; George W. Bush, Address to a Joint Session of Congress and the American People. White House Press Release, September 20, 2001.

7. "Robertson: Jihad at heart of Islam," CNN Access, www.cnn.com, November 26, 2002.

8. "India—Eight dead, 90 Hurt In Ongoing Anti-Falwell Riots," Agence France-Press, October 12, 2002; "Cleric demands death for three US Protestant pastors," Agence France-Presse, October 12, 2002.

9. Javeed Akhter, "Does Islam Promote Violence? Quoting the Qur'an (Koran) without context," The American Muslim, September–October 2002. Reprinted at http://www.ispi usa.org/currentarticles/violence.html.

10. Fedwa Wazwaz, "Does the Qur'an promote Violence?" Islamic Resource Group, http://www.islamicresourceonline.org/files/qv.html.

11. Ibn Warraq, editor, *Leaving Islam: Apostates Speak Out*, (Amherst: Prometheus Books, 2003), 400.

12. Osama bin Laden, "Declaration of War Against the Americans Occupying the Land of the Two Holy Places," www.terrorismfiles.org, August 23, 1996.

13. Osama bin Laden (?), "Letter to the American People, Observer Worldview Extra, November 24, 2002. http://www.observer.co.uk/worldview/story/0,11581,845725,00.html; Qassam Brigades Military Communiques found at Hamas: The Islamic Resistance Movement, Palestinian Information Center, http://www.palestine-info.co.uk/hamas/index.htm.

14. Ibn Warraq, editor, *Leaving Islam: Apostates Speak Out*, (Amherst: Prometheus Books, 2003), 401.

15. Ahmad Von Denffer, 'Ulum al-Qur'an: An Introduction to the Sciences of the Qur'an, The Islamic Foundation, 1994, 123.

16. Ibid., 136.

17. "Publishers Note," Tafsir Ibn Kathir (Abridged), Darussalam, 2000. Vol. 1, p. 5.

18. Sahih Bukhari, vol. 4, book 56, no. 2832.

19. Von Denffer, 'Ulum al-Qur'an.

20. "Hadith & Sunnah," www.islamonline.net.

21. See Ignaz Goldhizer, *Muslim Studies*, vol. 2, (London: George Allen & Unwin Ltd.), 1971.

22. Middle East Media Research Institute (MEMRI), "Bin Laden's Sermon for the Feast of the Sacrifice," MEMRI Special Dispatch No. 476, March 5, 2003.

23. Ibn Kathir, Tafsir Ibn Kathir (Abridged), Darussalam, 2000. Vol. 4, 370.

24. Imam Muslim, Sahih Muslim, translated by Abdul Hamid Siddiqi, Kitab Bhavan, revised edition 2000, book 37, no. 6670.
25. Ibn Kathir, Tafsir Ibn Kathir (Abridged), Darussalam, 2000. Vol. 4, 376.
26. Hazrat Moulana Sayyed Abul Hassan Ali Nadwi, The Seerah of Muhammad (The Last Prophet: A Model for All Time), Al-Islaah Publications, http://alislaah3.tripod.com/.
27. Ibn Kathir, Tafsir Ibn Kathir (Abridged), Darussalam, 2000. Vol. 4, 405.
28. Sahih Bukhari, vol. 5, book 64, no. 4364.
29. "Surat at-Tawba: Repentance," Tafsir al-Jalalayn, anonymous translation, reprinted at http://ourworld.compuserve.com/homepages/ABewley/tawba1.html.
30. Ibn Kathir, Tafsir Ibn Kathir (Abridged), Darussalam, 2000. Vol. 4, 377.
31. "Surat at-Tawba: Repentance," Tafsir Ibn Juzayy.
32. Von Denffer, 'Ulum al-Qur'an.
33. Ibid., 86-87.
34. Ibn Kathir, Tafsir Ibn Kathir (Abridged), Darussalam, 2000. Vol. 4, 376.
35. 'Abdullah bin Muhammad bin Humaid, "The Call to Jihad (Holy Fighting for Allah's Cause) in the Qur'an," Appendix III of Sahih Bukhari, vol. 9, 462.
36. S. K. Malik, The Qur'anic Concept of War, (New Delhi: Adam Publishers, 1992), 11.
37. Ibn Kathir, Tafsir Ibn Kathir (Abridged), Darussalam, 2000. Vol. 4, 376.
38. Ibid., 405.
39. Sahih Muslim, book 43, no. 7185.
40. Ibn Kathir, Tafsir Ibn Kathir (Abridged), Darussalam, 2000. Vol. 4, 406.
41. Sahih Muslim, book 26, no. 5389.
42. Ibn Kathir, Tafsir Ibn Kathir (Abridged), Darussalam, 2000. Vol. 4, 406.
43. Bat Ye'or, The Decline of Eastern Christianity Under Islam: From Jihad to Dhimmitude, (Rutherford: Fairleigh Dickinson University Press, 1996), 81.
44. Ibn Kathir, Tafsir Ibn Kathir (Abridged), Darussalam, 2000. Vol. 4, 405.
45. Ye'or, The Decline of Eastern Christianity Under Islam.
46. Ibn Kathir, Tafsir Ibn Kathir (Abridged), Darussalam, 2000. Vol. 4, 407.
47. Ye'or, The Decline of Eastern Christianity Under Islam.
48. "Lala Mustafa Pasha Mosque (St. Nicholas Cathedral)," http://www.cypnet.co.uk/ncyprus/city/famagusta/lala/index.html.
49. Ibn Kathir, Tafsir Ibn Kathir (Abridged), Darussalam, 2000. Vol. 4, 407.
50. Ibid.,404.
51. Middle East Media Research Institute (MEMRI), "Friday Sermons in Saudi Mosques: Review and Analysis," MEMRI Special Report No. 10, September 26, 2002. www.memri.org. This sermon is undated, but it appeared on the Saudi website www.alminbar.net in 2003.
52. Bob Harvey, "Christians in Iraq 'live like slaves': Ottawa cleric fears further hardships for non-Islamics," Ottawa Citizen, April 14, 2003.

53. Mark Baker, "Revealed: school that bred the Bali bombers," *The Age*, November 22, 2002, www.theage.com.au.

54. Against the Tides in the Middle East, International Evangelical Resource Centre, 1999, 35.

55. "UNC Qur'an Controversy," PBS Religion and Ethics Newsweekly, http://www.pbs.org/wnet/religionandethics/week551/sells.html.

Chapter 5

1. Al-Ajluni, Kashf al-Khafa', Cairo/Aleppo, no date, volume 1, no. 424.

2. See Suhaib Hasan, *An Introduction to the Science of Hadith*, Al-Quran Society, London, 1994. Reprinted at http://www.uh.edu/campus/msa/qurhad/suhaib.txt. Also Rudolph Peters, Islam and Colonialism: The Doctrine of Jihad in Modern History, (The Hague: Mouton Publishers, 1979), 120; and Abdullah Azzam, Join the Caravan, Azzam Publications, 2001, 51.

3. Sahih Bukhari, vol. 1, book 2, no. 25. The transliterated Arabic of the Muslim confession of faith has been omitted from this translation for ease of reading. The same statement is repeated in Bukhari, vol. 1, book 8, no. 392; vol. 4, book 56, no. 2946; vol. 9, book 88, no. 6924; and vol. 9, book 96, nos. 7284-7285.

4. Sahih Muslim, book 1, nos. 30-33; Abu Dawud, Sunan Abu Dawud, English Translation with Explanatory Notes, Ahmad Hasan, trans., Kitab Bhavan, 1990. Book 14, no. 2635.

5. Sunan Abu Dawud,book 14, no. 2497.

6. Sahih Bukhari, vol. 1, book 2, no. 26; cf. vol. 2, book 25, no. 1519 et al.

7. Sahih Bukhari, vol. 1, book 9, no. 527; cf. vol. 4, book 56, no. 2782 et al.

8. Sahih Bukhari, vol. 2, book 13, no. 969.

9. Sahih Bukhari, vol. 4, book 56, no. 2818.

10. Sahih Bukhari, vol. 1, book 2, no. 36.

11. Sunan Abu Dawud, book 14, no. 2510.

12. Sahih Muslim, book 19, no. 4294.

13. Sunan Abu Dawud, book 14, no. 2526.

14. Sahih Bukhari, vol. 5, book 64, no. 3949.

15. "Ibn Hisham's Notes," in A. Guillaume, translator, *The Life of Muhammad: A Translation of Ibn Ishaq's Sirat Rasul Allah*, (Oxford: Oxford University Press, 1955), 691.

16. Ibid., xl.

17. Ibid., xxxv.

18. Ibid., xxxvii.

19. My own copy bears the stamp of an Islamic bookstore in Lahore, Pakistan.

20. A. Guillaume, translator, *The Life of Muhammad: A Translation of Ibn Ishaq's Sirat Rasul Allah*, (Oxford: Oxford University Press, 1955), 516.

21. Ibid., 451.
22. Ibid., 289.
23. Ibid., 300.
24. Sahih Bukhari, vol. 4, book 56, no. 2817.
25. Sahih Muslim, book 20, no. 4639; cf. nos. 4640-4643.
26. Ibid., no. 4645.
27. Ibid., no. 4646.
28. Middle East Media Research Institute (MEMRI), "Friday Sermons in Saudi Mosques: Review and Analysis," MEMRI Special Report No. 10, September 26, 2002. www.memri.org.
29. Guillaume, *The Life of Muhammad*, 438.
30. Ibid., 452.
31. Ibid., 455.
32. Sahih Bukhari, vol. 4, book 56, no. 2813.
33. See Sura 5:59-60.
34. Guillaume, *The Life of Muhammad*, 461.
35. Ibid., 462.
36. Sahih Bukhari, vol. 4, book 56, no. 3043.
37. Guillaume, *The Life of Muhammad*, 464.
38. Ibid., 468-469.
39. Sunan Abu Dawud, book 38, no. 4390.
40. Guillaume, *The Life of Muhammad*, 468–469.
41. Sahih Bukhari, vol. 5, book 64, no. 4028.
42. Ye'or, *The Decline of Eastern Christianity Under Islam*.
43. 'Umdat al-Salik, o9.14.
44. Andrew G. Bostom, "The treatment of POWs," *Washington Times*, March 28, 2003.
45. Guillaume, *The Life of Muhammad*, 485.
46. Sahih Bukhari, vol. 5, book 64, no. 4091.
47. 'Umdat al-Salik, o9.16.
48. Guillaume, *The Life of Muhammad*, 515.
49. Ibid.
50. Ibid., 547.
51. Sahih Muslim, book 19, no. 4382.
52. Sahih Bukhari, vol. 1, book 1, no. 7.
53. Sahih Bukhari, vol. 4, book 56, no. 2924.

Chapter 6

1. Bernard Lewis, *The Arabs in History*, (Oxford: Oxford University Press, sixth edition, 1993), 55.
2. John Esposito, *Islam: The Straight Path*, (Oxford: Oxford University Press, third edition, 1998), 35.

3. Philip K. Hitti, *The Arabs: A Short History*, (Washington, D.C.: Regnery Publishing, revised edition, 1970), 59-60.
4. Ibid., 56.
5. Ibid., 205.
6. Sita Ram Goel, *The Story of Islamic Imperialism in India*, (New Delhi: Voice of India, revised edition, 1994), 70-71.
7. Ibid., 44.
8. Sunan Abu Dawud, book 14, no. 2610.
9. Sahih Bukhari, vol. 4, book 56, no. 3016.
10. Sayyid Qutb, *In the Shade of the Qur'an* (Fi Zilal al-Qur'an), M. A. Salahi and A. A. Shamis, translators, The Islamic Foundation, 1999. Volume 1, 211-2.
11. Sahih Bukhari, vol. 1, book 2, no. 53.
12. Al-Baladhuri, in Ye'or, *The Decline of Eastern Christianity Under Islam*, 272.
13. 'Umdat al-Salik, o10.2.
14. K. S. Lal, *The Legacy of Muslim Rule in India*, (New Delhi: Aditya Prakashan, 1992), 307-8.
15. Hitti, *The Arabs: A Short History*, 90.
16. Steven Runciman, *The Fall of Constantinople 1453*, (Cambridge: Cambridge University Press 1965), 124.
17. Ibn Abi Zayd al-Qayrawani, in Bat Ye'or, *The Decline of Eastern Christianity Under Islam: From Jihad to Dhimmitude*, (Rutherford: Fairleigh Dickinson University Press, 1996), 295.
18. Averroes, "Al-Bidaya," excerpted in Rudolph Peters, *Jihad in Classical and Modern Islam*, (Princeton: Markus Wiener Publishers, 1996), 40.
19. Ibn Taymiyya, "Jihad," Ibid.
20. Ibn Khaldun, *The Muqaddimah: An Introduction to History*, translated by Franz Rosenthal; edited and abridged by N. J. Dawood, (Princeton: Princeton University Press, 1967), 183.
21. Osama bin Laden, "Declaration of War Against the Americans Occupying the Land of the Two Holy Places," August 23, 1996. Reprinted at http://www.terrorismfiles.org/individuals/declaration_of_jihad1.html.
22. Habib C. Malik, "Christians in the Land Called Holy," *First Things*, January 1999.
23. For example, dhimmis "are distinguished from Muslims in dress, wearing a wide cloth belt (zunnar); are not greeted with 'as-Salamu 'alaykum' [the traditional Muslim greeting, "Peace be with you"]; must keep to the side of the street; may not build higher than or as high as the Muslims' buildings, though if they acquire a tall house, it is not razed; are forbidden to openly display wine or pork . . . recite the Torah or Evangel aloud, or make public display of their funerals or feastdays; and are forbidden to build new churches." 'Umdat al-Salik, o11.3, 5.
24. Lal, *The Legacy of Muslim Rule in India*, 302.
25. Ibid., 50; Ye'or, *The Decline of Eastern Christianity Under Islam*, 78.

26. Catharine Roehrig, *Fun with Hieroglyphs*, (New York: Metropolitan Museum of Art/Viking, 1990), 4.

27. Ibn Naqqash, in Bat Ye'or, *The Dhimmi: Jews and Christians Under Islam*, translated by David Maisel, Paul Fenton, and David Littman, (Rutherford: Fairleigh Dickinson University Press, 1985), 206.

28. Al-Asnawi, Ibid., 211.

29. Hitti, *The Arabs: A Short History*, 57.

30. Muhammad Marmaduke Pickthall, "Tolerance in Islam," 1927, abridged by Z. Haq. Reprinted at http://cyberistan.org/islamic/toleran1.html.

31. Ya'qub Abu Yusuf, in Bat Ye'or, *The Decline of Eastern Christianity Under Islam: From Jihad to Dhimmitude*, (Rutherford: Fairleigh Dickinson University Press, 1985), 274.

32. P. M. Holt, Ann K. S. Lambton, and Bernard Lewis, editors, *The Cambridge History of Islam, Volume 1A: The Central Islamic Lands from Pre-Islamic Times to the First World War*, (Cambridge: Cambridge University Press, 1970), 62-3.

33. John of Nikiou, in Bat Ye'or, *The Decline of Eastern Christianity Under Islam: From Jihad to Dhimmitude*, (Rutherford: Fairleigh Dickinson University Press, 1996), 272.

34. Malik ibn Anas, Muwatta' Imam Malik, translated by Muhammad Rahimuddin, Sh. Muhammad Ashraf, 2000, ch. 177, no. 661.

35. N. Leven, "Servitudes in Persia," in Bat Ye'or, *The Dhimmi: Jews and Christians Under Islam*, translated by David Maisel, Paul Fenton, and David Littman, (Rutherford: Fairleigh Dickinson University Press, 1985), 336.

36. Y. D. Sémach, Ibid., 341.

37. Hannah and Sa'adiya b. Shelomo Akiva, Ibid., 381-382.

38. P. D. Trotter, Ibid., 321.

39. Tudor Parfitt, "Dhimma Versus Protection in Nineteenth Century Morocco," in *Israel and Ishmael: Studies in Muslim-Jewish Relations*, Tudor Parfitt, editor, (New York: Palgrave Macmillan, 2000), 157-159.

40. 'Umdat al-Salik, o11.9, 11.

41. Vahakn Dadrian, *The History of the Armenian Genocide*, (Providence: Berghahn Books, 1995), 147.

42. Ye'or, *The Decline of Eastern Christianity Under Islam*, 197.

43. Andrew Bostom, "A Modern Jihad Genocide," FrontPageMagazine.com, April 28, 2003.

44. "Turkish Massacres: 47,000 Refugees Reach Mesopotamia," *Times of London*, October 11, 1918.

45. "Turks are Evicting Native Christians: Greeks and Armenians Driven From Homes and Converted by the Sword, Assert Americans," *New York Times*, July 11, 1915.

46. Samuel P. Huntington, *The Clash of Civilizations and the Remaking of World Order*, (New York: Touchstone, 1997), 256-8.

47. Bat Ye'or, "Myths and Politics: Origin of the Myth of a Tolerant Pluralistic Islamic Society," address to The International Strategic Studies Association, August 31, 1995. Reprinted at http://www.srpska-mreza.com/library/facts/Ye_Or.html.
48. "Arab Jews better off under Islamic rule," Gulf News, June 20, 2002.

Chapter 7

1. Karen Armstrong, "The curse of the infidel: A century ago Muslim intellectuals admired the west. Why did we lose their goodwill?" *The Guardian*, June 20, 2002.
2. Richard Fletcher, *Moorish Spain*, (Berkeley: University of California Press, 1992), 172.
3. Ibid.
4. Scott Bohlinger, "First U.S. Museum Devoted to Islam Based in Jackson, Mississippi: Museum Fosters Tolerance, Multicultural Understanding," U.S. Department of State, March 27, 2003. http://usinfo.state.gov/usa/islam/a032703.htm.
5. Scott Galupo, "Progress and Islam: The mini-enlightenment that was Andalusia," *National Review Online*, May 30, 2002.
6. Edward Said, "When will we resist? The US is preparing to attack the Arab world, while the Arabs whimper in submission," *The Guardian*, January 25, 2003.
7. Yossi Klein Halevi, jacket of María Rosa Menocal, *The Ornament of the World: How Muslims, Jews, and Christians Created a Culture of Tolerance in Medieval Spain*, (New York: Little, Brown, 2002).
8. María Rosa Menocal, *The Ornament of the World: How Muslims, Jews, and Christians Created a Culture of Tolerance in Medieval Spain*, (New York: Little, Brown, 2002), 281.
9. Harold Bloom, "Foreword," in Menocal, *The Ornament of the World*.
10. Menocal, *The Ornament of the World*, 5.
11. Ibid., 29–30.
12. Ibid., 72–3.
13. Kenneth Baxter Wolf, *Christian Martyrs in Muslim Spain*, (Cambridge: Cambridge University Press, 1988), 9–10. Reprinted at http://libro.uca.edu/martyrs/cm1.htm.
14. Ibid., 12.
15. 'Umdat al-Salik, o11.9, 11; see chapter five.
16. Richard Fletcher, *Moorish Spain*, (Berkeley: University of California Press, 1992), 172–3.
17. Wolf, *Christian Martyrs in Muslim Spain*, 12.
18. Menocal, *The Ornament of the World*, 70.
19. Wolf, *Christian Martyrs in Muslim Spain*, 12.

20. Menocal, *The Ornament of the World*, 70.
21. Wolf, *Christian Martyrs in Muslim Spain*, 34.
22. Menocal, *The Ornament of the World*, 135.
23. Fletcher, *Moorish Spain*, 108.
24. Mannaa K. al-Qubtan, "Saudi Arabia: Fatwa for non-Muslims," in Bat Ye'or, *The Decline of Eastern Christianity Under Islam: From Jihad to Dhimmitude*, (Rutherford: Fairleigh Dickinson University Press, 1996), 411.
25. Fletcher, *Moorish Spain*, 96–7.
26. Ibid., 172; Joseph Kenny, O.P., *The Spread of Islam Through North to West Africa*, Dominican Publications, Lagos, 2000, reprinted at http://www.op.org/nigeriaop/kenny/nwafr/DefaultNW.htm; 'Umdat al-Salik, o11.9, 11; see Chapter Six.
27. Fletcher, *Moorish Spain*, 172–3.
28. Bat Ye'or, "Myths and Politics: Origin of the Myth of a Tolerant Pluralistic Islamic Society," address to The International Strategic Studies Association, August 31, 1995. Reprinted at http://www.srpska-mreza.com/library/facts/Ye_Or.html.
29. Bat Ye'or Interview by Michael Cromartie, "The Myth of Islamic Tolerance: Muslim 'protection' of Christians and Jews has actually been oppression, says scholar Bat Ye'or," *Books & Culture*, September–October 1998. Reprinted at http://www.christianitytoday.com/bc/8b5/8b5038.html.
30. Ye'or, "Myths and Politics"
31. Bat Ye'or Interview by Michael Cromartie.
32. Ye'or, "Myths and Politics."
33. Bat Ye'or Interview by Michael Cromartie.
34. Interview with author, May 22, 2003.
35. Middle East Media Research Institute (MEMRI), "Friday Sermons in Saudi Mosques: Review and Analysis," MEMRI Special Report No. 10, September 26, 2002. www.memri.org.
36. Interview with author, May 22, 2003.
37. Habib C. Malik, "Christians in the Land Called Holy," *First Things*, January 1999.
38. Matt Rees, "The Saga of the Siege," *Time*, May 20, 2002.
39. Etgar Lefkovits, "Leading terrorists still located in Church of Nativity," *Jerusalem Post*, April 30, 2002.
40. Lauren Gelfond, "Church officials allege Bethlehem cover-up," *Jerusalem Post*, May 5, 2002.
41. Queen Noor, Leap of Faith, in Dick Morris, "Queen Noor's Anti-Semitism," *New York Post*, May 5, 2003.
42. "Christian converts imprisoned by Arafat: Coalition asks Israel to intervene to prevent torture, execution," WorldNetDaily.com, January 13, 2003.

43. Jonathan Adelman and Agota Kuperman, "Christian Exodus from the Middle East," Foundation for the Defense of Democracies, December 19, 2001. Reprinted at: http://www.defenddemocracy.org/publications/publications_show.htm?doc_id=155713.

44. Aliza Marcus, "Christian converts on the run from Arafat's men," *Telegraph*, December 21, 1997.

45. Palestinian Ministry of Information, "Reports in the Western Media, Palestine and the PNA, and Religion," December 1997, reprinted in the Palestinian Society for the Protection of Human Rights & the Environment, "The Myth of Christian Persecution by the Palestinian Authority," http://www.lawsociety.org/Reports/reports/1998/crz4.html.

46. Raphael Israeli, *Green Crescent Over Nazareth: The Displacement of Christians by Muslims in the Holy Land*, (London: Frank Cass, 2002), 60.

47. Middle East Media Research Institute (MEMRI), "A Friday Sermon on PA TV:...'We Must Educate our Children on the Love of Jihad...'" MEMRI Special Dispatch No. 240, July 11, 2001. www.memri.org.

48. Adelman and Kuperman, "Christian Exodus from the Middle East."

49. Ibid.

50. The Rev. Youngsook Kang, "The Situation of Christians in Pakistan," United Methodist Church General Board of Global Ministries, GBGM News, December 17, 2002. http://gbgm-umc.org/global_news/full_article.cfm?articleid=1311.

51. "Christians in Pakistan fear attack," The Associated Press, March 19, 2003.

52. "Hate Campaign Waged Against Christian Minority In Pakistan," International Christian Concern, March 12, 2003. http://www.persecution.org/news/press2003-03-12.html.

53. Patrick Sookhdeo, *A People Betrayed: The Impact of Islamization on the Christian Community in Pakistan*, (Fearn: Christian Focus Publications; Pewsey: Isaac Publishing, 2002), 130–131.

54. Ibid., 151–5, 183, 170.

55. U.S. Department of State Bureau of Democracy, Human Rights, and Labor, "Pakistan," Country Reports on Human Rights Practices—2000, February 23, 2001. http://www.state.gov/g/drl/rls/hrrpt/2000/sa/710.htm.

56. Sookhdeo, *A People Betrayed*, 152–3, 177, 178, 181, 231–2.

57. U.S. Department of State Bureau of Democracy, Human Rights, and Labor, "Pakistan," Country Reports on Human Rights Practices—2000, February 23, 2001. http://www.state.gov/g/drl/rls/hrrpt/2000/sa/710.htm

58. Ibid.

59. Sookhdeo, *A People Betrayed*, 239–240.

60. 'Umdat al-Salik, o11.10(5).

61. Sookhdeo, *A People Betrayed*, 248.

62. Ibid., 286.

63. Farajollah Parvizian, interview with author, May 9, 2003.

64. U.S. Commission on International Religious Freedom, Annual Report of the United States Commission on International Religious Freedom, May 2003.

Chapter 8

1. Rudolph Peters, *Islam and Colonialism: The Doctrine of Jihad in Modern History*, (The Hague: Mouton, 1979), 47-48.
2. Al-Ajluni, Kashf al-Khafa', Cairo/Aleppo, no date, volume 1, no. 424.
3. See Suhaib Hasan, *An Introduction to the Science of Hadith*, Al-Quran Society, London, 1994. Reprinted at http://www.uh.edu/campus/msa/qurhad/suhaib.txt. Also Rudolph Peters, Islam and Colonialism: The Doctrine of Jihad in Modern History, (The Hague: Mouton Publishers, 1979), 120; and Abdullah Azzam, Join the Caravan, Azzam Publications, 2001, 51.
4. Rudolph Peters, *Islam and Colonialism: The Doctrine of Jihad in Modern History*, (The Hague: Mouton, 1979), 51–2.
5. Ibid., 51.
6. Brynjar Lia, *The Society of the Muslim Brothers in Egypt*, (Reading: Ithaca Press, 1998), 28.
7. Ibid., 33.
8. Ibid., 68–9, 75–6.
9. Ibn Khaldun, *The Muqaddimah: An Introduction to History*, translated by Franz Rosenthal; edited and abridged by N. J. Dawood, (Princeton: Princeton University Press, 1967), 183.
10. Brynjar Lia, *The Society of the Muslim Brothers in Egypt*, (Reading: Ithaca Press, 1998), 79.
11. Middle East Media Research Institute (MEMRI), "Friday Sermon on Palestinian Authority TV," MEMRI Special Dispatch No. 370, April 17, 2002. www.memri.org.
12. Brynjar Lia, *The Society of the Muslim Brothers in Egypt*, (Reading: Ithaca Press, 1998), 80.
13. Martin Kramer, "Fundamentalist Islam at Large: The Drive for Power," *Middle East Quarterly*, June 1996.
14. Brynjar Lia, *The Society of the Muslim Brothers in Egypt*, (Reading: Ithaca Press, 1998), 153–4.
15. Ibid., 155.
16. Jonathan Raban, "Truly, madly, deeply devout," *The Guardian*, March 2, 2002.
17. Shaker El-sayed, "Hassan al-Banna: The leader and the Movement," Muslim American Society, http://www.maschicago.org/library/misc_articles/hassan_banna.htm.
18. Brynjar Lia, *The Society of the Muslim Brothers in Egypt*, (Reading: Ithaca Press, 1998), 116.

19. Tariq Ramadan, "Foreword," in Hassan al-Banna, Al-Ma'thurat, Awakening Publications, 2001. Reprinted at http://www.tariq-ramadan.org/document.asp?fichier=foreword&d=38.
20. Robert Irwin, "Is this the man who inspired Bin Laden?" *The Guardian*, November 1, 2001.
21. John Calvert, "'The World is an Undutiful Boy!': Sayyid Qutb's American experience," Islam and Christian-Muslim Relations, vol. 11, no. 1, 2000, 94.
22. Ibid., 95, 99, 100.
23. Sayyid Qutb, *Social Justice in Islam*, John Hardie, translator, Hamid Algar, translator of revised edition, (Oneonta: Islamic Publications International, 2000), 117.
24. Sayyid Qutb, *Milestones*, The Mother Mosque Foundation, undated, 7.
25. Ibid., 10–11.
26. Ibid., 9.
27. Ibid., 58.
28. Ibid., 21.
29. Ibid., 118–119.
30. Michael G. Knapp, "The Concept and Practice of Jihad in Islam," *Parameters*, Spring 2003, 83.
31. Sayyid Qutb, *Milestones*, The Mother Mosque Foundation, undated, 58.
32. David Pryce-Jones, *The Closed Circle: An Interpretation of the Arabs*, (Chicago: Ivan R. Dee, 2002), 251–2.
33. Sayyid Qutb, *Milestones*, The Mother Mosque Foundation, undated, 55.
34. Ibid., 58–9.
35. Ibid., 61.
36. Ibid., 53.
37. Ibid., 64.
38. Ibid., 53–4.
39. Ibid., p. 55.
40. Ibid., 57.
41. Ibid., 56.
42. Ibid., 57.
43. Ibid., 61–2.
44. Ibid., 62.
45. Majid Khadduri, "Translator's Introduction," in *The Islamic Law of Nations: Shaybani's Siyar*, Majid Khadduri, translator, (Baltimore: The Johns Hopkins Press, 1966), 58.
46. Sayyid Qutb, *Milestones*, The Mother Mosque Foundation, undated, 75–6.
47. Ibid., 62–3.
48. Ibid.,64.
49. Ibid.,71–2.
50. Ibid.,59–60.

51. Sayyid Qutb, *In the Shade of the Qur'an* (Fi Zilal al-Qur'an), M. A. Salahi and A. A. Shamis, translators, The Islamic Foundation, 1999, Volume 1, 210.
52. Sayyid Qutb, *Milestones*, The Mother Mosque Foundation, undated, 63.
53. Ibid., 73.
54. Sayyid Qutb, *In the Shade of the Qur'an* (Fi Zilal al-Qur'an), M. A. Salahi and A. A. Shamis, translators, The Islamic Foundation, 1999, Volume 1, 208, 328.
55. Sayyid Qutb, *Milestones*, The Mother Mosque Foundation, undated, 63.
56. Fiona Symon, "Analysis: The roots of jihad," BBCNews, October 16, 2001.
57. Sayyid Qutb, *Milestones*, The Mother Mosque Foundation, undated, 65.
58. Sayyid Qutb, *In the Shade of the Qur'an* (Fi Zilal al-Qur'an), M. A. Salahi and A. A. Shamis, translators, The Islamic Foundation, 1999, Volume 1, 328.
59. Zafar Bangash, "Remembering Sayyid Qutb, an Islamic intellectual and leader of rare insight and integrity," *Muslimedia*, September 1, 1999. Reprinted at http://www.muslimedia.com/archives/features99/qutb.htm.
60. Robert Irwin, "Is this the man who inspired Bin Laden?" *The Guardian*, November 1, 2001.
61. "Muslim Brotherhood—Egypt," Encyclopedia of the Orient, http://lexicorient.com/cgi-bin/eo-direct-frame.pl?http://i-cias.com/e.o/mus_br_egypt.htm.
62. "Muslim Brotherhood Movement Homepage," http://216.239.39.104/ search?q=cache:IQW-JimlYqoC:www.ummah.org.uk/ ikhwan/ 1 %22Muslim 1 Brotherhood%22&hl=en&ie=UTF-8.
63. Not to be confused with former Afghan President Burhanuddin Rabbani's Muslim Party, which is usually rendered in English Jamiat-e-Islami.
64. Syed Ubaidur Rahman, "Jamaat-e-Islami: where it stands today?" *Milli Gazette*, January 15, 2002.
65. Syed Abul Ala Maududi, "Jihad in Islam," Address at the Town Hall, Lahore, April 13, 1939. Reprinted at http://host06.ipowerweb.com/~ymofmdc/books/jihadinislam/.
66. Sayyid Abul A'la Maududi [here, Mawdudi], *Towards Understanding the Qur'an*, Zafar Ishaq Ansari, translator, The Islamic Foundation, revised edition 1999, Vol. 3, 202.
67. Qazi Hussain Ahmed, "Ijtihad," Jamaat-e-Islami Pakistan, http://www.jamaat.org/qa/ijtihad.html.
68. Khurram Murad, "Revolution: Through Bullet or Ballot," Tarjuman Al Quran, January 1996. Reprinted at http://www.jamaat.org/Isharat/archive/0196.html.
69. "'Al-Qaeda brain' praised as hero," BBCNews, March 4, 2003.
70. Paul Haven, "Al-Qaeda has changed, but it's still at the epicenter of anti-Western terrorism," The Associated Press, March 5, 2003.

71. Gretchen Peters, "Al Qaeda-Pakistani ties deepen: Khalid Sheik Mohammed was nabbed at the home of a parliamentary official," *Christian Science Monitor,* March 6, 2003.
72. Ibid.
73. Phil Hirschkorn, Rohan Gunaratna, Ed Blanche, and Stefan Leader, "Blowback," *Jane's Intelligence Review,* August 1, 2001.
74. 'Umdat al-Salik, k29.5; r40.1-3.
75. "Who was Abdullah Azzam?" in Abdullah Azzam, *Join the Caravan,* Azzam Publications, 2001, 8.
76. Ibid., 9.
77. Ibid., 10.
78. Ibid., 11.
79. Ibid., 7.
80. Interestingly, this was one of the books on jihad found in the possession of the American Muslim Jeffrey Leon Battle, who is charged with attempting to go to Afghanistan to fight American troops alongside al-Qaeda and the Taliban.
81. Abdullah Azzam, *Join the Caravan,* Azzam Publications, 2001, 51.
82. Sahih Bukhari, vol. 4, book 56, no. 2790; cf. Abdullah Azzam, *Join the Caravan,* Azzam Publications, 2001, 40.
83. Tawfiq Tabib, "Interview with Sheikh al-Mujahideen Abu Abdel Aziz," *Al-Sirat Al-Mustaqeem* (The Straight Path), August 1994. Reprinted at http://www.seprin.com/laden/barbaros.html.
84. Abdullah Azzam, *Join the Caravan,* Azzam Publications, 2001, 25. "SAWS" is an abbreviation for an Arabic phrase that Muslims utter after speaking the name of a prophet. It is usually rendered in English "peace be upon him"; its literal meaning is more or less "may the blessings (or prayers) and peace of Allah be upon him."
85. Ibid., 30.
86. Ibid., 39.
87. Abdullah Azzam, *Defence of the Muslim Lands,* Mohammed Taqi-ud-Oin AI-Hilali and Mohammed Muhsin Khan, translators. Maktaba Dar-us-Salam, 1993. Reprinted at http://www.religioscope.com/info /doc/jihad/azzam_defence_1_table.htm.
88. Abdullah Azzam, *Join the Caravan,* Azzam Publications, 2001, 23.

Chapter 9

1. Hamid Algar, Letter to the Editor, *New York Times Magazine,* April 20, 2003.
2. Ibn Taymiyya, "Jihad," in Rudolph Peters, *Jihad in Classical and Modern Islam,* (Princeton: Markus Wiener Publishers, 1996), 49.
3. Osama bin Laden (?),"Letter to the American People," November 24, 2002. http://www.observer.co.uk/worldview/story/0,11581,845725,00.html.

4. Middle East Media Research Institute (MEMRI), "Friday Sermons in Saudi Mosques: Review and Analysis," MEMRI Special Report No. 10, September 26, 2002. www.memri.org.
5. Sahih Bukhari, vol. 2, book 23, no. 1365.
6. Middle East Media Research Institute (MEMRI), "An Interview with the Mother of a Suicide Bomber," MEMRI Special Dispatch No. 391, June 19, 2002.
7. Amir Taheri, "The Truth About Jihad," *New York Post*, April 20, 2003.
8. Amir Taheri, "Libya's Future? Talking to Muammar Kaddafi's son," *National Review Online*, January 2, 2003.
9. Middle East Media Research Institute (MEMRI), "Saudi Opposition Sheikhs on America, Bin Laden, and Jihad," MEMRI Special Dispatch No. 400, July 18, 2002. www.memri.org.
10. Middle East Media Research Institute (MEMRI), "Saudi Government-Controlled Daily Praises Passover and Jerusalem Supermarket Suicide Bombers," MEMRI Special Dispatch No. 367, April 12, 2002. www.memri.org.
11. Sarah El Deeb, "Al-Qaida Operative Warned of Attacks," The Associated Press, May 13, 2003.
12. Middle East Media Research Institute, "Leading Egyptian Government Cleric Calls For: 'Martyrdom Attacks that Strike Horror into the Hearts of the Enemies of Allah,'" MEMRI Special Dispatch No. 363, April 7, 2002. www.memri.org.
13. David Brooks, "Among the Bourgeoisophobes: Why the Europeans and Arabs, each in their own way, hate America and Israel," *The Weekly Standard*, April 15, 2002.
14. Letters to the editor, "The Roots of Mideast Terror," *New York Times*, May 7, 2003.
15. Khaled Abou El Fadl, "The Place of Tolerance in Islam," in Khaled Abou El Fadl, et al., *The Place of Tolerance in Islam*, (Boston: Beacon Press, 2002).
16. "Interview Khaled Abou el-Fadl," Faith and Doubt at Ground Zero, PBS Frontline, 2002. Reprinted at http://www.pbs.org/wgbh/pages/front-line/shows/faith/interviews/elfadl.html.
17. Farajollah Parvizian, interview with author, May 9, 2003.
18. Philip K. Hitti, *The Arabs: A Short History*, (Washington, D.C.: Regnery Publishing, revised edition, 1970), 137.
19. Syed Abul Ala Maududi, "Jihad in Islam," Address at the Town Hall, Lahore, April 13, 1939. Reprinted at http://host06.ipowerweb.com/~ymofmdc/books/jihadinislam/.
20. M. Amir Ali, "Jihad Explained," About Islam and Muslims, http://www.unn.ac.uk/societies/islamic/jargon/jihad2.htm.
21. "Muhammad and . . . Violence and Jihad," Muhammad: Legacy of a Prophet, http://www.pbs.org/muhammad/ma_violence.shtml.
22. "What Jihad Means," Reuters News Service, September 18, 2001.

23. Council on American Islamic Relations, "About Islam and American Muslims," www.cair-net.org/asp/aboutislam.asp; International Institute of Islamic Thought, Q & A on Islam and Arab Americans, 2002.

24. Council on American Islamic Relations advertisement, *New York Times*, February 16, 2003.

25. Muhammad Hisham Kabbani, "Islamic Extremism: A Viable Threat to U.S. National Security," speech at U.S. Department of State, January 7, 1999. For some time this speech was available at the website of the Islamic Supreme Council: http://www.islamicsupremecouncil.org/extremism/islamic_extremism.htm. However, it has recently been taken down after Kabbani himself was subjected to threats and abuse from Muslim radicals because of his statements. See Pat McDonnell Twair, "Dispute Between Kabbani Followers and Hosts Disrupts Forum at Islamic Center of Southern California," Washington Report On Middle East Affairs, July/August 1999.

26. MSNBC, Nachman, February 25, 2003. http://www.msnbc.com/news/877675.asp.

27. Dave Eberhart, "Muslim Moderate Kabbani Firm on Terrorist Nuclear Threat," NewsMax.com, November 19, 2001.

28. Mary Jacoby and Graham Brink, "Saudi form of Islam wars with moderates," *St. Petersburg Times*, March 11, 2003.

29. Lisa Gardiner, "American Muslim leader urges faithful to spread Islam's message," *San Ramon Valley Herald*, July 4, 1998.

30. Art Moore, "Should Muslim Quran be USA's top authority?" WorldNet-Daily.com, May 1, 2003.

31. United States District Court, Eastern District of Virginia, *United States of America v. Randall Todd Royer, Ibrahim Ahmed El-Hamdi, Masoud Ahmad Khan, Yong Ki Kwon, Mohammed Aatique, Seifullah Chapman, Hammad Abdur-Raheem, Donald Thomas Surratt, Caliph Basha Ibn Abdur-Raheem, Khwaja Mahmood Hasan, Sabri Benkhala.* June 2003. http://news.find-law.com/hdocs/docs/terrorism/usroyer603ind.pdf. See also Terry Frieden, "'Jihad network' suspects plead not guilty," www.cnn.com, July 3, 2003.

32. "100 Questions and Answers About Arab Americans," *Detroit Free Press*, http://www.freep.com/jobspage/arabs.htm, 2001. Linked from http://www.adc.org/index.php?id=247.

33. For taqiyyeh among al-Qaeda cell members, see Charles M. Sennott, "Exposing Al Qaeda's European Network," *Boston Globe*, August 4, 2002.

34. John Perazzo, "The Meaning of Jihad," FrontPageMagazine.com, November 26, 2002.

35. Jessica King, "Clarifying Islam misconceptions: Jihad and peace defined under Muslim faith," *Northern Star Online*, January 28, 2003, http://www.star.niu.edu/campus/articles/012803-islam.asp.

36. Karen Armstrong, "The True, Peaceful Face of Islam," *Time*, October 1, 2001.

37. Daniel Pipes, "Jihad and the Professors," *Commentary*, November 2002.

38. Chris Arabia and Jean Pearce, "The Unpatriotic University: Duke," FrontPageMagazine.com, May 7, 2003.
39. Martin Kramer, *Ivory Towers on Sand,* Washington Institute for Near East Policy, 2001, 56.
40. Ibid., 51.
41. Noah Feldman, *After Jihad: America and the Struggle For Islamic Democracy,* (New York: Farrar, Straus and Giroux, 2003).
42. Julia Duin, "Islamic dissidents warn humanists to beware radicals," *Washington Times,* April 13, 2003.
43. Paul M. Barrett, "How a Chaplain Spread Extremism To an Inmate Flock," *Wall Street Journal,* February 5, 2003.
44. Yancey Roy, "Schumer rips prison officials over 'radical' cleric," Gannett News Service, February 7, 2003.
45. Michael Gormley, "State bans former head imam from prison for 9-11 remarks," The Associated Press, February 6, 2003.
46. Stephen Schwartz, "Lying About Islam," *New York Post,* March 3, 2003.
47. Sohail H. Hashmi, "Jihad," in *Encyclopedia of Politics and Religion,* Robert Wuthnow, editor. Congressional Quarterly, Inc., 1998, 425–426.

Chapter 10

1. Abdus Sattar Ghazali, *Islam in the Post-Cold War Era,* Eagle Enterprises, 1999. Reprinted at http://www.ghazali.net/book2/.
2. Ibid.
3. Noam Chomsky, "What Americans have learnt—and not learnt—since 9/11," *The Age,* September 7, 2002.
4. Noam Chomsky, *9-11,* (New York: Seven Stories Press, 2002), 61.
5. Ibid., 31.
6. Ibid., 21.
7. Carrie Benzschawel, "The Homegrown Nuclear Threat," Common Dreams News Center, February 26, 2002.
8. Student Peace Action Network, http://www.studentpeaceaction.org/.
9. Ibid.
10. "Anti-U.S. Prof Enrages Columbia Alums," NewsMax.com, March 31, 2003.
11. Thomas Bartlett, "The Most Hated Professor in America," *Chronicle of Higher Education,* April 18, 2003.
12. International Solidarity Movement, "ISM Statement on the Killing of Rachel Corrie and Its Aftermath, March 21, 2003. http://www.rachel-corrie.org/ism.htm.
13. "IDF: International Solidarity Movement hid senior Palestinan terrorist" The Associated Press, March 27, 2003.

14. Sam Skolnik, "Activist's death focuses spotlight on Mideast struggle," *Seattle Post-Intelligencer*, March 20, 2003.

15. Columbus Progressive Alliance, "Events For Monday, April 14th, 2003," http://cpanews.org/events/2003/04/14/.

16. Isioma Daniel, "The World at Their Feet . . ." *This Day*, November 16, 2002.

17. Andrew Sullivan, "Beauties and the beasts," Salon.com, November 27, 2002.

18. Ibn Warraq, "Introduction: The Allah That Failed," in Ibn Warraq, editor, *Leaving Islam: Apostates Speak Out*, (Amherst: Prometheus Books, 2003), 136.

Chapter 11

1. "Arab sermons: O Lord, deal with your enemies . . . Americans, British . . . kill them one by one," Independent Media Review Analysis (IMRA), June 5, 2003. http://www.imra.org.il/story.php3?id=17134.

2. David Gollust, "US Report Says Terror Attacks Declined Sharply Last Year," VOANews.com, April 30, 2003.

3. "President Returns to Land to Talk Economy, National Security," FoxNews.com, May 2, 2003.

4. Charles Hays Burchfield, "Saudi Official Says Saudi Arabia is 'Mobilized' to Fight Terrorism," U.S. Department of State International Information Programs, June 12, 2003.

5. "Saudi sermon after Sharm: 'O God . . . destroy Islam's enemies, including the vile Jews,'" Independent Media Review Analysis (IMRA), June 9, 2003. http://www.imra.org.il/story.php3?id=17183.

6. For Rahman at al-Farooq, see J. Bowyer Bell, *Murders on the Nile: The World Trade Center and Global Terror*, (San Francisco: Encounter Books, 2003), 121.

7. Nisa Islam Muhammad, "FBI continues to target mosques," FinalCall.com, March 4, 2003.

8. Michelle Malkin, "Grateful for Patriot Acts," CNSNews.com, July 2, 2003.

9. Kati Cornell Smith and Marsha Kranes, "A Jihad Grows in Brooklyn," *New York Post*, March 5, 2003.

10. Council on American Islamic Relations, "Readers of right-wing web site threaten Muslims," April 29, 2003.

11. William McGowan, "Covering Terrorism: Tracking the media," *National Review Online*, May 15, 2003.

12. Joseph D'Agostino, "7,000 Men Recently Entered from Al Qaeda 'Watch' Countries," *Human Events*, December 17, 2001.

13. Joseph D'Agostino, "Immigration fraud 'out of control,'" WorldNet-Daily.com, February 25, 2002.

14. William McGowan, "Covering Terrorism: Tracking the media," *National Review Online*, May 15, 2003.
15. Mark O'Keefe, "Has the United States Become Judeo-Christian-Islamic?" Newhouse News Service, 2003.
16. Abdulwahab Alkebsi, "Human dignity, the rule of law and limits on the power of the state are clearly mandated by Islam's holy book," *Insight*, April 1, 2003.
17. "'Terrorism Is the Most Dangerous Challenge,'" *Arab News*, May 18, 2003.
18. Joyce M. Davis, "Muslim scholars decry extremism," *San Jose Mercury News*, July 9, 2002.
19. Kevin Murphy, "Federal raids on charities anger U.S. Muslim leaders," Knight Ridder Newspapers, March 21, 2002.
20. Jaime Laude, "1995 Raid in Philippines Unearthed Plot to Use Civilian Airliners in Terrorist Attack," *Philippine Headline News Online*, September 13, 2001.
21. Middle East Media Research Institute (MEMRI), "Friday Sermon on Palestinian Authority Television," MEMRI Special Dispatch No. 490, April 2, 2003.
22. Josette Alia, "Islam: le temps de l'autocritique: Musulmans Le choc du 11septembre," *Nouvel Observateur*, October 4, 2001.
23. Middle East Media Research Institute, "A Tunisian Intellectual on The Arab Obsession with Vengeance," MEMRI Special Dispatch No. 499, May 4, 2003. www.memri.org.
24. Craig S. Smith, "Cleric in Iran says Shiites must act," *New York Times*, April 26, 2003.
25. Richard Norton-Taylor, "Terror crackdown has not reduced al-Qaida threat, warns thinktank," *The Guardian*, May 14, 2003.
26. Middle East Media Research Institute (MEMRI), "Friday Sermons in Saudi Mosques: Review and Analysis," MEMRI Special Report No. 10, September 26, 2002. www.memri.org.
27. "Moroccan Islamist: Time to globalise Jihad," Middle East Online, May 17, 2003. http://www.middle-east-online.com/english/?id=5600.
28. United Nations, Universal Declaration of Human Rights, December 10, 1948. Reprinted at http://www.un.org/Overview/rights.html.

INDEX

Abbas, Mahmoud, 94–95
Abdallah, 36
Abdullah, Mirza, 108
Abdullah, Prince, 98–99
Abidin, Abdul Hamid Zainal, 37
Ablah, Ibrahim bin Abi, 247
Ablaj, Abu Mohammed al-, 109–10
abrogation (*naskh*), 135–36
Abyat, Ibrahim Muhammed Salem, 198
Abyssinia, 163
Achille Lauro, 279
ACLU, 99
ADC. *See* American Arab Anti-Discrimination Committee
adultery: in Saudi Arabia, 54; Sharia and, 277
AEL. *See* Arab European League
Afghanistan, 11, 23, 44, 102, 116, 171; al Qaeda training camps in, 22; anti-terror war in, 85–86; jihad in, 247–49; Soviet Union and, 43, 280; Taliban in, 85; United States and, 21
Africa, 24
After Jihad (Feldman), 274
Ahmad, Nasser Muhammad Al-, xi, 96, 303
Ahmed, Omar, 269
Ahmed, Qazi Hussain, 243
Aisha, 78, 157
Akbar, Hasan, 15, 19–20, 26, 63, 292; Kuwait attack and, 3–5, 12, 21; trial of, 4, 12
Akhdar, Al-' Afif Al-, 302
Akhtar, Hamida, 57

Akhtar, Mohammad, 57
Akhter, Javeed, 125
Alabama, x
Al-Ahram Center for Political and Strategic Studies, 31
Al-Anfal, 144
Alaoui, Fouad, 82
Al-Azhar University, 29–30, 77, 144, 231, 245
Albani, Muhammad Naasir ud-Din Al, 259
Albani, Nasir ad-Din al-, 102
Albanian National Army, 107
Albright, Madeleine, 103
Al-Damam, 14
Alexandria, University of, 260
Alexandria, 17
al-Farooq mosque, 47, 293, 296
Algar, Hamid, 253–54
Algeria, 43
Ali, Abdullah Yusuf, vi, 121
Ali, M. Amir, 265, 266
Ali-Hamoud, Farouk, 48
Al-Jama'ah al-Islamiyyah, 102
Al-Jazeera, 35, 109, 131, 246, 258
Al-Jazirah, 259
Alkebsi, Abdulwahab, 300
Al-Khobar, xi
Allah. *See also* Qur'an; Christians and, 18; Jews and, 16, 18; jihad and, 5–6, 7–8, 33, 50, 118; Muslim allegiance and, 20; women and, 78. *See also* Muhammad; Qur'an
All Pakistan Minorities Alliance, 205
al-Muhajiroun, 55, 58, 60

337